# Programming in Dylan

Springer
*London*
*Berlin*
*Heidelberg*
*New York*
*Barcelona*
*Budapest*
*Hong Kong*
*Milan*
*Paris*
*Santa Clara*
*Singapore*
*Tokyo*

Iain D. Craig

# Programming in Dylan

Springer

Dr Iain D. Craig
Department of Computer Science
University of Warwick
Coventry, CV4 7AL, UK

ISBN-13: 978-3-540-76053-5 e-ISBN-13: 978-1-4471-0929-7

DOI: 10.1007/978-1-4471-0929-7

British Library Cataloguing in Publication Data
Craig, Iain D.
Programming in Dylan
1.Dylan (Computer program language) 2.Programming
(Electronic computers)
I.Title
005.1'33
ISBN 3540760539

Library of Congress Cataloging-in-Publication Data
A catalog record for this book is available from the Library of Congress



Softcover reprint of the hardcover 1st edition 1997



Typesetting: camera ready by author

34/3830-543210 Printed on acid-free paper

*To my number one chum.*

# Preface

This book is intended for programmers who have experience with programming languages like Pascal, Fortran and C; that is, who have no experience with object-oriented languages. The intention was to write a relatively accessible book which introduces object-oriented programming and makes the transition from the older to the newer approach relatively painless. I have therefore included two extended examples, one much more comprehensive than the other.

The examples were developed using Carnegie-Mellon University's mindy system (version 1.3). mindy is a relatively full implementation of the Dylan language, but contains a number of extensions that are not in the *Dylan Interim Reference Manual*, which I took as the defining text for this book. In particular, the *Interim Reference* contains no mention of I/O routines, although mindy provides them. As a result, I did not mention them in the text, and only included relatively primitive I/O calls in the example programs. It is possible that incompatibilities exist between mindy-1.3 and subsequent versions, and it is possible that they exist between it and other implementations. As far as possible, I have tried to keep the constructions in the programs as standard as possible.

While writing the book, the *Dylan Interim Reference Manual* was the basis for all constructs and information about the language. As I was preparing the camera-ready copy, the final *Dylan Reference Manual* became available on the Internet. Unfortunately, it became available too late to include in this book. However, the *Dylan Reference Manual* is about to be published by Addison-Wesley. Its ISBN is 0-201-44211-6. I suggest that dedicated readers purchase a copy.

Some readers might complain that I have not addressed the issue of highly structured data types (e.g. the types derived from `<vector>`, `<string>` and `<table>`. This is a deliberate move on my part and is motivated by a couple of issues. First, it is quite possible for small differences to be introduced in the language after the *Interim Reference*. Secondly, and perhaps more important, these types introduce complexities (e.g. iteration protocols) which can be avoided in an introductory text. I decided that it was better to avoid any such problem and to refer the reader to their installation-specific documents.

The choice of Dylan for this book was my own idea. At the time I began the text (July 1995), Dylan seemed to have a very bright future. As a well-designed language, it had lots of appeal. Unfortunately, it does seem to have been somewhat eclipsed by the appearance of Java and the various Web devices that it has spawned. Dylan, to my mind, is still very elegant and (dare I say it!) far more elegant than Java. It is my hope that Dylan will not submerge like so many other fine programming languages.

I would like to conclude this Preface by thanking Beverley Ford, my editor, for her constant support and advice, and also by thanking my brother Adam for drawing the figures. All errors in the text are my own.

*Iain Craig*
*Acock's Green,*
*August 1996*

# Contents

# Chapter 1

# Introduction

## 1.1 Introduction

Object-oriented programming is an approach to the construction of programs hich has grown in application over the past few years. This rise has been contemporaneous with the adoption of the C++ programming language. C++ [20] extends C [11] in a variety of ways, some of which make for safer programming. The primary extension afforded by C++ is that of object-oriented programming. Object-oriented programming did not start with C++, however, and it will not end with it, either.

The roots of object-oriented programming can be traced in part to the Simula-67 langauge [2]. Simula-67 was based on Algol-60 [14] and was intended for use in the construction of simulation programs. It introduced the concept of the class, a construct that described the behaviour of objects. The ideas of classes and objects were adopted by the Smalltalk team at Xerox Parc in the early 1970s, and culminated in the development of the Smalltalk80 programming language and its environment [7]. Thereafter, interest in object-oriented programming increased with the development of languages such as Loops [3], the CLOS [17] object-oriented extension to LISP [18], and others. At about the same time, C++ was developed by Stroustrup as an extension to C. More recently, languages like Java [21] have appeared, and the Dylan language [6] was defined by Apple Computer, Inc.

Apple developed Dylan as an application-development language for personal computers. It is a language designed around the concept of object orientation. This makes it somewhat different from C++, which is defined as an object-oriented extension to an existing language, and, as such, had to take on boad all those undesirable or outmoded features of its base language. With Dylan, the situation was different and a language was designed from scratch with object orientation as its central concept. The result is much cleaner and semantically clearer. Initially, Dylan had a syntax similar to that of LISP, but this has changed, and an algebraic syntax with infix operators is now the standard.

Dylan was intended for the development of applications on personal computers. The applications to be developed will be object-oriented in the sense that they are structured around the concept of the class. Classes and their instances constitute objects which are made to interact in various ways in order to produce the behaviour desired of the program. Access to standard libraries such as graphics, databases, and communications software is also required so that Dylan programs can be seamlessly integrated with existing software and applications. Unlike Java, [21] which is designed for a specific application within a specific environment, Dylan is conceived as a programming language which can be implemented in any environment; in particular, current implementations of the language run on Unix workstations, on Apple Macintoshes and PowerPCs, and on MS-DOS machines under Windows. Current Dylan implementations are of a programming language, and they make few assumptions about the uses to which programs are to be made or about the details of the environments in which they will operate. In particular, nothing is assumed about network interfaces or about World-Wide Web interfaces.

Dylan is semantically clean and has some properties in common with modern dialects of LISP. This should be seen as a positive property of the language, because it has adopted some of the cleaner and well-motivated aspects of LISP, in particular static scoping and tail-recursion optimisation. Dylan is a dynamically typed language which also allows the programmer to assign types to variables; this makes things easier for the compiler, and it also makes things easier for the user. A number of loop constructs are included, and they make programming easier as well as allowing for compilation into efficient code. The object-oriented facilities of Dylan also afford the programmer opportunities to annotate and provide typing information, as well as indications about storage allocation. Dylan is an excellent example of a modern object-oriented language.

## 1.2 The Aim of this Book

This book is intended as an introduction to the Dylan programming language, and is intended for use by those who know a language like C or Pascal, but who do not know any object-oriented programming. As a consequence, object-oriented concepts are emphasised in the presentation. As part of the book, a relatively extended program is given as an example. It is hoped that the reader will learn the fundamentals of object-oriented programming from the text and the example program. It is further to be hoped that the reader will develop a taste for object-oriented programming and will adopt the approach in his or her programming. Formal exercises are not included in the text; instead, a number of suggestions are made for the extension of the example program.

## 1.3 The Organisation of this Book

The book is organised as follows. In Chapter 2, the fundamental concepts of object-oriented programming are presented. The chapter introduces and explains the concepts of class, instance, inheritance, method, overloading and polymorphism. It also includes a short section on object-oriented design.

Chapter 3 contains the example program. The program is presented intact and with considerable amounts of explanatory material. Often readers must wait until the later chapters of a book in order to see an extended program. By that time, the reader is jaded and perhaps a little bored. Here, it has been decided to show the reader the details of a moderately sized program at the start of the book. Later on, it is possible for the reader to flip back to the example program and to relate the more detailed descriptions of the programming language's constructs to the example program. The program has been compiled without error and run on a real computer, so is not a paper exercise.

In the following chapters, the constructs of the Dylan language are described in detail. The constructs are often presented together with examples of their use. The examples are described and are commented upon in detail. As noted above, the reader can flip back to the main example and relate the constructs to a real program.

Chapter 4 deals with the basic data types and values. Any programming language relies upon a collection of simple or standard types. The aim of this chapter is to acquaint the reader with these types and with some of the more unusual features of Dylan (in particular the role of the value 'false' written `#f`).

Chapter 5 introduces the reader to some of the main conventional program structures. In particular, it deals with Dylan variables, expressions, assignment, and control structures. Dylan is expression-oriented, so every construct notionally returns a value. Sometimes a construct returns a meaningless value; sometimes, indeed, more commonly, the value returned is of value. This is important because control structures in languages like Pascal do not return values; C is similar (although it has some features in common with expression languages). In Pascal, Ada and C, control structures like while loops and conditionals do not return values; in Dylan, they do. A conditional or a loop construct in Dylan can be used for its effect (as in a statement-oriented language) as well as for its value (as in an expression or in a functional language). It is also possible to supress the values returned by an expression by means of a call to a function (called values).

Chapter 6 describes the Dylan procedure construct. In Dylan, procedures and functions are similar. Procedures are mainly called for effect, while functions are called for their value. Because Dylan is expression-oriented, the distinction is blurred. However, Dylan procedures are intimately bound to classes and the name 'method' has been adopted to denote the function concept. Dylan methods can be recursive (the compiler must implement the tail optimisation method to convert tail recursion into iteration). Methods have zero or more input values and can return zero or more values. It is possible to assign types to input and output values, a property of Dylan which makes for safer code. Dylan methods are organised around 'generic' methods, and this concept is also described.

Chapter 7 deals with Dylan's object-oriented programming constructs. Dylan is based entirely upon the concept of object-oriented programming, and is used in the production of such programs. This chapter is, then, the most important. The chapter contains a self-contained example which illustrates the definition of classes and the inheritance of values. The chapter also includes descriptions and explanations of the various annotations that affect instantiation, storage allocation and initialisation of objects.

Chapter 8 is about conditions and errors. Programs in Dylan are able to deal with errors and are able to signal exceptional conditions, as well as handle exceptional cases. This chapter outlines the standard exception-handling methods provided by Dylan.

Finally, Chapter Nine describes the features in Dylan for programming in the large. In addition to the other constructs, Dylan provides modules and libraries. These facilities allow programmers to collect classes and methods into modules, thereby restricting visibility to some of the constructs employed in the production of an abstraction. Libraries collect modules and other libraries into larger collections of code. Components can be collected into libraries for future use. For example, a library might contain the components of a compiler, but lots of them. For example, a compiler library might contain a library of parsers, code generators, optimisers and code representation methods. A library might provide a database systems components which can be composed and integrated with larger applications.

Appendix A contains the complete code of the example program without annotation. Appendix B gives the class diagrams for the example programs.

# Chapter 2

# Object-Oriented Programming

## 2.1 Introduction

Having seen the main components of an object-oriented program, it is necessary to say a thing or two about how to design programs with this paradigm. Many authors have written on this subject (see [4]) for one wide-ranging example), and what follows is only an introduction to the area. In addition, what follows is just the current author's approach to the design and construciton of programs. What will be described has the advantage that it works, and that it has worked for something like 15 years, even though it does not contain large amounts (even any) of formalisms and diagrams, and even though it is based upon simple observations about the paradigm and about programs in general.

## 2.2 Encapsulation and Abstraction

For a long time, modular programming has been advised. This approach requires the programmer to group related operations and data structures into a module. The modules thus defined are also required to have a well-defined interface. Modules can be composed to form subsystems simply by connecting their interfaces together. Given the definition of the interface, it should not be necessary, usually, to inspect the contents of a module in order to understand its function and its use.

Modules are intended as an abstraction from the details of the operations and data that they contain. For example, a compiler can have a lexical analysis module or a code generator module; for the user of one of these modules, the exact details of what goes on, and the way data are represented inside, are of no importance. What matters is that the module performs the advertised operation correctly.

Increasing abstraction has been an almost constant trend in software for more than thirty years. Initially, the procedure or subroutine was identified as the unit of abstraction for code; operations need be defined once and the procedure implementing the operation is called with different parameters at different places in the program's code. Next came the module concept which, as has been seen, collects procedures (operations) and data within a well-defined interface. Data has also been considered the subject of abstraction, and the concept of the abstract data type has resulted.

Many modules define, in effect, new data types. The type is defined in terms of a collection of data and a collection of procedures and functions. The interface to the data type is provided by the procedures and functions; access to the data items is typically prohibited. This view of data type, the abstract data type, is one of the foundations of object-oriented programming.

In object-oriented programming, the programmer defines new data types and new modules. Some languages tend to bias the programmer to one or the other of these views, but it is common to find that both approaches are supported. When defining new data types, the programmer composes existing types to form new types and also provides new operations that form the interface. The details of how the new type is implemented are hidden from the user; typically, the details are made totally invisible by the encapsulation mechanisms of the object-oriented programming language.

The types that can be created vary enormously. For example, bit strings can be created, as can lists and hash tables. More abstractly, sets can be defined, as well as trees and forests; tasks and the constructs employed by graphical user interfaces (e.g. menus, windows, and buttons), and even a relational database system can be described in terms of abstract data types.

Because abstract data types are encapsulated, users cannot see their internal workings. This means that the data types used in their definition, as well as the workings of the operations used to provide the interface and fundamental operations of the new type, are all hidden from the user. This implies that the implementation of an abstract type can be changed without altering the interface to it. For example, the abstract data type representing a set of integers might be defined in terms of a singly linked list of integers. The set type will provide operations to create a new set; test for membership; operations to perform union, intersection and set difference; and test to see whether the set is empty. One user might be quite satisfied by this type, but might find that it is very slow when sets become large. Given the encapsulated property of an abstract data type, the implementation of the integer set type can be changed. For example, if it is known that sets never have more than a certain number of elements, an array can be used in place of the list; if the upper bound on cardinality (number of elements) is not known, some form of tree-based representation could be used. The operations provided by the abstract type do not change; if the singly linked list is changed to a binary tree, the type will still have operations to create a new set; test for membership; perform union, intersection and set difference and test to see whether the set is empty. The interface remains the same; the implementation is what changes, and it changes in a way that is totally invisible to the user. What the user might notice is improved speed, but the code which uses integer sets does not change because that code is written in terms of the operations provided by the set type (the operations define the set type, in fact); all that has changed is the implementation of the type, not the interface provided by it.

Encapsulation prevents users from seeing inner details. Whether we choose to view an object in an object-oriented programming language as a kind of module or as an abstract data type, the property of encapsulation still holds. The interface to an object is all that is visible. The difference between what is normally construed as a module and what is construed as a data type tends to merge in an object-oriented conception of the world. Editors are typically viewed as modules, as are syntax analysers and code generators; in the object-oriented view of things, editors, syntax analysers and code generators are objects that provide an interface; in practice, the view of them is identical to that of an abstract data type, so the thinking carries over—everything that was said about the set of integers carries over to these three subsystems or modules or system components or objects (one difference is, though, that an editor is very much more complex than an integer set type, and would itself be defined in terms of a number of component abstract data types). The way an editor implements a string-matching operation is irrelevant to the user. If the string representation used by an editor is structured as an object, a slow algorithm (e.g. the simple linear-time one in which comparisons start at the left-hand end of the string and continue rightwards until either the end of the string is reached or a mismatch is detected) can be replaced by a faster one (e.g. one that changes the representation of the string to a tree to allow log-time performance) without changing any of the code that uses the string or the string matcher.

Encapsulation also prevents errors from propagating and allows the programmer to find them more easily. If the interface to an abstract data type or to an object remains the same, and if the encapsulated object has been changed internally, and if the program which uses it stopped working immediately after the change to the encapsulated type, that type must be the source of the error. This boils down to investigating the changed implementation and to investigating the interface to ensure that the right things have been passed. This is far better than inspecting thousands of lines of code. Dylan considers objects as types. When an object is defined, a new abstract data type is defined.

## 2.3 Classes and Inheritance

### 2.3.1 Classes

There are two fundamentally different ways of viewing the concept of 'object-orientation.' One views objects as 'prototypes' which are extended to form new objects. Encapsulation can be relatively weak under this view, and inheritance is replaced by a concept called 'delegation.' The programming language SELF [22] and the frame/unit knowledge representation frameworks (e.g., Stefik's UNITS [19], Roberts, *et al.'s* FRL [16], for example) exemplify this approach. The other view is 'class-based.' Class-based object-orientation is by far the more common view; it is the view upon which Dylan is based.

The class-based approach assumes a division between classes and their instances. Programmers define classes. Programs create instances of classes (or 'instantiate classes'). The objects manipulated by programs are instances of classes. This needs a little explanation.

The definition of a class is the definition, at least in Dylan, as in C++, of a new data type. The class is defined in terms of its component data structures (and types), as well as a collection of operations which comprise the class's interface. The class is, in essence, a template which is used to create instances. When creating instances of a class, the components are used to allocate storage for the instance, each component's definition in the class being used to allocate storage for the right kind ofobject. For example, if a class states that it has a data component (called a 'slot' in Dylan) called **counter** of type **<integer>** (in Dylan, by convention, types have names that start with '<' and end with '>'), instances of the class will also have a component which is referred to by counter and which holds an integer. The information about the counter slot held in the class's definition is used to create instances upon demand.

Sometimes, a class will contain the definition of a slot which specifies some initial value. That value will be stored in every instance of the class when that instance is created. Sometimes, a function is associated with a slot; this function is used to compute an initial value when the instance is created. Initial values and initialisation functions must result in the slots being initialised to a value of the correct type. Both initial values and initial values returned by initialisation functions are used when creating instances of classes.

Classes are defined by programmers and are typically not modified when the program runs. Dylan allows programmers to change the structure of classes, but these facilities are best ignored, at least until the reader has considerable experience with the paradigm, and has extremely good grounds for performing such operations. Classes, in a way, are similar to procedure definitions; a class is defined once in a program and is instantiated whenever the program requires an object of that type. A procedure is defined once and is instantiated once (there can be exceptions to this—for example, if the procedure is open-coded, or if it is a generic procedure—but single instantiation is by far the most common process). In many object-oriented programming languages, the class is a textual construct which is used by the compiler in the creation of code to create instances; this is precisely the view of classes in C++ and Modula-3 [8]. Given this view, changes to a class require the recompilation of the program which instantiates it. The Dylan model, as has been noted, is more flexible (but not as flexible—or dangerousas CLOS or Telos), but the reader should regard it as having a model similar to that of C++, at least for the time being.

Instances are the things manipulated by programs. In an object-oriented program, the programmer defines classes and then creates instances. Instances have the structure defined by their class; they have slots of the types defined in the class definition. Instances are created and destroyed; they can be manipulated in the ways delineated by their class's interface specification. In class-based programs, instances are run-time objects, whereas classes are not. We will see some more differences between classes and instances when we discuss methods.

### 2.3.2 Inheritance

In an object-oriented program, classes are grouped to form an inheritance hierarchy . In its simplest form, this is a tree of classes, the root of which is the most general class and the leaves of which are the most concrete classes.

When defining an application program, classes are defined. These classes define structures that are general in the sense that they omit specific information. For example, a class might be defined that represents sets of integers. This class will have an interface that is defined in terms of operations to create a new set, perform union, perform intersection, test for membership and test for the empty set. The interface that is thus defined will be used by all classes that represent sets of integers. This class might be fine for most uses. If it is found that the cardinality (number of members of the set) of the set is required, the class as originally defined cannot perform this task. What can be done is either to modify the original class definition or to define a new class with an extended interface to allow the cardinality to be returned to users. There are two ways to extend the class definition. One is to add an integer counter which is incremented whenever a new element is added and decremented whenever an element is removed; the value of this counter can be returned via the class's interface. The second way is to define an operation which will compute the number of elements. Either extension is possible. It is not a good idea to redefine the original class, because it will make the extension available to every piece of code that uses the set abstraction; in the present case, giving this code the ability to determine cardinalities is not a problem, but in other cases an extension might be desirable for some parts of a program but not for others (it might expose or compute things that should be left hidden or unknowable in some parts of the program).

The new class is called a subclass of the original. The subclass inherits all those operations that were defined for the original class (which is called its superclass). Thus, the subclass inherits the operations for union, intersection, membership test, empty set test, and so on; these operations can be performed on instances of the newly defined class. The slots that are in the definition of the superclass are also inherited by the subclass; the slot which holds the collection of integers will be inherited by the subclass.

When one class inherits slots from a superclass, the slots are accessible to the subclass. The subclass can update the slot and can read its contents. If a subclass inherits an operation from a superclass, that operation can be performed on the subclass; there is no need to redefine operations.

When one class is a subclass of another, the subclass extends the superclass either by the addition of slots or by the definition of operations, or by a combination of both.

For example, if we have a class that represents a FIFO queue, it will be defined in terms of:

- a slot to hold the elements of the queue
- an operation to add an element to the end of the queue
- an operation to remove the first element of the queue
- an operation to test whether the queue is empty

This queue class can be extended so that the length of the collection of elements can be made available to users of the queue. This queue is defined by adding a new operation which computes the length of the collection of elements in the slot; the operation is added to a newly defined subclass of the queue class. Alternatively, using facilities introduced in Chapter 7, the operations for adding and deleting elements can be extended so that the addition operation increments a counter and the removal operation decrements it. The counter will be stored in a new slot in the class. The class which contains the new slot and which has the extended operations is a subclass of the original queue class. In both cases, the original queue class still exists in its original form, so it can be used without problem when the need arises; for cases where the queue's length must be known, the subclass is used, but when this information is irrelevant the superclass can be instantiated. This means that extensions (subclasses) are used wherever they are needed, and they do not affect the status of superclasses. Once a class has been defined, it can be instantiated at any point in a program, even if it has had subclasses defined from it.

Next, imagine a queue in which elements can be added to the front as well as to the back, and in which the last element to be removed is remembered. This class will be very similar to the original queue class. The new class will extend the FIFO queue class by:

- a slot to hold the previously removed element
- an operation to add an element to the front of the queue

This new class can be used wherever it is needed, and it will make available all those operations defined for the FIFO queue classthe operations defined for the FIFO queue are inherited by this new subclass. When the program requires an instance of the original FIFO queue, it is still there to be used; when the program needs an instance of the DE-queue (which, in one form, is what has been defined by the new subclass), it can also be produced.

Inheritance is the process of obtaining information and operations (slots and operations) from more general classes by their subclasses. Inheritance can be simple in the sense that the subclass has only one superclass, or it can be multiple in the sense that a subclass can have more than one superclass. For the purposes of this book, multiple inheritance is ignored; it is somewhat controversial and involves complications which are best left until the reader has more experince of class-based programming.

An issue which can often cause problems is that of containment. Containment is a property of objects such that objects contain instances of other objects. In the case of the FIFO queue we might want to store the queue's elements in a singly linked list. This list is an instance of a singly linked list class. The FIFO queue class, when instantiated, contains instances of the singly linked list class; the FIFO contains the list. Components (values stored in slots, or slot 'fillers') that are contained in classes are just objects that can be manipulated—there is nothing strange about them. However, contained objects have nothing to do with their container's inheritance hierarchy; contained objects are just values, whereas inheritance is a relation between classes. A contained object can be defined by inheritance, but inheritance is defined in terms of its superclasses, not the superclasses of its container. An object can contain objects of any type or class provided that their containing slots are declared.

Inheritance makes programs very much shorter because it shares information between classes. It avoids the problem of requiring the programmer to rewrite operations when a small change in data type occurs. For example, consider the case of strings in Pascal. Frequently, Pascal implementations allow a type called 'array of character,' but not one that represents variable length strings. When declaring an array of character in Pascal, the array bounds must be provided. Two arrays with different bounds are considered to be of distinct types by the Pascal type-checking procedure. If a set of Pascal procedures is written to manipulate strings as arrays of character, the set must be rewritten if the bounds of the array are altered. If a program requires strings of two different lengths (say, one of 80 characters and one of 32), the procedures dealing with the 80 character string must be rewritten to handle those of length 32. In an object-oriented program this does not occur. Instead, a general string class is defined. The class can be specialised to deal with strings of different lengths (actually, in most object-oriented languages, such specialisation is not required because dynamic storage allocation is provided); the specialisation will automatically take care of the procedures defined for the string type (upper and lower bound information must be provided in the form of slots in the basic class).

Encapsulation and inheritance are two primary characteristics of object-oriented programs.

## 2.4 Abstract and Concrete Classes

Above, it was implied that every class can be instantiated. This is, in fact, incorrect. Sometimes, it makes no sense to instantiate a class. For example, if we are building a graphics program, we will need to represent polygons. Some operations will be performable on all polygons: for example, computing interior points, returning the coordinates of vertices or filling the polygon with colour. Polygons come in different flavours; there are polygons with three, four, five, ..., sides. The details of the representation of each flavour will be a little bit different (the vertices coordinates might be recorded in an array, and the length of the array will depend on the number of sides). The most general operations apply to all polygons and are independent of the number of sides or colour; these operations can be collected together and represented in a most general polygon class (the 'root' class for polygons). However, because it makes no sense to create an instance of a polygon without a specification of the number and coordinates of its vertices, it makes no sense to instantiate the root polygon class.

A class for which it makes no sense to create instances is called an abstract class. The root polygon class is an abstract class. Classes which can be meaningfully instantiated are called concrete classes.

It makes sense to define subclasses for both abstract and concrete classes. It can make sense to define an abstract class for red polygons if they are going to be used enough. An abstract red polygon class can be specialised to red triangles, red rectangles, red squares and so on. Concrete classes can also be specialised via the definition of subclasses. The queue classes in the last section were all concrete classes.

As will be seen, Dylan allows programmers to annotate classes to inform the system that an abstract or concrete class is being defined. This allows the compiler to trap attempts at instantiating abstract classes.

## 2.5 Methods and Overloading

So far, we have seen that classes are defined in terms of data elements (slots) and operations. A class encapsulates the slots from which it is defined; slots are private data storage and represent the current state of a class. The operations allow users access to the slots of a class, and they also serve as functions which implement the abstract functions that the class's specification requires. For example, the class representing a set has operations to perform (among other things) the following actions:

- union

- intersection
- difference
- membership test
- add a new member
- test for emptiness
- calculate the cardinality
- iterate over the set

These operations define, in part, what it is for something to be a set. Something is a set if and only if it is an unordered collection of objects (its members) and which permits the above-listed operations (and some others) to be performed on it. The results of many of the above operations are new sets (union, intersection, difference).

It is the methods of a class that perform the operations the class requires. A FIFO queue is defined as a linear sequence of elements and the following operations:

- add an element to the back
- remove the front element
- test for emptiness

In addition, operations can be defined to calculate the length of the queue and to empty the queue of all its elements.

A FIFO queue is a collection of elements that are organised in a particular way, together with a set of operations which act upon the collection. The operations, in a way, animate the collection and allow it to be used in ways that the collection alone cannot.

Methods (operations) are inherited in a way identical to slots. Thus, a method defined for a superclass can be directly used by one of its subclasses. Consider a class which implements a set of integers and which does not have a method for computing the cardinality of the set. The class has the following methods:

- union
- intersection
- difference
- membership test
- add a new member
- test for emptiness

but no method to calculate cardinality. A subclass of the set class can be defined in which cardinality is provided. One way to do this is to add a slot to count the elements as they are added (there is no way to remove elements if the difference and intersection create new sets, an approach which is entirely reasonable). This would require an addition to the method which adds new members, and we will discuss this shortly. Meanwhile, the simpler approach is employed. A new method is defined which iterates over the collection of members that the class holds (uses to implement the collection); every time the method encounters a new element, it adds one to its counter. In Dylan, we might represent the class as:

```
define class <set> (<object>)
      slot elems :: <list>, init-value: #()
end class <set>;
```

and the counted version can be defined as:

```
define class <counted-set> (<set>)
      slot card :: <integer>, init-value: 0
end class <counted-set>;
```

So **<counted-set>** inherits the elems slot from **<set>**. It extends **<set>** by the addition of the slot **card** which records the cardinality whenever it is computed. The cardinality method might be implemented as:

```
define method cardinality (s :: <counted-set>)
      card(s) := 0;
      for (e in elems(s))
          card := card + 1
      end for;
      card
end method cardinality;
```

The cardinality method is in addition to the other methods defined for class **<set>**. Thus it is possible to compute the union of two instances of **<counted-set>** by calling the union method defined for **<set>**. In an identical fashion, the intersection of to instances of **<counted-set>** can be computed via a call to the intersection method for **<set>**.

There are two alternatives to this scheme. One alternative involves a complete redefinition of the method which adds elements to instances of **<set>**; this redefined method is attached to class **<counted-set>**. The other involves the definition of a new method, but very little other work. We will look at these alternatives in order.

The first alternative involves the redefinition of the method which adds elements to the set. We can assume that **<counted-set>** is defined as above. The add element method first tests to see if the element to be added is already in the set; if it is, no further action is performed. If the element is not present, it is added to the collection and the card counter is incremented by one. The method in Dylan might look like:

```
define method add-element (e ::  <integer>,
                           s ::  <counted-set>)
      if (~member?(e,elems(s),test:  \==))
         elems := pair(e,elems);
         card := card + 1
      end if
end method add-element;
```

This scheme requires sets to be constructed an element at a time; a constructor method (the operation which creates instances of the class) for sets which took, say, a list of elements and converted it into a list, would require a call to a function to compute the cardinality. This would require some redefinition of the constructor, and it could involve some redefinition of the other methods defined for **<set>** and which need adjusting to cater for **<counted-set>**.

The second alternative is considerably more elegant. It requires the language to provide a way of calling methods that are defined for superclasses. In Dylan, as in Smalltalk, CLOS and Telos, this function is provided. The name of this function is next-method in Dylan. What **next-method** does is to search upwards in the inheritance chain from the class in which it is called. It finds the closest method with the same name as the one in which it was called and supplies its caller's arguments to that method. In other words, next-method calls the next most general method with the same name in the class's inheritance chain.

If we were to define the add-element method for **<set>** as:

```
define method add-element (e ::  <integer>, s ::  <set>)
      if (~member?(e,elems(s),test:  \==))
         elems := pair(e,elems)
         end if
end method add-element;
```

we could now define a corresponding method for **<counted-set>** as:

```
define method add-element (e ::  <integer>,
                           cs ::  <counted-set>)
      next-method();
      card := card + 1
end method add-element;
```

What happens now is the following. If we want to add an element to an instance of **<counted-set>**, we call add-element, supplying it with appropriate values. The add-element method calls next-method and passes its parameters to it. The next-method function searches along the chain of superclasses of **<counted-set>** until it finds the add-element method defined for **<set>**; this version of the method (which is defined for a more general class than **<counted-set>**) is then applied to the arguments passed to the original call.

Remember that an instance of a class counts as an instance of all and any of its superclasses; the slots that are to be acted upon by the more general method will be present (the more general method knows nothing about the slots added in the definition of the subclass). Thus, in the **next-method** call above, the element **e** will be added to the **elems** slot of **cs** because **cs** inherits that slot from **<set>**.

By means of calls to next-method, methods for subclasses can be defined in a simple manner, and in a manner which does not require the programmer to know about the internals of the superclass. The next-method operation allows subclasses to be defined while maintaining abstraction and encapsulation. The next-method approach to subclass method definition is to be preferred whenever alternatives are presented to the programmer. A multiset is a set which allows duplicate elements. A multiset is sometimes called a bag. An example of a multiset is:

$$\{1, 2, 3, 1, 25\}$$

Another is:

$$\{\{1, 2\}, \{3, 4, 5\}, \{\}, \{2, 1\}\}$$

Multisets and sets are very closely related. Indeed, many of the operations defined over sets have direct analogues in terms of multisets. Thus it is possible to define union, intersection, difference, membership tests and so on. In a similar fashion, it is possible to add two integers, add two floating point numbers and add two complex numbers. The operations just mentioned are given similar names, but they operate on different types. The input types of set union are two sets, and the result is a set; the inputs to set intersection must be a pair of sets, and the result is a set. The inputs to multiset union are two multisets, and the result is a multiset. The inputs to integer addition are two integers, and the result is an integer. And so on.

The definition of a function, operation or method with the same name but different input and output types is called overloading. In Dylan syntax, we can have:

```
define method union (s1 :: <set>, s2 :: <set>) ...
define method union (m1 :: <multiset>,
                     m2 :: <multiset>)
      ...
define method \+ (i1 :: <integer>, i2 :: <integer>) ...
define method \+ (r1 :: <real>, r2 :: <real>) ...
define method \+ (c1 :: <complex>, c2 :: <complex>) ...
```

The first pair of methods overload the union method by requiring it to operate on pairs of sets and on pairs of multisets. The three following methods overload the addition operator, first by defining it for integers, then for reals, and finally for complex numbers.

When a method is overloaded, the types of its arguments are used to determine which algorithm will be applied. In the case of the plus method, which takes two integers, the fact that plus is being applied to a pair of integers determines that the method with two input integers is called, not the one which applies to pairs of reals.

The methods for adding elements to a set—the one which does not count the number of elements and the one which does—are an example of overloading. In this case, the method is specialised for the **<counted-set>** subclass of **<set>**; this is a mild form of overloading.

Overloading is an important and powerful property of a programming language. It allows the programmer to employ the same name for a cluster of methods that have some semantic property in common. In the case of union, what the various methods have in common is that they join two collections together; in the case of plus, the methods all perform addition (but on objects of different types and which require different arguments). Overloading allows methods to be polymorphic. Polymorphism is a powerful facility and allows namespaces to be kept uncluttered.

## 2.6 Static and Dynamic Binding

The issue of static versus dynamic binding is concerned with how methods are associated with classes and how they are looked up at run-time. Methods are associated with classes; they take classes as arguments and return them as results. As has been seen, a method can be defined in one class and specialised in one of that class's subclasses. In such a circumstance, when a method is called it is necessary to determine which method is required; is the one defined for the subclass required or is it the one defined for the superclass?

Under a static binding regime, methods are statically associated with classes. This is the kind of binding method employed in C++, for example. If we have a class which defines a print method and we define subclasses which also define methods to print their contents on the screen, static binding will always force the system to select the root class's print routine. What is wanted is the print method for the particular calling class. In other words, the subclasses need to override the method for printing. The reason why the wrong method is called is that the compiler cannot know about other methods when it is compiling the print method for the superclass. This method becomes available for use by all subclasses.

What is very often required is dynamic binding. In this scheme, a search is made at run-time for the most appropriate method to apply. The rule is that the method to be found closest to the calling class is the one that is applied.

If we had static binding, a call to add-element with two instances of **<counted-set>** would end up with a call to the method defined for **<set>**. What we want, and what polymorphism (overloading) requires, is that the version for **<counted-set>** should be called. Since the arguments are both of type **<counted-set>**, a run-time search starts with that class to determine the closest method. In this case, **<counted-set>** itself defines a method and this is the one that is used. Now, suppose we define another kind of set, one that counts its elements as they are added, but which also provides another kind of difference operation called symmetric difference. This class, `<sd-counted-set>`, is a subclass of `<counted-set>`, and it inherits the add-element method from `<counted-set>`.

Under dynamic binding the following will happen. If we now have an instance of `<sd-counted-set>` and we add an element to it, the search begins with `<sd-counted-set>`. Class `<sd-counted-set>` does not define an add-element method, but inherits it. The search then proceeds to the superclass of `<sd-counted-set>`, which is class `<countedset>`. This time, an add-element method is defined, and this is the one that is used to add the new element to the instance of `<sd-countedset>`; this is what we want because it increments the counter by one as well as adding the element.

Dylan uses dynamic binding, so no problems will be encountered.

## 2.7 Building Object-Oriented Programs

A fundamental observation which is borne out by experience is that once a program's data structures have been designed, the rest follows with relative ease. Thus, the starting point for the design of an object-oriented program is the data structures. However, the data structures are the program's classes. The main data structures also correspond to the primary concepts in the program. For example, when building a window-based interface, one of the primary concepts is that of the window; the window is also a major data structure. When building a compiler, one of the major concepts is the representation of the program's syntactic form—the parse tree can also be one of the most important data structures in the program. When simulating aircraft, the individual aircraft must be represented by data structures of some kind; it is also the case that aircraft comprise one of the central concepts of an airspace simulation.

The process begins by identifying the primary concepts for the problem to be solved. Once they have been identified, they can be recorded and related. These diagrams depict how classes are related to each other in terms of the sub/superclass relationships; that is, they record the derivation of specialised classes from more general ones.

The class hierarchy diagram will almost certainly be revised a number of times during design, particularly as subclasses are combined and isolated. The process which follows from the identification of the primary concepts (classes) is the refinement of these classes. The question to be asked at this stage is 'what are the concepts which, when combined, form the primary ones?'

The answer to this question yields a set of classes which combine to form the primary one. Some of the second set of classes might be primitive ones (integer, boolean etc.), but some might not (for example, sets or other collections not directly provided by the language). The question 'what are the concepts which, when combined, form the primary ones?' should be asked until all the classes identified can be constructed directly from the classes provided by the programming language being used (so, a program in C++ might involve the definition of a list type, but one in CLOS or Dylan will not; similarly, a Dylan or CLOS program might employ the built-in table classes, while a C++ program will have an explicit programmer-defined class for tables).

This refinement process is applied to every primary concept. The relationships between the classes derived by the refinement process can be recorded. For example, it might be found that classes C and D both require the composition of class E with some other structures. In this case, classes C and D have a common component. When common components occur, it is essential to record the fact because the interfaces presented by common components must be such that they can be appropriately used in possibly widely differing contexts. For example, classes C and D might make different assumptions about what kinds of object class E deals with. For example, C might construe the interface in terms of strings, while D construes it in terms of a pointer to some kind of structure. Common components are important because they afford the programmer the opportunity to reduce work by providing more general objects. Common components must be reduced in the same way as other classes.

During the refinement process, account should be taken of the methods defined for each class. At this stage, it does not amount to a detailed definition, only to recording the operations that must be performed. For example, when defining a set class, a record of the fact that union must be provided could be made. When defining a symbol table class, it might be noted that an insertion but no deletion method is required. Common operations can also be detected as the refinement process continues; common operations might have different signatures (input and output type specifications), but they might be indicative of an underlying concept that needs to be made explicit—what happens will vary.

Sometimes, more than one class will have methods in common. If the classes are related by inheritance there is no problem, but in other cases there might be an issue to resolve. This can sometimes be a simple consequence of the nature of the classes. For example, container classes often have methods to insert and deleter elements; this is just a fact about containers. Sometimes, inspection and analysis reveal that there are common operations which can be represented by a common data structure (involving representation chagne across the interface, perhaps). This could indicate that a new class or set of classes should be defined.

Once a collection of hierarchy diagrams has been produced, the detailes of the classes thus exposed can be determined. In the author's experience, this has often been a relatively straightforward matter, closely related to standard programming methods. The overall structure of the prgoram can be determined from the relationship between the primary concepts. It is important to maintain modularity, but it is a desirable goal to reduce the number of classes (i.e., the number of concepts—this is called 'Occam's razor'). One way to do this is to identify common concpets and to design their class representation in as general a way as possible. If this proves difficult of impossible, a class can be defined which captures the general case and subclasses defined for particulars; the general case will include a representation of what is common to all the particular cases. This is, in general, an approach to the design of classes, secondary classes in particular.

Finally, when programming individual classes, modularity should be respected. This does not imply, however, that auxilliary functions should be used. Good programming methods should always apply, and code shoul dbe written in as clear and concise a fashion as possible.

The example program in Chapter 3 was designed along the above lines. Implementation, because of various deadlines, some of which relate to the publication of this book, required that the analysis proccess be curtailed sooner than the author would have ideally preferred. However, primary concepts were first indentified. For the most part, thre were no interactions between the concepts. Next, the concepts were refined. Refinement was, for the most part, relatively simple; Dylan provides a good many high-level concepts which can be included immediately in the program. Where theprogram would benefit is in a more detailed and careful design of the underlying 'database' structure. It is, we believe, somewhat messy and perhaps a little inflexible. The reader might care to take the outline design and refine it to a more careful result.

# Chapter 3

# An Example Dylan Program

## 3.1 Introduction

This chapter contains an example Dylan program of moderate size. The aim is to present a Dylan program which exploits a number of features of the language so that the reader can derive an overall impression of it. Dylan is an object-oriented language, so classes are thoroughly exploited and methods attached to classes as a matter of course; one generic method is explicitly declared. The focus of the example is on object-oriented programming; the other types and primitives are considered to be relatively straightforward and should be appreciated by the reader after consultation of the language reference manual.

The example program implements a very simple database system. The database is intended to record information about the weekly or monthly food purchased by a family. The idea is that a shopping list is made out and the food purchased. From the receipt, the prices of the various items can be recorded in the database, together with the date and the name of the shop where the food was bought. This information allows a family to calculate the differences in costs between the various shops visited, as well as providing trend information about costs and calculating the rate of inflation. Other information can be extracted from the database as and when required (e.g. the amount of butter purchased over a given period).

The program implements the main data storage structures together with methods for their manipulation. This component is simply referred to as the 'database'.

The 'database' component is relatively completely defined in the program. Facilities (methods) are defined that allow the user to write queries, but no explicit queries are included. It is left as an exercise to the reader to complete the various query methods and to run them.

The example program was designed to allow optimisations and alterations of a number of kinds. These modifications can be used as exercises by the reader, either as re-workings of the current program or as extensions to it (some are noted in the text). The program does not employ the module construct provided by Dylan, and this is an omission which should be rectified as a matter of urgency. In addition, access to disk files should be provided. These two issues are left to the reader.

Because of the size of the example, it has not been possible to include uses of all the data types provided by the language. For example, vectors and arrays are not used at all, and strings receive only a cursory glance. No use is made of introspection, nor is there any modularisation, nor use of libaries. If all of these facilities were included, the example program would be some orders of magnitude larger than it is.

Furthermore, I/O is not included, and this for a number of reasons, the most significant being that the [6] does not specify I/O primitives, a fact which allows implementers complete freedom in the way in which they treat this area.

The example program was written using Carnegie-Mellon University's mindy-1.3 implementation of Dylan, running on a Sun SparcStation 2 under SunOS. The program was fully tested and judged to be functioning correctly. It is conceivable that differences between mindy 1.3 and other implementations of Dylan (including differences between releases of mindy) will entail changes to the program text.

The chapter is organised as follows. In the next section, the details of the program's specification are given. Following that, the class hierarchy of the resulting program is depicted. This hierarchy shows how the various classes which comprise the program are related. In addition to this hierarchy, information is included about the inclusion relationships between the program's classes. It is common in object-oriented programs for classes to have components whose values are classes; this constitutes important structural information about the program. Thereafter, the various classes and their associated methods are described in detail. The descriptions relate to the implementation details and some discussion of the options available. Each section can be considered a separate module.

## 3.2 Specification

Most UK families buy their food from supermarkets, typically making one trip each week. Some families buy their food on a monthly basis, but the norm appears to be weekly. The choice of supermarket from which the food is bought varies from region to region, but nationally there is a more restricted choice. Depending upon one's definition, there are about five supermarket chains with national coverage, and prices are roughly the same, with variation occurring between individual lines. For example, butter might be a bit cheaper in supermarket A than in B, but washing powder might be cheaper in B than in A.

The retail price index (the measure of inflation) computed by the UK government is viewed by people as a little unreliable. It is an average and omits a number of items which are commonly purchased by families and it also includes items which are rarely purchased; the omitted items tend to be expensive, while the additional ones tend to be cheap. The subjective impression that one has is that prices are rising more steeply than is officially claimed. In order to plan expenditure, more accurate information, and information more closely tailored to an individual family's purchasing patterns, must be maintained.

The program in this chapter was written in response to the above requirements. The program assumes that a family goes to one supermarket per week (or per month) and makes all purchases there. A list of items to be purchased is either constructed prior to the shopping expedition, or is reconstructed from the receipt issued by the supermarket, which lists all the items purchased, as well as their cost; the receipt is more important, but the information will be referred to as the 'shopping list'. The shopping list, together with the costs of the items purchased, are entered into the program. The information on the receipt is entered into the program so that it has a complete and accurate record of what was bought and what it cost.

The items purchased naturally fall into categories of various kinds. Categories can be defined along the lines of meat, fish, dairy products, vegetables and so on. In addition, information on packaging is useful. Packaging affects the amounts purchased, and differences in packaging can lead to differences in price. For example, it is not possible to buy 550 g of borlotti beans if the standard can sizes are 250 and 440 g. The price of fresh, unpacked cheese can be considerably lower than that of the processed, vacuum-sealed form. Eggs are sold in packs of six; it is usually impossible to buy eggs in anything other than multiples of six. Canned vegetables and fresh also differ; canned fruit often comes with lots of syrup which can get in the way of a number of recipes.

The database is designed so that packaging information is recorded. Packaging also affects the way in which unit costs are computed. Cheese is bought by mass; milk is bought by volume; haddock fillets are often bought by number. In many cases, canned goods are sold in two standard sizes—small and large—so the mass is, in a sense, irrelevant. The unit by which an item is bought is also recorded by the program. The program has representations for volume (in litres), mass (in kilograms), and in units (e.g. for eggs, frozen haddock fillets, and cans). From this information, the unit cost of a food item is computed. Packaging information must be added to the item type and cost on the receipt when entering the data into the program.

The shopping list and item costs (the receipt, that is) are entered into the program. The items are classified according to the information on the shopping list. The unit cost is calculated and the information stored in the program's data structures. The program must be organised in such a way that information of a variety of different kinds can be extracted. For example, calculation of the total cost of a particular foodstuff can be performed, and the difference between the cost of an item purchased three months ago and that of one purchased this week can also be calculated. Because the program records the name of the shop at which items were purchased, it is possible to perform these calculations and to see how they differ between stores. These calculations can be performed across a variety of foodstuffs, so an overall comparsion between supermarkets can be performed.

The program must be able to check its input and to be extensible. For example, the program should be given information about what counts as a foodstuff. For example, we might want to exclude shoe polish as an item because it is an incidental which is purchased only occasionally (and which is relatively inexpensive anyway). In addition, the packaging and unit must be supplied so that the program can check that ten litres of lamb chops have not been bought. These types and associated information must be represented in a form which is extensible, so facilities for extending the range of foods must be provided. In addition, it is necessary to be able to add new supermarkets to the program.

## 3.3 Amounts and Time

In this section, we describe two simple but important classes used in the program. The two classes represent amounts of money and purchase dates. Every item purchased from a shop has a cost, and is bought on a particular day. If one wants to perform analyses of the family's rate of inflation for the range of foods and other items one purchases (which differ from those in the Government's 'Shopping bag', and hence give a different inflation rate) this information must be maintained. In addition, if one wants to compare the prices of similar items purchased from different shops, the difference in time between the two purchases might be significant. Finally, the database holds information about weekly shopping, so the date and cost of the shopping each week must be recorded.

The first class to be considered is the **<amount>** class. This class represents an amount of money in pounds sterling (with a minor adjustment of the code it can be made to represent any decimal currency). The class must hold an amount represented in numbers of pounds and numbers of pence. Its definition is:

```
define class <amount> (<object>)
       slot pounds ::  <integer>, init-keyword:  pounds:,
                                  init-value:  0;
       slot pence ::  <integer>,
                      required-init-keyword:  pence:;
end class <amount>;
```

The class is an immediate descendent of **<object>**, and can, therefore, inherit every operation defined on **<object>**. In particular, inheritance from **<object>** allows such necessary things as generic function dispatch to work. The **<amount>** class has two slots: **pounds** and **pence**, each of which is of type **<integer>**. It was decided that a type would be associated with the slots. One reason for this is that it should be impossible to represent fractions of pounds because they are represented by the value of the **pence** slot; equally, fractions of a penny must be prohibited because the UK penny does not have any legal subdivisions (the halfpenny was withdrawn from circulation some years ago). These semantic considerations led to the decision to specialise the class's slots; furthermore, by specialising the slots to **<integer>**, the semantic constraints just outlined are enforced by the code.

The slots are associated with initialisation keywords (init-keywords). The **pounds** slot has an init-keyword **pounds:**, and it has also been given a default initial value (**init-value:**), the reason for which being that it is still possible to buy something which costs less than one pound. When such an item is bought, it would be extremely tiresome to have to represent the cost as zero pounds and the number of pence. The init-keywords assist in this as follows.

Init-keywords are used when creating instances of a class. A required init-keyword must always be used when creating an instance; an init-keyword can be omitted, particularly if an init-value is also provided. Thus, it is possible to create an instance of class **<amount>** omitting the number of pounds but specifying the number of pence. In every case of **<amount>** instance creation, the number of pennies must be mentioned. For example, the following is a legal call to make for **<amount>**:

```
make(<amount>,pence: 72)
```

The instance created as a result of this call represents the amount of 72 pence. The following call creates an instance which represents the sum of £1.81:

```
make(<amount>,pounds: 1,pence: 81)
```

The following call is, however, illegal:

```
make(<amount>,pounds: 10)
```

The reason that it is illegal is that there is no parameter to specify the number of pence; the number of pence must always be explicitly stated in the call to **make**. The correct form of the last call is:

```
make(<amount>,pounds: 10,pence: 0)
```

It is tiresome to call **make** every time we need an amount of money to be represented. Also, when calling **make**, there are no checks on the actual values passed to the program. The following method is defined to create instances of **<amount>**:

```
define method make-amount (#key pounds (0), pence (0))
       if (pounds < 0)
          error("Cannot make amount with negative pounds")
       elseif (pence < 0)
          error("Cannot make amount with negative pence")
       end if;
       make(<amount>,pounds:  pounds, pence:  pence)
end method make-amount;
```

Note that the method checks that the amounts of pounds and pence are not negative. A negative amount would represent a refund in some conditions. For the application considered here, amounts represent costs, and negative costs are not permitted. Hence, the two tests

The **make-amount** method has two parameters, both of which are keyword parameters which have default values of zero. The keywords can be passed to the method in either order, or can be omitted altogether. An instance of **<amount>** can be created by:

```
make-amount(pounds: 1, pence: 81)
```

or by:

```
make-amount(pence: 81, pounds: 1)
```

An amount in pence only can be created:

```
make-amount(pence: 72)
```

An amount representing nothing can be created with:

```
make-amount()
```

(this uses the default values for both parameters).

Now, a word is in order about the use of keyword arguments in **make-amount**, and the requirement that one of the parameters to make is a required init-keyword, while the other is not required. It would seem that everything can be handled simply by use of the **make-amount** function; all the stipulations are enforced by it, and this fact makes the constraints on the **<amount>** class's slots redundant.

The approach adopted above places constraints upon calls to **make**. If within this module, or within some other module, there is a direct call to **make** which has **<amount>** as its first parameter, the protocol defined above will ensure that the sum must be expressed in whole pence at the very least. Anyone who attempts to provide values which do not conform to the protocol will cause an error. It can be argued that every instance of **<amount>** must be created via a call to **make-amount**. This is what should be the case, but there is nothing to prevent someone from ignoring **make-amount** in favour of the primitive call. Furthermore, within the code which implements the **<amount>** class, the **make-amount** method is not always used (the reason being that it is quicker at run-time to call the make primitive direct, and for the reason that where such calls are made, the relevant constraints hold); the protocol which has been defined for **<amount>** makes it possible only to specify a negative sum, and this is unlikely, given that amounts are entered into the database via calls to make-amount (**make-amount** should be an exported method which users employ; since we are not exploiting the module system, we are not making use of the export facility). Finally, the protocol that we have chosen also exemplifies more of the Dylan language in use—this is a minor point as far as the code is concerned, however.

The next method is a little utility. It is a predicate which is true if the sum represented by an instance of **<amount>** is less than one pound.

```
define method pence-only? (amount :: <amount>)
      pounds(amount) = 0
end method pence-only?;
```

The method takes a single parameter which is specialised to **<amount>**. It tests the pounds slot (notice how we use the functional representation for slotnames) to see whether it is equal to zero. The predicate exemplifies the convention that Dylan methods which implement predicates have names ending with '?'

The above method could also have been written:

```
define method pence-only? (amount :: <amount>)
      amount.pence = 0
end method pence-only?;
```

using the so-called 'functional' notation for slot access. In the actual code, all accesses to slots are written in the form:

```
<slotname>(<instance-name>)
```

This is a convention which is adopted uniformly. The reason for adopting this convention is that it resembles standard function application more than does the alternative. The notation adopted here is, we believe, clearer and more intuitive; it also has the advantage of not containing small punctuation characters which can easily be lost when quickly reading a method.

The following two methods convert between pounds and pence. The first routine converts an amount in pounds and pence to an amount expressed in pence. There are 100 pennies to a pound, so the calculation is extremely simple:

```
define method pounds-to-pence (amount :: <amount>)
      (100 * pounds(amount)) + pence(amount)
end method pounds-to-pence;
```

The second conversion method is a little more complex. It takes an amount expressed in pennies and converts it into an instance of class **<amount>** which represents that same sum in terms of pounds and pence. The method employs a loop which terminates when the number of pence is less than 100 (i.e. when the amount is less than one pound). Until that occurs, the number of pence is decremented by 100 (by one pound) and the number of pounds incremented by one. Finally, the method creates and returns an instance of class **<amount>** to represent the calculated amount.

```
define method pence-to-pounds (amount :: <integer>)
      let pounds = 0;
      let pence = amount;
          while (pence > 99)
                pence := pence - 100;
                pounds := pounds + 1;
          end while;
          make(<amount>,pounds: pounds,pence: pence)
end method pence-to-pounds;
```

An alternative to the above would be a method which does not return an instance of **<amount>**, but, rather, returns two values: one representing the number of pounds, another representing the number of pence. In this case, the last line would be:

```
values(pounds,pence)
```

It was decided that an instance of **<amount>** would be returned in the interests of uniformity. The program as a whole deals with instances of class **<amount>** whenever it deals with money, and a case in which a sum of money was represented by two integers would break this uniformity down.

It is also possible to remove the **while** loop from the **pence-to-pounds** method. Instead, an integer division by 100 and a remainder by 100 could have been used. The **while** loop was used for expository reasons, as an example of how such a loop looks. If we wanted to write a real database application for the shopping problem, the division and remainder approach would have been preferred.

The next four methods are examples of relational operations defined over class **<amount>**. In each case, they overload the corresponding relation which is defined over numbers. The four methods show that methods can be defined which extend those already provided by the Dylan language, and can be defined for any suitable classes. The examples also show that the operator being overloaded must be quoted when used to name the method. Thus, instead of writing:

```
define method < (amount1 etc.
```

We must write:

```
define method \< (amount1 etc.
```

The '\' before the '<' acting as a quotation character.

The methods for the relational operators are as follows:

```
define method \< (amount1 :: <amount>, amount2 :: <amount>)
       pounds-to-pence(amount1) < pounds-to-pence(amount2)
end method \<;

define method \= (amount1 :: <amount>, amount2 :: <amount>)
       pounds-to-pence(amount1) = pounds-to-pence(amount2)
end method \=;

define method \~= (amount1 :: <amount>, amount2 :: <amount>)
       ~(amount1 = amount2)
end method \~=;

define method \<= (amount1 :: <amount>, amount2 :: <amount>)
       (amount1 < amount2) | (amount1 = amount2)
end method \<=;
```

With the addition of a few extra methods for performing comparisons, the file defining class `<amount>` is complete.

The class representing times is used to express the purchase dates of items of shopping. Everything that is bought is bought on a particular day, and this information is recorded in the database so that costs can be compared across time.

The class representing purchase dates is defined as:

```
define class <purchase-date> (<object>)
       slot day :: <integer>, init-keyword: dd:;
       slot month :: <symbol>, init-keyword: mm:;
       slot year :: <integer>, init-keyword: yy:;
       slot dayno :: <integer>;
       slot monthno :: <integer>;
end class <purchase-date>;
```

The class is a subclass of `<object>`, so standard things will work with it. Time is represented within instances of `<purchase-date>` in one of two forms: in terms of day, month, year (where day and year are numbers, and month is a symbol); thus `02 #"feb" 96` is a valid date, and in terms of day number, month number and year number (thus `33 89` is a valid date in this second format). (The month number is also computed, so `33 89` would have `monthno` set to 02.) The second format can be used when making certain numerical calculations.

It is always useful to be able to read the contents of a class's instances in some useful and legible format, so a method is defined to perform this task

```
define method show (pd :: <purchase-date>)
```

```
        print(format("Date:  %d/%s/%d.",
                day(pd),as(<string>,month(pd)),year(pd)))
end method show;
```

The method uses the function **print** (provided by the mindy implementation) to perform the actual printing, and uses the **format** function (again, a mindy intrinsic) to format the date into a convenient form. The form that is printed is the one in which months are represented by symbols. The format directive states that the date is printed as the string 'Date:' followed by a decimal number (specified by the **%d**) directive, a string (specified by the **%s** directive), and a second decimal number (the format directives are roughly the same as in C). The format string is followed by the required number of parameters, each of which extracts the appropriate slot from the instance of **<purchase-date>** supplied as the parameter to the entire method. Worthy of note is the call:

```
as(<string>,month(pd))
```

which converts a symbol (the contents of **month(pd)**) into a string; the Dylan intrinsic function as converts the type of its second argument to the type specified as its first argument. In this case, the symbol representing the month is converted to a string before printing (format appears not to handle symbols directly, at least in mindy-1.3).

Next, there is a method for comparing purchase dates. This method overloads the Dylan = method as follows:

```
define method \= (pd1 ::  <purchase-date>,
                  pd2 ::  <purchase-date>)
        (year(pd1) == year(pd2))
            & (dayno(pd1) == dayno(pd2))
            & (monthno(pd1) == monthno(pd2))
end method \=;
```

Note again that the quoting convention is employed. The method performs comparison on the basis of the numerical form of the date; this has the clear implication that some kind of checking or automatic conversion must be performed when entering dates so that the two representations remain correctly aligned (i.e. a mechanism must be provided to prevent the user writing **26 #"feb" 96** as **26 10 96**).

The process of ensuring that such mismatches cannot occur is as follows. First, a table is defined which records the name of each month, its ordinal number in the year, and the number of days it contains. This table is implemented as a list of triples (each triple represented by a list rather than a vector—this is purely a convenience); the entire table is defined as a constant:

```
define constant $year-info =
        #( #(#"january",1,31),
        #(#"february",2,28),
```

```
        #(#"march",3,31),
        #(#"april",4,30),
        #(#"may",5,31),
        #(#"june",6,30),
        #(#"july",7,31),
        #(#"august",8,31),
        #(#"september",9,30),
        #(#"october",10,31),
        #(#"november",11,30),
        #(#"december",12,31));
```

Note that the Dylan convention of starting a constant with a '$' sign. (In a similar fashion, global variables start and end with '*').

Next, an interface to the table is defined in terms of a number of access methods. The first method returns the symbolic name of a month, the second the ordinal number of the month, and the third the number of days in the month (note that the case of 29 days for February when it is a leap year has been ignored). In each case, the method takes a parameter which is bound to a list; the list is one of the triples stored in **$year-info**:

```
define method month-name (minfo :: <list>)
       head(minfo)
end method month-name;

define method month-number (minfo :: <list>)
       head(tail(minfo))
end method month-number;

define method days-in-month (minfo :: <list>)
       head( tail( tail(minfo)))
end method days-in-month;
```

The next method checks that the symbolic name of the month is valid. This method is called when creating a new instance of **<purchase-date>**; the creation method expects the month to be given as a symbol.

```
define method valid-month? (month-name :: <symbol>)
       member?(month-name,
               #( #"january", #"february",#"march",
               #"april", #"may", #"june",
               #"july", #"july", #"august",
               #"september", #"october", #"november"),
               test: \=)
end method valid-month?;
```

The **valid-month?** predicate calls the Dylan intrinsic function **member?** to determine whether **month-name** is valid; if **month-name** occurs in the list which is **member?**'s second argument, it is valid. Note that **member?** in Dylan is a second- order function; its third argument is an equality predicate (in this case identity). In this case, the name of the equality is quoted because it is an operator symbol.

The next thing to do is to calculate the ordinal number of the month in the year. The argument to the method is a symbol which represents the month's name (e.g. **#"feb"**) and the result should be a number in the range 1 to 12.

```
define method calc-monthno (m-name :: <symbol>)
  if (~valid-month?(m-name))
     error(
     "Cannot calculate month number: unknown month %s.",
     as(<string>, m-name))
  end if;
  let mno :: <integer> = 0;
  let year-data = $year-info;
  let month-data = head(year-data);
      while (month-name(month-data) ~= m-name)
            year-data := tail(year-data);
            month-data := head(year-data)
      end while;
  month-number(month-data)
end method calc-monthno;
```

The method first checks that the symbol is the name of a real month. If this test (implemented by a call to **valid-month?**) fails, an error is signalled. Notice that the symbol '~ appears immediately before **valid-month?**; this symbol represents logical negation and the condition-part of the initial **if**-expression is read '*not valid-month?(m-name)*'. The error is raised by the standard function **error**, which takes a format string as its first argument and a **#rest** parameter which is bound to the arguments required by the format string.

If the symbol correctly names a month, the main part of the method is executed. The body of the main part of the method is a while loop which iterates over (a copy of) the **$year-info** table until an entry has been found whose symbolic month name is identical to the method's parameter. Given that the month name has already been verified, it is impossible, short of a system error, for this loop not to return a triple containing month information. When the loop terminates, the **month-number** is extracted by means of a call to the selector function.

Next, it is necessary to compute the number of the day. This calculation returns the number of the day within the year (in this case, dates are represented in ISO format). Here, the fact that the year is a leap year is taken into account by having a keyword parameter **leap-year?** which is set to true by the user when the year is a leap year (otherwise, the default value supplied in the method's parameter list is employed). The method uses a local method in order to perform the main calculation; there is no particular need for this, but it does exemplify the definition and call of a local method.

```
define method calc-dayno (m-name :: <symbol>,
                          day :: <integer>,
                          #key leap-year?(#f))
  local method calc ()
        let month-infos = tail($year-info);
        let month-data = head($year-info);
        let days-tot = 0;
            while (month-name(month-data) ~= m-name)
                  if (month-name(month-data) == #"february")
                     if (leap-year?)
                        days-tot := days-tot + 29
                     else
                        days-tot := days-tot + 28
                     end if
                  else
                     days-tot :=
                       days-tot + days-in-month(month-data)
                  end if;
                  month-data := head(month-infos);
                  month-infos := tail(month-infos)
            end while;
        days-tot + day
  end;
  if (~valid-month?(m-name))
     error(
     "Cannot calculate day number: unknown month %s.",
     as(<string>,m-name))
  end if;
  calc()
end method calc-dayno;
```

The method works as follows. Given the month name, the triple is looked up in **$year-info**. The triple contains the number of days in each month. The method then loops over the months in the year which occur before the input month and adds the number of days to a running total. If it is a leap year and the month comes after February, 29 is added to the running total, otherwise the running total is incremented by 28. The running total production is stopped when the input month is reached; the day within the input month is then added to the running total and returned as the result of the calculation.

Finally, the method for creating instances of **<purchase-date>** can be stated:

```
define method make-purchase-date (day :: <integer>,
                                  month :: <symbol>,
```

```
                                        year :: <integer>,
                                        #key leap-year?(#f))
  if (year < 1995)
     error(
     "Cannot make date:  year must start at 1995 (%d).",
     year)
  end if;
  if ((day < 1) | (day > 31))
   error(
   "Cannot make date:  days must be in range 1..31 (%d).",
   day)
  end if;
  let mnumber = calc-monthno(month);
  let dynumber = calc-dayno(month,day,
                              leap-year?:
                              leap-year?);
  let pdate = make(<purchase-date>,
                   dd:  day,
                   mm:  month,
                   yy:  year);
      dayno(pdate) := dynumber;
      monthno(pdate) := mnumber;
      pdate
end method make-purchase-date;
```

The method has a **#key** parameter for determining whether the year is a leap year (the keyword parameter defaults to false). The method checks that the year is valid (it was written in 1995, so it assumes that any date before that is invalid), and it checks that the day is in the correct range. The method continues by calculating month and day numbers and then creating an instance of **<purchase-date>**. The instance is created with the symbolic form of the month's name (notice how keywords are used). Then the day number and month numbers are assigned to their corresponding slots and the result is returned.

(The above process is incomplete. What has been omitted? Write a piece of Dylan code to rectify the problem and incorporate it with the remainder of the code.)

Finally, two predicates, **before?** and **after?** are defined. Method **before?** returns true when the date represented by its first parameter is before the date represented by the second parameter. Method **after?** returns true in the opposite case.

```
define method before? (time1 :: <purchase-date>,
                       time2 :: <purchase-date>)
      if (year(time1) < year(time2))
         #t
```

```
        elseif (year(time1) == year(time2))
                dayno(time1) < dayno(time2)
        else #f
        end if
end method before?;

define method after? (time1 :: <purchase-date>,
                      time2 :: <purchase-date>)
        if (year(time1) > year(time2))
           #t
        elseif (year(time1) == year(time2))
                dayno(time1) > dayno(time2)
        else #f
        end if
end method after?;
```

Both methods employ the same approach. They first compare year numbers. If there is an inequality, the corresponding truth value is returned. Otherwise, the two instances of `<purchase-date>` refer to the same year, so the day numbers are compared. The day numbers represent the ordinal of the day within the year, so permit comparison (this was one reason why they were also computed.)

## 3.4 Quantities

Food is always purchased in quantities. Quantities can be numbers, weights or volumes. For example, eggs are bought by number (six, twelve, or ten), beef is bought by the kilogram, and milk by the litre. Quantities must be represented in the program to permit comparison, and they are also used in the calculation of unit costs. Unit costs permit objective comparison between purchases, so must be computed. The file containing the definitions of the classes representing quantities is complicated by the fact that there are three kinds of quantity, but they all have some common operations.

The classes used to represent quantity are called:

- `<number-quantity>`. This class represents a number. It is used to count food items. For example, six tins of soup would have their quantity (six) represented by an instance of this class.

- `<mass-quantity>`. This quantity represents weights (masses) in kilograms (actually, the representation is in grams so that integer operations can be used). If a purchase of 1500g of beef were made, the quantity would be an instance of ¡mass-quantity¿.

- `<volume-quantity>`. This class represents a volume in litres.

In addition to these classes, there is an abstract class, **<quantity>**, which is a root for the three other classes. By rooting the three quantity classes under an abstract class **<quantity>**, the three concrete classes are separated off from any other classes in the program (or even in Dylan); they comprise an isolated little system of their own, and all instances can easily and logically be distinguished. The **<quantity>** class is *abstract* because there are to be no direct instances of it; it is impossible for there to be an instance of a quantity without the dimensions of that quantity being taken into account.

Thus, we define:

```
define abstract class <quantity>(<object>)
end class <quantity>;
```

This is the definition of the **<quantity>** class. It is abstract and is marked as such. It has no slots; it is possible for abstract classes to have slots—they are inherited by the concrete classes which are derived from the abstract one—but we do not require them here. More significantly, there is no constructor method for class **<quantity>**; indeed, any call to **make** specifying **<quantity>** as its first argument will cause an error (**make** checks that its argument class is not abstract).

Next, every subclass of **<quantity>** will have a method called compute-unit-cost. Every instance of this method will take a quantity (a subclass of **<quantity>**) and an instance of **<amount>** (a cost) as parameters and will compute the price per unit. In order to document this fact and to make the interface known to the compiler, a generic method is defined:

```
define generic compute-unit-cost (quant, cost);
```

This establishes the generic function.

With these preliminaries out of the way, it is possible to begin the definition of the concrete quantity classes and their methods. The process starts with class **<number-quantity>**, whose definition is:

```
define class <number-quantity> (<quantity>)
      slot amount :: <integer>, init-keyword: amnt:;
end class <number-quantity>;
```

The class defines one slot called **amount** (this is not to be confused with the class representing sums of money whose name is **<amount>**—the angle brackets are significant). The slot is initialised by means of an init-keyword (which is optional). The slot holds integer values (strictly, it ought to contain positive integral values).

The first method for class **<number-quantity>** is one which prints the number in a readable form:

```
define method show (a :: <number-quantity>)
      print(format("No. = %d.",amount(a)))
end method show;
```

Next, a constructor method is defined. This method takes an integer value as input and creates an instance of class **<number-quantity>**:

```
define method make-number-quantity (q :: <integer>)
       if (q <= 0)
          error("Cannot make negative quantity -- %d", q)
       else
          make(<number-quantity>,amnt: q)
       end if
end method make-number-quantity;
```

Note that if the input, **q**, is non-positive, an error is signalled. If all instances of **<number-quantity>** are created using this method (which they should be), there will never be problems with zero or negative numbers of purchased items (which could cause problems when computing unit costs).

A method for testing the equality of numbers is required. This method overloads the equality method defined by Dylan; comparison is in terms of numerical equality:

```
define method \= (nq1 :: <number-quantity>,
                  nq2 :: <number-quantity>)
       amount(nq1) == amount(nq2)
end method \=;
```

Finally, the unit cost must be computed. This is done in the obvious way by the following method:

```
define method compute-unit-cost (quant :: <number-quantity>,
                                 amnt :: <amount>);
       let pence = pounds-to-pence(amnt);
       let rounded = round(pence / amount(quant));
           pence-to-pounds(rounded)
end method compute-unit-cost;
```

Notice that rounding is performed so that fractions of a penny can be discounted. The accuracy we desire from the program is one penny; this routine achieves this level of accuracy by calling the **round** intrinsic function on the result of computing the unit cost.

The remaining subclasses of **<quantity>** are defined in a similar fashion, and they have similar methods defined for them. The definitions for **<mass-quantity>** are as follows:

```
define class <mass-quantity> (<quantity>)
       slot mass-in-grams :: <integer>, init-keyword: mig:;
end class <mass-quantity>;
```

The class is initialised by keyword, and mass is expressed in grams (to make arithmetic more efficient).

A display method is defined so that the mass can be shown to users:

```
define method show (mq :: <mass-quantity>)
      print(format("Amount = %= kg.",
                   mass-in-grams(mq) / 1000.0))
end method show;
```

Comparison is numerical comparison and overloads the standard Dylan numerical equality for integers:

```
define method \= (mq1 :: <mass-quantity>,
                  mq2 :: <mass-quantity>)
      mass-in-grams(mq1) == mass-in-grams(mq2)
end method \=;
```

The creation method is defined as:

```
define method make-mass (mass)
      if (mass < 0)
         error("Cannot make mass: mass negative (%d)", mass)
      else
         make(<mass-quantity>,mig: mass)
      end if
end method make-mass;
```

The mass input to the creation routine is expressed in grams.

Finally, the unit cost computation is defined as:

```
define method compute-unit-cost (quant :: <mass-quantity>,
                                 amnt :: <amount>)
      let pence = pounds-to-pence(amnt);
      let rounded = round(pence / mass-in-grams(quant));
         pence-to-pounds(rounded)
end method compute-unit-cost;
```

Note that rounding occurs when performing this computation. The reasons for this are exactly the same as for `<number-quantity>`.

Finally, there is class `<volume-quantity>`. Although this class introduces nothing new from the perspective of algorithms or Dylan constructs, it is included here for the sake of completeness.

```
define class <volume-quantity> (<quantity>)
      slot mil :: <integer>, init-keyword: milvol:;
end class <volume-quantity>;

define method show (vq :: <volume-quantity>)
      print(format("Volume = %=.", mil(vq) / 1000.0))
end method show;

define method \= (vq1 :: <volume-quantity>,
                  vq2 :: <volume-quantity>)
      mil(vq1) == mil(vq2)
end method \=;
```

```
define method make-volume (vol)
      if (vol < 0)
         error("Cannot make volume:  volume negative (%d)",vol)
      else
         make(<volume-quantity>,milvol:  vol)
      end if
end method make-volume;

define method compute-unit-cost (quant ::  <volume-quantity>,
                                 amnt ::  <amount>)
      let pence = pounds-to-pence(amnt);
      let rounded = round(pence / mil(quant));
         pence-to-pounds(rounded)
end method compute-unit-cost;
```

At this point, the program has classes for the representation of:

- sums of money
- dates
- numbers of objects
- weights of objects
- volumes of liquids

and can compute the unit costs of purchases. These representations and their associated methods provide the foundation on top of which it is possible to construct the higher-level concepts required by the shopping database. We next need to represent the various kinds of food which can be purchased from a supermarket, and we need a representation for shopping lists (it is assumed that most, if not all, families construct a list of items to be purchased prior to entering upon the weekly/monthly/quarterly expedition to the supermarket). It is to these matters that we now turn our attention.

## 3.5 Foodstuffs

The whole purpose of shopping is to buy food. This section is concerned with the representation of foodstuffs and the representation of the concept of a purchase. The shopping database is centred around what has been bought and where it was bought. Lists of purchases made in a particular shop are what the database stores. In this section, we concentrate on what can be bought (ignoring questions about whether a particular supermarket has it in stock); the information represented in this section deals entirely with what to buy and with recording what has been bought. This information is later sorted and stored within a record containing information about the shop where the purchases were made.

The first task to be performed is the representation of the various classes (types, in this case) of food which can be bought. To keep things simple, the types of food are represented by symbols and are stored in a global constant called **$food-category**:

```
define constant $food-category =
       > #( #"meat",
       #"fish",
       #"vegetable",
       #"fruit",
       #"bread",
       #"dairy-product");
```

There are other classes which could be mentioned, but the above is general enough for current purposes.

Food comes in different kinds of packaging. Differentiating between packages can be a significant process. For example, frozen beef might be cheaper than fresh; canned peaches might be more costly than fresh. There is a difference between canned milk and fresh. The food packaging kinds are also stored in a global constant called **$packing-kind**:

```
define constant $packing-kind =
       #( #"fresh",
       #"canned-product",
       #"dairy-product",
       #"bread",
       #"frozen-food",
       #"paper-goods");
```

Having set up the basic categories of food and the kinds of packaging or presentation that are possible, it is necessary to define instances of the foodstuffs in each category. This information is provided so that the program can check the assignment of foods to categories. Information on individual foodstuffs is maintained in global variables, one for each food category. Note that global variables have named beginning and ending with '*' by convention; thus the global list of vegetables is called ***vegetables***, that for bread ***breads***, and so on. The lists given below are fairly comprehensive and were derived from a number of sources, including real shopping lists and recipe books. In each case, the name of the list (the name of the global variable) should be sufficient to indicate the food category.

```
define variable *vegetables* =
       #( #"potatoes",
       #"onions",
       #"carrots",
       #"cabbage",
       #"cauliflower",
```

```
        #"parsnips",
        #"leeks",
        #"lettuce",
        #"artichoke",
        #"chillies",
        #"garlic",
        #"root-ginger",
        #"turnip",
        #"swede",
        #"fennel",
        #"celery",
        #"celeriac",
        #"broad-beans",
        #"string-beans",
        #"french-beans");

define variable *fruit* =
        #( #"apple",
        #"orange",
        #"banana",
        #"grapefruit",
        #"melon",
        #"lemon",
        #"lime",
        #"apricot",
        #"peach",
        #"nectarine",
        #"tomato",
        #"pepper",
        #"aubergine",
        #"strawberry");

define variable *dairy-products* =
        #( #"milk",
        #"cheese",
        #"creme-fraiche",
        #"single-cream",
        #"double-cream",
        #"yoghurt");

define variable *breads* =
        #( #"loaf",
        #"rolls",
        #"baguettes",
        #"biscuits");
```

```
define variable *meat* =
      #( #"beef",
      #"lamb",
      #"pork",
      #"veal",
      #"liver",
      #"kidney",
      #"pork-chops",
      #"lamb-chops",
      #"sausages");

define variable *fish* =
      #( #"cod",
      #"haddock",
      #"sole",
      #"coli",
      #"kipper",
      #"salmon",
      #"trout",
      #"sea-bass",
      #"monk-fish",
      #"sardines",
      #"tuna",
      #"pichards",
      #"anchovies",
      #"crab",
      #"lobster");
```

Given the above, a method can be defined to classify an item of food. The method takes a symbol as input and returns one as output. The input symbol denotes the name of the foodstuff; the output is its category. The category of foodstuff is used in the representation of a week's shopping (Section 3.8). If a foodstuff is unknown, an error is raised.

```
define method type-of-food (x :: <symbol>)
  case
      member?(x,*meat*,test: \==) => #"meat";
      member?(x,*fish*,test: \==) => #"fish";
      member?(x,*vegetables*,test: \==) => #"vegetable";
      member?(x,*fruit*,test: \==) => #"fruit";
      member?(x,*breads*,test: \==) => #"bread";
      member?(x,*dairy-products*,test: \==)
                                          => #"dairy-product";
  otherwise =>
      error("type-of-food: unrecognised food kind %d.",
           as(<string>,x))
  end case; end method type-of-food;
```

Notice, again, how the **member?** method is higher-order. Its third argument is an equality predicate. Since we are dealing with symbols and lists of symbols, the test required here is identity (`==`). The first argument to **member?** in the above method is the name of the foodstuff, and the second is the list in which to test membership. The body of the method is a case expression which has a default (**otherwise**) clause. The case expression (which is akin to cond in Lisp) is interpreted as follows. The expression is formed from a number of clauses, each clause being composed of a test expression and an action, the two being separated by the '`=>`' symbol. Execution of the case expression proceeds as follows. The first clause is selected and its test evaluated; if the test evaluates to true, the action is executed and control passes out of the case expression. If the test fails, control passes to the second clause, and its test is evaluated. If that test fails, control passes to the third clause, and so on. If none of the tests is satisfied, the otherwise clause (if present) is evaluated. In the above example, the action consists of simply returning the symbol on the right-hand side of the `=>` as the result of the **case** (and of the method).

In order to define a purchase, it is necessary to state what was purchased. A good percentage of the code in this file is concerned with that representation, a process which begins with the definition of an abstract class to represent a foodstuff.

```
define abstract class <foodstuff-info> (<object>)
      slot packing-kind :: <symbol>;
      slot food-category :: <symbol>;
      slot foodname :: <symbol>;
end class <foodstuff-info>;
```

This class is an abstract one and cannot be directly instantiated. Unlike the abstract class for quantities (class **<quantity>**), this class has slots. These slots are inherited by all of **<foodstuff-info>**'s subclasses. Thus, although **<foodstuff-info>** cannot be instantiated, it can still define slots which are useful to other classes. The abstract class again serves to root a hierarchy of other classes and to divide them off from the rest of the system.

The slots provided by **<foodstuff-info>** represent the kind of packaging (fresh, canned etc.), the category of foodstuff (meat, dairy product, bread etc.), and the name of the food (chicken, milk, trout etc.). These slots are common to all of the foodstuffs that can be purchased, and are, therefore, defined in the most abstract class which is relevant. In this case, the classes which represent foodstuffs are clearly rooted in **<foodstuff-info>**, so these three slots are best defined in **<foodstuff-info>** to be inherited by everything else that is derived from it.

The first method defined for **<foodstuff-info>** and its subclasses is one which prints the three slots in any instance of **<foodstuff-info>**. The method is:

```
define method show (fs :: <foodstuff-info>)
      print(format("Packaging: %s.",
```

```
                    as(<string>,packing-kind(fs))));
    print(format("Category:  %s.",
                    as(<string>,food-category(fs))));
    print(format("Name:  %s.",
                    as(<string>,foodname(fs))))
end method show;
```

Given the fact that abstract classes cannot be instantiated, this might appear a little contradictory. It must be remembered that a method defined for a class is applicable to all of the subclasses of that class. Thus, **show** can be applied to any instance of any concrete class derived from **<foodstuff-info>**, and it will print the **packing-kind**, **food-category** and **foodname** slots of that instance.

In a similar fashion, equality can be defined for the abstract class and inherited by all derived classes; if any of the derived classes are concrete, they can be tested for equality using the root class's equality method.

```
define method \= (fsi1 ::  <foodstuff-info>,
                  fsi2 ::  <foodstuff-info>)
    (packing-kind(fsi1) == packing-kind(fsi2))
     & (food-category(fsi1) == food-category(fsi2))
     & (foodname(fsi1) == foodname(fsi2))
end method \=;
```

At this point, concrete classes can be defined. The classes derived from **<foodstuff-info>** are:

- **<foodstuff-with-mass>** This represents foodstuffs which are measured in terms of their mass (e.g. legs of lamb).
- **<foodstuff-with-volume>** This represents foodstuffs which are measured in terms of their volume (e.g. litres of milk).
- **<counted-foodstuff>** This represents foodstuffs which are counted (e.g., cans of beans).

In addition, it can be useful to make a distinction between those items of each category which bear a brand name. Often there is a clear difference in price between items which bear the supermarket's brand and those which bear another brand (one which is not specific to the supermarket). For example, cornflakes which bear the market-leader's brand can often cost significantly more than those which bear the supermarket's own brand (even though they might be indistinguishable in terms of quality or nutritional value). Each of the classes described in the last paragraph has a derived form which represents the branded form (e.g. **<branded-foodstuff-with-mass>**). The extension in each **<branded-** case is by the inclusion of a brand name, as will be seen.

Each of the immediate descendants of **<foodstuff-info>** has a similar structure, and similar methods are defined for each.

Class **<foodstuff-with-mass>** is a subclass of **<foodstuff-info>**, specialising it by the inclusion of a slot which represents the mass of the item. The mass is an instance of **<mass-quantity>**, and the slot, **mass**, is correspondingly specialised:

```
define class <foodstuff-with-mass> (<foodstuff-info>)
      slot mass ::  <mass-quantity>;
end class <foodstuff-with-mass>;
```

The **show** method extends the one defined for **<foodstuff-info>** in that it also displays the contents of the slot mass. The method uses **next-method** in order to invoke the show method defined for **<foodstuff-info>**:

```
define method show (fsm ::  <foodstuff-with-mass>,
                    #next next-method)
      next-method();
      show(mass(fsm))
end method show;
```

When called with an instance of **<foodstuff-with-mass>**, **show** first prints those slots defined in its superclass (slots defined in **<foodstuff-info>**, that is) by means of the **next-method()** call; it then prints the contents of the mass slot (by means of a **show** method defined for class **<mass-quantity>**). The parameter list of **show** contains the **#**-word **#next** with argument **next-method**; this is required by the mindy-1.3 implementation and is not standard Dylan.

The remaining methods for this class also employ **next-method** to obtain the functionality upon which they are based. Consequently, they all mention **next-method** in their parameter lists.

```
define method \= (fsm1 ::  <foodstuff-with-mass>,
                  fsm2 ::  <foodstuff-with-mass>,
                  #next next-method)
      (mass(fsm1) = mass(fsm2))
          & next-method()
end method \=;
```

The class **<foodstuff-with-volume>** is a subclass of **<foodstuff-info>** and specialises it in the provision of a volume slot. This class is directly analogous to **<foodstuff-with-mass>**, so no detailed comments will be made.

```
define class <foodstuff-with-volume> (<foodstuff-info>)
      slot volume ::  <volume-quantity>;
end class <foodstuff-with-volume>;
```

The methods for class **<foodstuff-with-volume>** are defined in ways directly analogous to those for **<foodstuff-with-mass>** and all call **next-method** in their bodies.

```
define method show (fsv :: <foodstuff-with-volume>,
                    #next next-method)
      next-method();
      show(volume(fsv))
end method show;

define method \= (fsv1 :: <foodstuff-with-volume>,
                  fsv2 ::<foodstuff-with-volume>,
                  #next next-method)
      (volume(fsv1) = volume(fsv2))
           & next-method()
end method \=;
```

The final class in this group is <counted-foodstuff>. It is similar to the other two classes, so we have no more to say about it.

```
define class <counted-foodstuff> (<foodstuff-info>)
      slot number :: <number-quantity>;
end class <counted-foodstuff>;

define method show (cf :: <counted-foodstuff>,
                    #next next-method)
      next-method();
      print(number(cf))
end method show;
define method \= (cf1 :: <counted-foodstuff>,
                  cf2 :: <counted-foodstuff>,
                  #next next-method)
     (number(cf1) = number(cf2))
          & next-method()
end method \=;
```

We now come to the classes which add a brand name. There are three classes which add a brand name:

- <branded-foodstuff-with-mass>
- <branded-foodstuff-with-volume>
- <counted-branded-foodstuff>

Each of these is a subclass of the unbranded subclass of <foodstuff-info>. So, for example, <branded-foodstuff-with-volume> is a subclass of <foodstuff-with-volume>, and <branded-foodstuff-with-mass> is a subclass of <foodstuff-with-mass>. In each case, the new class defines a slot called brandname (which must be filled by an instance of class <string>); this slot extends the superclass.

There are two methods defined for each of the branded classes, one to show the contents of instances of the class (show their slots), and one to perform equality tests. These methods are specialisations of the methods defined for the superclasses, and rely upon those defined for **<foodstuff-info>** to print and compare the slots which are common to all classes. (Note that the slots are common, but their instances are not shared; we have not marked the slots so that they are only instantiated once per class and held in the class, which we could have done. Instead, the slots are replicated in each subclass.)

We will describe the first of these branded classes in a little detail and leave the reader to complete the description of the remaining two.

Class **<branded-foodstuff-with-mass>** represents a foodstuff, or food item, which is measured in terms of its weight and which has a brand name. The class is a subclass of **<foodstuff-with-mass>**, and specialises it by the addition of a brand name slot. This slot is intended to hold a filler which is a string; the string is the name of the food's brand. Instances of this class have slots to represent the following:

- the foodstuff's kind
- the foodstuff (what precisely the item is—e.g. cheese, canned beans)
- the foodstuff's packing kind (e.g. tinned, fresh)
- the foodstuff's weight

With the addition of the brand name, the make of food is also represented. The class's definition is:

```
define class <branded-foodstuff-with-mass>(<foodstuff-with-mass>)
      slot brandname :: <string>
end class <branded-foodstuff-with-mass>;
```

Clearly, this is a simple extension of the class's superclass. Note that there is no initialisation keyword for the brand name; it is possible to omit the brand name unless care is taken to include it in calls to **make**.

Next, the show method is defined. The method first prints all the information inherited from the superclass (kind, category, packaging, weight), and then prints the brand name. The method calls **next-method** in order to call the **show** method defined for its superclass (which in turn calls next-method to run its superclass's **show** method). The method is defined as:

```
define method show (bfm :: <branded-foodstuff-with-mass>,
                    #next next-method)
      next-method();
      print(format("Brand: %s.",brandname(bfm)))
end method show;
```

Finally, the equality method. Here, it is necessary for the two brand names to be the same as well as all the other information. The test of the brand name is used as a precondition to the test of all the other slots. If the two brand names are equivalent, next-method is called to test the mass and other slots (the other slots are tested via another call to **next-method**). The method's definition is:

```
define method \= (b1 :: <branded-foodstuff-with-mass>,
                  b2 :: <branded-foodstuff-with-mass>,
                  #next next-method)
      (brandname(b1) = brandname(b2))
                 & next-method()
end method \=
```

The remaining classes and methods are defined in ways directly analogous to those for **<branded-foodstuff-with-mass>**. The two classes and their methods are now presented without comment. If you compare them with those just described, you will see their common structure.

```
define class <branded-foodstuff-with-volume>
                  (<foodstuff-with-volume>)
      slot brandname :: <string>
end class <branded-foodstuff-with-volume>;

define method show (bfv :: <branded-foodstuff-with-volume>,
                    #next next-method)
      next-method();
      print(format("Brand: %s.",brandname(bfv)))
end method show;

define method \= (b1 :: <branded-foodstuff-with-volume>,
                  b2 :: <branded-foodstuff-with-volume>,
                  #next next-method)
      (brandname(b1) = brandname(b2))
                 & next-method()
end method ;

define class <counted-branded-foodstuff>(<counted-foodstuff>)
      slot brandname :: <string>
end class <counted-branded-foodstuff>;

define method show (cfm :: <counted-branded-foodstuff>,
                    #next next-method)
      next-method();
      print(format("Brand: end method show;

define method \= (b1 :: <counted-branded-foodstuff>,
                  b2 :: <counted-branded-foodstuff>,
                  #next next-method)
```

```
        (brandname(b1) = brandname(b2))
                  & next-method()
end method \=;
```

Finally, we come to the **<purchase>** class. This class represents the purchase of an individual item of food. The class is a subclass of **<object>**, and is, therefore, totally disjoint from the classes defined above in this section. However, the **<purchase>** class also defines a show method and an equality predicate (the latter overloading the standard method **=**), but, beyond their intention and their names, there is little in common between them and the foodstuffs classes just defined.

The instances of the **<purchase>** class represent individual purchases of food. The class's definition is:

```
define class <purchase> (<object>)
        slot shopname :: <string>;
        slot item-purchased :: <foodstuff-info>;
        slot date-purchased :: <purchase-date>;
        slot total-cost :: <amount>;
        slot unit-price :: <amount>,
             init-function:
                  method()
                        make(<amount>,pence: 0)
                  end
end class <purchase>;
```

The class records the name of the shop in which the purchase was made, the item which was purchased, the date of the purchase, the cost of the purchase, and the unit price.

The slot **item-purchased** is specialised to **<foodstuff-info>**, so can hold any instance of a subclass of **<foodstuff-info>** (since that class is abstract). For example, slot **item-purchased** can contain an instance of **<counted-branded-foodstuff>** or it can contain an instance of **<foodstuff-with-mass>**, depending upon exactly what was purchased. Whenever a slot is specialised to a type (class), it can legally be filled by an instance of that class or one of its subclasses.

Slot **date-purchased** must be filled by an instance of **<purchase-date>**, and slots **total-cost** and **unit-price** must be filled with instances of the **<amount>** class.

None of **<purchase>**'s slots have initial values specified. When created, they are uninitialised, so their initial contents cannot be relied upon. The exception to this is the **unit-price** slot. **unit-price** is equipped with an init-function; when instances of **<purchase>** are created, the init-function is called if there is no default value supplied (and is called before any values are bound to the slot as a result of performing **make**). The value to which **unit-price** is initially bound is the sum of zero pounds and zero pence.

The **show** method for **<purchase>** is straightforward. It prints the slots in the instance of **<purchase>** passed to it as an argument. In the case of slot **shopname**, there is no **show** method defined for its class, so a formatted print is used. All the other slots have a method defined for them, so that method is called with the appropriate slot. In two cases, additional material is printed; the total cost and unit price are flagged in the output.

```
define method show (p ::  <purchase>)
       print(format("Shop:  %s.",shopname(p)));
       show(item-purchased(p));
       show(date-purchased(p));
       print("Total cost:");
       show(total-cost(p));
       print("Unit price:");
       show(unit-price(p));
end method show;
```

Class **<purchase>** has an equality defined for it. The equality predicate overloads the standard = method and is defined in a straightforward manner:

```
define method \= (p1 ::  <purchase>, p2 ::  <purchase>)
       (shopname(p1) = shopname(p2))
                 & (total-cost(p1) = total-cost(p2))
                 & (unit-price(p1) = unit-price(p2))
                 & (date-purchased(p1) = date-purchased(p2))
                 & (item-purchased(p1) = item-purchased(p2))
end method \=
```

What is going on here is that either standard methods are being called to test equality (as is the case with **shopname**—it contains a string), or else equality methods defined for the slot's class are being called. Equality methods are defined for **<amount>**, **<purchase-date>**, and for **<foodstuff-info>** and its subclasses; these user-defined predicates are called when **total-cost**, **unit-price**, **date-purchased** and **item-purchased** are compared.

At this point, we have a representation of what was purchased, where it was purchased, its cost and its unit cost. We next need to define structures which will store this information in an easily accessible form for long-term reference. This involves representing the shop at which the item was purchased as well as the shopping list from which the decision to make the purchase was formed.

## 3.6 The Database Structure

The database holds the records of what was purchased and where. This structure is of central importance to the program. The database should be organised so that it can easily be queried and easily updated. For the current application, updates of existing information are not permitted (because what is already in the database is of an historical nature), so only queries and additions are permitted. Records and results of queries should be printed, either on the screen or in hard copy form, but here significant problems were encountered with mindy-1.3; it was found to be impossible to open and use the I/O libraries defined by it as an extension to the Dylan language. As a consequence, detailed I/O routines could not be defined. However, I/O is not defined by the DIRM, so any routines that might have been used would not necessarily have been portable. This section does show, though, how to use hash tables in Dylan; they are an important data structure, and knowledge of their use is at least highly useful.

The implementation of the database is relatively straightforward, as will be seen. The code as presented below does not support all possible queries; in fact, it does not support any particular queries, either. Instead, it provides facilities which support the writing of query-performing code; such code must be written by the user in Dylan. In some ways, this appears to be closer in spirit to the way in which some object-oriented databases are queried—instead of a query language like SQL, the user is required to write code in the databases object-oriented language.

The database's central class is called `<food-table>`. A single instance of this class comprises the storage area for the database. Class `<food-table>` records a list of foodstuffs, `valid-food-kinds`, which can legally be entered into it, and it contains a table, `entries`, which records the actual purchases. The idea is that if a foodstuff is present in `valid-food-kinds`, the purchase can be added to the database; otherwise, the purchase cannot be processed. The motivation for this approach is that many different things can be bought at a supermarket these days, not just food; the restriction of purchases to food items is necessary because this database is all about food. In addition, the purpose of establishing a database is to see how the standard foods that one buys from week to week change in price, and also how the shopping lists vary with time. A one-time purchase of red mullet or of two pounds of asparagus should not really affect the trend information. However, new foods can be added to the valid-food-kinds list, so matters can be adjusted.

```
define class <food-table> (<object>)
      slot entries :: <object-table>,
           init-function: // no setter needed
                method () make(<object-table>) end;
      slot valid-food-kinds :: <list>,
           init-keyword: valid-foods:; // constant slot
end class ¡food-table¿;
```

The `<food-table>` class is relatively simple, but the `entries` slot has an init-function modifier whose function creates an instance of the table type `<object-table>`. The valid-food-kinds slot is provided with an init-keyword initialiser to make initialisation more readable (and also to serve as a reminder that the slot must be initialised—preferably to `#()`).

The database class is instantiated by method **make-food-table** which takes a list of valid foods as input and creates an instance of **<food-table>** using this list; the list is supplied as the value of the keyword argument **valid-foods:** to the **make** primitive. When the foods acceptable to the database have been initialised, a loop is entered. This loop creates an entry for each valid food kind and sets that entry to the empty list.

```
define method make-food-table (kinds :: <list>)
      let ft = make(<food-table>,valid-foods: kinds);
          for (fk in valid-food-kinds(ft))
              element(entries(ft),fk) := #()
          end for;
      ft end method make-food-table;
```

The intention is that when a purchase of a valid foodstuff is made, information about that purchase is added to the list in the corresponding entry. Thus, if one purchases two kilos of lamb, the information about that purchase is added to the entry for lamb (the addition is by using the primitive **pair** function to add elements to the front of the list held in the entry—other storage methods could have been used, but the one adopted is easy to understand and does not involve great amounts of index construction and traversal).

The database program would be extremely inflexible if it did not permit the user to add to the program's repertoire of foods. Tastes and availabilities change; people can become vegetarian or vegan, or they can move house to a neighbourhood where new foods become available and old ones are no longer can be purchased. The following method is included so that additions to the database can be made (old foods which are no longer of interest remain in the database just in case one needs to refer to them again). The method destructively updates the database (in particular, slot **valid-food-kinds**), and so, following convention, its name ends with '!'.

```
define method add-valid-food! (ft :: <food-table>,
                               fk :: <symbol>)
      if (~valid-food?(ft,fk))
         valid-food-kinds(ft) := pair(fk,valid-food-kinds(ft));
         element(entries(ft),fk) := #()
      end if
end method add-valid-food!;
```

The method first checks that the new food kind (parameter **fk**) is not already one of the foods considered valid (this is done by means of the call to the predicate **valid-food?** which is defined next). If the food is already known to the database, control drops out of the method and nothing is done. If, on the other hand, the food kind is unknown, the **valid-food-kinds** list is updated by adding the new kind to the front of its list, and by creating a new entry in entries with an empty list of purchases. Once this method returns, the foodstuff is valid and purchases of it can be recorded in the database.

A food is valid for the database if it is recorded in the list held in slot **valid-food-kinds**. The next method, which is a predicate (hence its name ends with '?'), tests a food kind to determine whether it is valid. The **member?** predicate is testing symbols, so identity is used as the comparison function.

```
define method valid-food? (ft :: <food-table>,
                           food-kind :: <symbol>)
      member?(food-kind,valid-food-kinds(ft),test: \==)
end method valid-food?;
```

Now we can turn our attention to the addition of purchases to the database. Thereafter, we will see some code for the construction of queries.

When a purchase is added to the database, the method **add-food-purchase!** is used. This method takes an instance of **<food-table>**, a statement of the food's kind and the information about the food as inputs. The information is about the purchase and is specialised to **<object>**—any type—for the present; it would be better if info were of some more specialised type, but we have not yet encountered it.

```
define method add-food-purchase! (ft :: <food-table>,
                                  food-kind :: <symbol>,
                                  info :: <object>)
      if (~valid-food?(ft,food-kind))
         error("Cannot add purchase: invalid food (%s).",
               as(<string>, food-kind))
      endelement(entries(ft),food-kind)
         := pair(info,element(entries(ft),food-kind))
end method add-food-purchase!;
```

The method works by checking that the food's kind is one that can validly be stored in this database (instance of **<food-table>**). If it cannot, an error is signalled. If the food's kind is valid, the information about the purchase (in info) is added to the entries of the table, indexed under the food's kind. Note here that the accessor function, **element**, appears on the left-hand side of the assignment. This is because **element** is being used to update the table. When it appears on the right-hand side of an assignment or on its own, element returns the entry in its first argument that is indexed by its second argument (a default value is returned if there is nothing stored). Thus:

```
element(entries(ft),food-kind)
```

returns all those items in the table entries(**ft**) which are indexed by food-kind, whereas:

```
element(entries(ft),food-kind) := #(1, 2, 3)
```

assigns the list **#(1, 2, 3)** to the table entry indexed by **food-kind**. The accessing of table entries will be encountered more than once in the methods that follow.

The methods that follow are mainly concerned with providing support for queries. The method **purchases-of-kind** returns the list which is stored in the table's entries. Recall that instances of **<food-table>** contain a table data structure called **entries**; this holds the information in the instance. The **purchases-of-kind** method is intended to be called whenever the user wants to know about those items of food of a particular kind which have been purchased. The method checks that the food kind is valid, and then indexes the table to extract the list of purchases (buys); that list is returned.

```
define method purchases-of-kind (ft :: <food-table>,
                                 food-kind :: <symbol>)
  if (~valid-food?(ft,food-kind))
     error(
       "Cannot retrieve purchases of kind %s -- invalid kind.",
       as(<string>,food-kind))
  end if;
  let buys = element(entries(ft),food-kind);
      buys
end method purchases-of-kind;
```

The next method returns the names of all the food kinds that are currently stored in the instance of **<food-table>** supplied as input. Food kinds are the keys under which purchases are indexed, so returning the food kinds in the table amounts to returning the table's keys; this is done via a call to the intrinsic function **key-sequence**:

```
define method current-food-kinds (ft :: <food-table>)
       key-sequence(entries(ft))
end method current-food-kinds;
```

Method **purchased-food-kinds** returns the names of all those food kinds under which at least one purchase is recorded. If the food kind is present in the database, but nothing of that kind has yet been bought, the entry will be empty (equal to the empty list—**entries** was initialised to this value when the **<food-table>** instance was created).

```
define method purchased-food-kinds (ft :: <food-table>)
       let kinds = #();
           for (kind in current-food-kinds(ft))
               if (element(entries(ft),kind) ~= #())
                  kinds := pair(kind,kinds)
               end if
           end for;
           kinds end method purchased-food-kinds;
```

In the method, there is a **for** loop which iterates over the keys of the table contained in it. If the key's entry is not equal to nil (the empty list), it is consed onto the list of food kinds for which purchases have been made (**kinds**). When the **for** loop terminates, **kinds** is returned.

The next method, **all-purchases**, iterates over the database and returns all the purchases that are recorded in it. To do this, it determines which food kinds are associated with purchases, and then sets a list of purchases to empty. Then, the method iterates over these kinds, concatenating the list of purchases for each kind with the collecting list (purchases) which is the value returned by the method.

```
define method all-purchases (ft :: <food-table>)
       let kinds = purchased-food-kinds(ft);
       let purchases = #();
           for (kind in kinds)
               purchases :=
                          concatenate(purchases,
                                      purchases-of-kind(ft,kind))
           end for;
           purchases
end method all-purchases;
```

The **all-purchases** method is used whenever the user wants to access all of the purchases that have been recorded in the database. One reason for this might be that a total for the costs of the purchases is required. The method returns all purchases in a totally indiscriminate fashion; sometimes, it is better to return only those purchase records which have some property. The next method, **filter-purchases**, performs this task. **filter-purchases** is an example of a second-order method because its last parameter, **filter**, must be an instance of a function. The other arguments are the **<food-table>** instance and the kind of foodstuff to be checked.

```
define method filter-purchases (ft :: <food-table>,
                                kind :: <symbol>,
                                filter :: <function>)
       let purchases = purchases-of-kind(ft,kind);
       let filtered = #();
           for (purchase in purchases)
               if (filter(purchase))
                  filtered := add(filtered,purchase)
               end if
           end for;
           filtered
end method filter-purchases;
```

The method works by extracting the purchases of the kind specified by the **kind** parameter. A list, called **filtered**, is declared and initialised to **#()**. Next, a **for** loop iterates over the list of purchases of the specified kind. The body of the loop is where the filtering process occurs; the **filter** function is applied to the purchase data and, if the function returns true, the purchase is added to the end of **filtered**. List **filtered** is returned at the end.

Finally, method **filter-all-purchases** is defined. The idea is that all the purchases held in the database are examined to see if they satisfy the predicate **filter** (**filter-all-purchases** is another second-order method); those which satisfy the **filter** predicate are stored in a list which is returned at the end of the method. The actual algorithm employed in the definition is really very slow!

```
define method filter-all-purchases (ft :: <food-table>,
                                    filter :: <function>)
      let all-purchased-items = all-purchases(ft);
      let filtered = #();
          for (purchase in all-purchased-items)
              if (filter(purchase))
                 filtered := add(filtered,purchase)
              end if
          end for;
          filtered
end method filter-all-purchases;
```

The last two methods we have defined run over the database and find purchases which have some property or properties in common. They could be used, for example, to find all those items of a particular kind (or just all those items) which were bought on a particular day; they could be used to find items which cost over, or below, a certain amount; they could be used to find items bought at a specific shop. The results of the two methods are sets, so intersections, unions and differences can be taken, very much in the spirit of a conventional query language like SQL.

## 3.7 The Shopping Database

All records of purchases are stored in a single global database. This database is called **<shopping-info>**. All queries, updates, calculations, etc. are performed on the information stored in this central database. The database is defined as a class as follows:

```
define class <shopping-info> (<object>)
      slot shops :: <list>, init-value: #();
      slot meat-items :: <food-table>,
           init-function:method ()
                           make-food-table(*meat*)
           end;
      slot fish-items :: <food-table>,
           init-function:method ()
                           make-food-table(*fish*)
```

```
          end;
     slot veg-items ::  <food-table>,
          init-function:method ()
                             make-food-table(*vegetables*)
          end;
     slot fruit-items ::  <food-table>,
          init-function:method ()
                             make-food-table(*fruit*)
          end;
     slot dairy-items ::  <food-table>,
          init-function:method ()
                             make-food-table(*dairy-products*)
          end;
     slot bread-items ::  <food-table>,
          init-function:method ()
                             make-food-table(*breads*)
          end;
end class <shopping-info>;
```

Class **<shopping-info>** records the names of the shops which are to be visited. Most people regularly visit only a few shops to buy food, and the names of these shops are recorded in the shops slot. The slot is used to check that the names of shops are correct, thus enabling the database to maintain a certain degree of consistency across shops. A method called **add-shopname!** allows users to add more shops as and when the need arises. Initially, there are no shops known to the database (the slot has an **init-value:** of **#()**).

Thereafter, the class defines a collection of slots, each of which contains an instance of **<food-table>**. Each instance records the purchases of a different kind of food. When a purchase of a food item is recorded, the code surrounding the database determines the category of the food item and places the record in the most appropriate instance of **<food-table>**. The reason for arranging the database in this way was that it is common to compare the cost of something, for example herrings, across time, but not to compare the cost of mackerel and bread together; the cost of bread has little bearing (or little direct bearing) on the cost of mackerel (when computing the average increase in the cost of bread over a six-month period, the cost of mackerel is completely irrelevant). Furthermore, it is sometimes useful to be able to determine how much of a particular foodstuff was bought at a particular time; for example, when guests return for dinner, it can be useful to look back and see how much of a particular foodstuff was bought for their last visit. By collecting information by food type, searches are obviated and time is saved.

The first method determines whether the shop names in a purchase record are known to the system.

```
define method known-shop? (sn ::  <string>,
                           si ::  <shopping-info>)
```

```
        member?(sn, shops(si), test: \ =)
end method known-shop?;
```

Method **add-shopname!** destructively modifies the shops slot of the input instance of **<shopping-info>** when the shop is not already known to the database. If the shop is known, no action is taken.

```
define method add-shopname!  (sn ::  <string>,
                              si ::  <shopping-info>)
       if (~ known-shop?(sn,si))
          shops(si) := pair(sn,shops(si))
       end if;
       sn
end method add-shopname!;
```

The next method, **add-purchased-item!** updates the database. It takes as input a variety of information about the purchase, as well as a shopping database (**si**—an instance of **<shopping-info>**). The first thing the method does is to check that the shop is known; if the shop is not known, the transaction is aborted by raising an error. Otherwise, the update can proceed. The value of item-kind (which denotes the kind or category of foodstuff) is used to determine the region of the database to update; it does this by determining which slot will be updated (the slots in question hold instances of **<food-table>**). If the food category is not recognised, an error is raised.

```
define method add-purchased-item!
                            (purchased-item ::  <purchase>,
                            shop-where-purchased ::  <string>,
                            item-kind ::  <symbol>,
                            food-kind ::  <symbol>,
                            si ::  <shopping-info>)
  if (~known-shop?(shop-where-purchased,si))
     error("Do not know this shop:  %s.",shop-where-purchased)
  end if;
  select (item-kind)
       #"meat"=>
              add-food-purchase!(meat-items(si),
                                 food-kind,
                                 purchased-item);
       #"fish" =>
              add-food-purchase!(fish-items(si),
                                 food-kind,
                                 purchased-item);
       #"vegetable" =>
                   add-food-purchase!(veg-items(si),
                                      food-kind,
                                      purchased-item);
```

```
        #"fruit" =>
                 add-food-purchase!(fruit-items(si),
                                    food-kind,
                                    purchased-item);
        #"bread" =>
                 add-food-purchase!(bread-items(si),
                                    food-kind,
                                    purchased-item);
        #"dairy-product"=>
                        add-food-purchase!(dairy-items(si),
                                           food-kind,
                                           purchased-item);
        otherwise =>
         error("add-purchased-item!:  cannot recognise %s.",
               as(<string>,item-kind))
  end select
end method add-purchased-item!;
```

Methods which support queries are now defined. The reader should note that we have not defined every method which would be needed in reality; instead, we have provided a few examples and suggest that those sufficiently motivated might care to extend them as an exercise.

The method **purchases-of-kind** takes a database and a specification of a food kind (represented by a symbol). It then uses **fk** to determine which food kind to examine, and returns all the purchases currently recorded under that kind. If the food kind is unknown, an error is signalled.

```
define method purchases-of-kind (si :: <shopping-info>,
                                 fk :: <symbol>)
  let purchases = #();
      select(fk)
           #"meat" =>
             purchases := all-purchases(meat-items(si));
           #"fish" =>
             purchases := all-purchases(fish-items(si));
           #"vegetable" =>
             purchases := all-purchases(veg-items(si));
           #"fruit" =>
             purchases := all-purchases(fruit-items(si));
           #"bread" =>
             purchases := all-purchases(bread-items(si));
           #"dairy-product" =>
             purchases := all-purchases(dairy-items(si));
      otherwise =>
       error(
         "purchases-of-kind:  unrecognised food kind %s.",
```

```
        as(<string>,fk))
  end select;
end method purchases-of-kind;
```

The **purchases-of-kind** method returns every purchase of a particular kind of food that is stored in the database. This information can be used to calculate the increase in unit cost, or to determine which shop is consistently cheaper, or to find out where purchases of this particular foodstuff are most commonly made; these are examples of this method's use—others can probably be found. (The reader might care to define some more as an exercise.)

The next method, **every-purchase**, returns a list of all the purchases in the database.

```
define method every-purchase (db :: <shopping-info>)
  let all-purchases = #();
      for (kind in #( #"meat", #"fish",
          #"vegetable", #"fruit",
          #"bread", #"dairy-product"))
          let purchases = purchases-of-kind(db,kind);
          if (purchases ~= #())
            all-purchases := add(all-purchases,purchases)
          else
            all-purchases :=
                add(all-purchases,list("nothing for",kind))
          end if
      end for;
  all-purchases
end method every-purchase;
```

It iterates over all the kinds in the database and produces a list of all the purchase records stored in the database.

Finally, we define a method which applies a predicate to the purchases stored in the database. This allows the formation of sets of records which can be subjected to further processing; for example, it can find the set of all purchases at a particular shop, all purchases within a specified period, all purchases below a given cost and so on. Method **filter-purchases** is a second-order function.

```
define method filter-purchases (si :: <shopping-info>,
                                food-kind :: <symbol>,
                                filter :: <function>)
      let purchases-of-kind = purchases-of-kind(si,food-kind);
      let filtered = #();
          for (purchase in purchases-of-kind)
              if (filtered(purchase))
                filtered := add(filtered,purchase)
              end if
```

```
            end for;
            filtered
end method filter-purchases;
```

The algorithm chosen for the definition of the method is an extremely slow one (but one that is extremely simple to implement!). As an exercise, the reader is asked to improve upon the speed with which the method performs the filtering operation.

## 3.8 The Shopping List

Most people make a list of items to be purchased before they go to the shops. The shopping list is then used to determine what to buy (and sometimes where); it can be adjusted as the shopping expedition progresses, with items being added and others omitted. Here, we define structures to represent the shopping list and the specification of the purchases to be made. The list is not dynamic as far as we are concerned; after all, when the list is entered into the database, all the shopping has been done.

The code in this section relies upon the existence of the classes **<purchase>**, **<quantity>**, **<amount>** and **<purchase-date>**, the most significant for processing being **<purchase>**.

The shopping list is defined as a class, called, surprisingly enough, **<shopping-list>**. The shopping list, here, is a record of what has been purchased at a single shop; it also records the date on which the shopping was purchased, and the list of items that were purchased. The class definition is as follows:

```
define class <shopping-list> (<object>)
       slot shop ::  <string>, init-keyword:  shop-name:;
       slot date ::  <purchase-date>,
                     init-keyword:  shopping-date:;
       slot items-purchased ::  <list>, init-value:  #()
end class <shopping-list>;
```

Note that every slot of the class is specialised, and that slots **shop** and **date** have associated init-keywords; perhaps these init-keywords should be required, rather than being optional (exercise for the reader—discuss the merits of this proposal). The list of purchased items, **items-purchased**, is initialised to nil (**#()**) when instances of **<shopping-list>** are created.

The first method defined for **<shopping-list>** is a print routine:

```
define method show (sl ::  <shopping-list>)
       print(format("Shop:  %s.",shop(sl)));
       show(date(sl));
       for (item in items-purchased(sl))
           show(item)
       end for
end method show;
```

Next, we have to define a shopping item and a routine to print it on the screen. Shopping items are the objects stored in the **items-purchased** slot of instances of **<shopping-list>**. A shopping item has to record the name of the item (e.g. spaghetti), the quantity purchased, the cost, the packaging (canned or loose for spaghetti), and the brand name if applicable. The class definition is:

```
define class <shopping-item> (<object>)
   slot item-name :: <symbol>, init-keyword: item-name:;
   slot quantity :: <quantity>, init-keyword: amount-bought:;
   slot cost :: <amount>, init-keyword: item-cost:;
   slot packing :: <symbol>, init-keyword: packaging:;
   slot brandname :: <string>, init-value: ""
end class ¡shopping-item¿;
```

Again, most of the slots have associated init-keywords. The **brandname** slot is just initialised to the empty string. Brand names are completely optional, so an initialisation keyword would not be appropriate.

We need, if only for testing, to print instances of **<shoppingitem>** on the screen, so a method is defined:

```
define method show (si :: <shopping-item>)
      print("-------------------");
      print(format("Item name: %s.",
                   as(<string>,item-name(si))));
      show(quantity(si));
      show(cost(si));
      print(format("Packaging: %s.",
                   as(<string>,packing(si))));
      if (brandname(si) ~= "")
         print(format("Brand: %s.",brandname(si)));
      end if
end method show;
```

(The workings of this method should be clear.)

The next method looks completely forbidding. It is interesting because it makes use of the **select** expression in a particular way and to a particular end. The purpose of the method is to convert an instance of **<shopping-item>** into one of **<purchase>** in order that it can be stored on the database. The shopping list maintains a different representation for purchases than the database, and the external representation needs to be converted into the internal one; this involves testing the types of objects and performing operations on the basis of type. The inputs to the method are a shopping item, the name of the shop at which the purchase was made and the date on which si was bought.

The first few lines of the method deal with the creation of an instance of **<purchase>**, the extraction of the food's name and its packaging. A flag called **branded?** is initialised to false (**#f**); this flag will be used when creating instances of the subclasses of **<foodstuff-info>**, in particular in deciding whether to create a subclass with a brand or not. Next, information about the shop, the purchase date, and the cost is stored in the instance of **<purchase>** (purchase-record). Also at this point, the **branded?** flag is set if the instance of **<shopping-item>** has a brand name. The unit price is computed before moving to the **select** expression.

The aim of the **select** expression is to store the unit and amount in the most appropriate type of object. For example, if the purchase was of a product which is bought by number (e.g. two melons or five cans of tomatoes), and the product has a brand name, it is most appropriate to create an instance of **<counted-branded-foodstuff>** in order to hold the information about the number and brand of the product. Determining whether the information should be held in an instance of a class whose name is prefixed by **branded-** is easy enough; it is sufficient to see whether the **branded?** flag has been set (then the brand name string can be extracted from **si**). It is harder to determine what the unit of the purchase is. To do this, the **select** expression tests the quantity slot of **si** to determine its type; this is done by adding a test to the **select** expression. The presence of the test is denoted by the word by in the expression, and we have used **instance?** to obtain the type of the value of **quantity(si)**. When using **by instance?**, Dylan extracts the value of the preceding expression (here **quantity(si)**) and determines its class. The branches of the **select** expression are differentiated by class names, not ordinary values (select by **instance?** is akin to **typecase** in Lisp).

For each appropriate quantity type, an instance of one of the quantity-representing classes is created, a test being made to see if a branded version is required. An otherwise clause is used to trap illegal contents of the **quantity** slot of **si**.

```
define method shopping-item-to-purchase
                    (si ::  <shopping-item>,
                     shop ::  <string>,
                     date ::  <purchase-date>)
  let purchase-record = make(<purchase>);
  let food-name = item-name(si);
  let branded?  = #f;
  let how-packed = packing(si);
  let item = #f;
      shopname(purchase-record) := shop;
      date-purchased(purchase-record) := date;
      total-cost(purchase-record) := cost(si);
      if (brandname(si))
         branded?  := #t
      end if;
      unit-price(purchase-record)
           := compute-unit-cost(quantity(si),cost(si));
      // Now store the item, unit and amount
```

```
    // in the most appropriate object.
    select(quantity(si) by instance?)
      <number-quantity> =>
        if (branded?)
          item := make(<counted-branded-foodstuff>);
          brandname(item) := brandname(si)
        else
          item := make(<counted-foodstuff>)
        end if;
        number(item) := quantity(si);
      <mass-quantity> =>
        if (branded?)
          item := make(<branded-foodstuff-with-mass>);
          brandname(item) := brandname(si)
        else
          item := make(<foodstuff-with-mass>)
        end if;
        mass(item) := quantity(si);
      <volume-quantity> =>
        if (branded?)
          item := make(<branded-foodstuff-with-volume>);
          brandname(item) := brandname(si)
        else
          item := make(<foodstuff-with-volume>)
        end if;
        volume(item) := quantity(si);
      otherwise =>
        error(
          "Unrecognised quantity.  %=")
    end select;
    food-category(item) := type-of-food(food-name);
    foodname(item) := food-name;
    packing-kind(item) := how-packed;
    item-purchased(purchase-record) := item;
    purchase-record
end method shopping-item-to-purchase;
```

Once the **select** has completed, the remaining slots of the new instance of **<purchase>** are filled in, and it is returned as the value of the method.

The next method interfaces the shopping list to the shopping database (the one composed of many instances of **<food-table>**—that is, the class **<shopping-info>**). The method **store-shopping-list** performs the operation of storing a shopping list in the shopping database. Its inputs are a shopping list and a shopping database (an instance of **<shopping-info>**). The method iterates over the shopping list, adding each item to the database, having first converted it to the form required by the database. The method

**add-purchased-item!** performs the actual addition of the purchase record to the database. Note that the name of the shop where the purchases were made and the date of purchase are extracted from the shopping list before entering the loop which updates the database; this is done in order to avoid repeatedly extracting these items from each record of a purchase.

```
define method store-shopping-list (sl :: <shopping-list>,
                                   db :: <shopping-info>)
  let shopname = shop(sl);
  let date = date(sl);
      for (item in items-purchased(sl))
          let purchase =
              shopping-item-to-purchase(item,shopname,date);
              add-purchased-item!
                 (purchase,
                  shopname,
                  food-category(item-purchased(purchase)),
                  foodname(item-purchased(purchase)),
                  db)
      end for;
  values() end method store-shopping-list;
```

We need a method to create an item to be added to the shopping list. We could just call **make** and get it to do all the work, but that would be tedious and error-prone. The solution adopted is to have a method do the work and to do a little checking for us. The method has parameters for the usual things: foodstuff name, quantity, cost and packing type, and a **#key** parameter to represent the brand name; if a food is not branded, this parameter can simply be omitted, and its default value (the empty string) will be used in its place.

The method first checks that the packing is valid, and then creates an instance of **<shopping-info>**. It then uses the fact that an initial value is defined for the brandname slot of **<shopping-info>** for setting the value of that slot. The instance of **<shopping-item>** is returned for addition to the shopping list.

```
define method make-shopping-item (name :: <symbol>,
                                  quantity :: <quantity>,
                                  cost :: <amount>,
                                  packing :: <symbol>,
                                  #key brand-name(""))
      if (~member?(packing,$packing-kind,test: =))
         error("Unknown packaging (%s).",
               as(<string>,packing))
      end if;
      let food-kind = type-of-food(name);
      let sitem = make(<shopping-item>,
```

```
                         item-name: name,
                         amount-bought: quantity,
                         item-cost: cost,
                         packaging: packing);
      if (brand-name ~= "")
         brandname(sitem) := brand-name
      end if;
      sitem
end method make-shopping-item;
```

Method **add-shopping-item** creates an instance of **<shopping-item>**, and adds it to the shopping list. The method returns no value of any interest (signalled by the call **values()**).

```
define method add-shopping-item (sl :: <shopping-list>,
                                 name :: <symbol>,
                                 quantity :: <quantity>,
                                 cost :: <amount>,
                                 packing :: <symbol>,
                                 #key brand-name (""))
  items-purchased(sl)
      := add(items-purchased(sl),
             make-shopping-item(name,quantity,cost,packing,
             brand-name: brand-name));
  values()
end method add-shopping-item;
```

Finally, we must consider how the shopping list is input to the program to begin with. For the sake of simplicity, it was decided that the user would create lists of lists in the specification of a shopping list. If a menu-based interface were available, calls to the constructor of **<shopping-item>** would be perfectly in order. However, we cannot assume such an interface, and one which is easy (or relatively easy) to type was adopted.

The format of the list input to the program is as follows:

```
#(shopname, #(dd month yy,)
  #(foodname, quantity, cost, packing, | brandname))
```

The list is composed of the name of the shop where the purchases were made, with a sublist denoting the date of purchase, and another sublist containing the details of the purchase. (Note that the items in *italics* are *meta*-items.)If the length of the second sublist is four, there is no brand name; otherwise a brand name is present. The code which follows is concerned with converting the above representation into the shopping list representation (which will eventually be converted into the internal database representation).

The following methods unpack the data.

Method **list-shopname** returns the name of the shop at which the purchases were made.

```
define method list-shopname (sl :: <list>)
      head(sl)
end method list-shopname;
```

Method **list-date** extracts the date of purchase from the input list.

```
define method list-date (sl :: <list>)
      head(tail(sl))
end method list-date;
```

Method **list-purchases** extracts the sublist containing the details of the purchase (cost, amount, etc.).

```
define method list-purchases (sl :: <list>)
      tail(tail(sl))
end method list-purchases;
```

The details of the sublist returned by list-purchases are handled by the method **add-list-item**, whose definition now follows.

```
define method add-list-item (sl :: <shopping-list>,
                             li :: <list>)
      let name = head(li);
      let quant = head(tail(li));
      let cost = head(tail(tail(li)));
      let packing = head(tail(tail(tail(li))));
      local method convert-quant(q)
            let units = head(q);
            let num = head(tail(q));
                select (units)
                #"kg" => make-mass(num);
                #"num" => make-number-quantity(num);
                #"ltr" => make-volume(num);
                otherwise =>
                   error("unrecognised physical unit: %s.",
                         as(<string>,units))
                end select
      end;
      if (size(li) == 5)
         add-shopping-item(sl,name,convert-quant(quant),
                           make-amount(pounds: head(cost),
                           pence: head(tail(cost))),
                           packing,
                           brand-name: last(li))
      else
          add-shopping-item(sl,name,convert-quant(quant),
                            make-amount(pounds: head(cost),
                            pence: head(tail(cost))),
```

```
                                        packing)
        end if
end method add-list-item;
```

Method add-list-item adds a new purchase record to the shopping list. It first extracts the information about foodstuff name, quantity, cost and packaging. Quantities are expressed in a more 'user-friendly' form than inside the program:

- mass is denoted by the symbol `#"kg"`
- number is denoted by the symbol `#"num"`
- volume is denoted by the symbol `#"ltr"`

Thus, for example, in:

```
#("SuperFoods" #(26 #"feb" 96)
  #(#"milk" #(#"ltr" 2) ... ))
```

two litres of milk have been purchased on 26 February 1996. In:

```
#("MegaNosh" #(03 #"mar" 96)
  #(#"beef" #(#"kg" 3.4) ...  ))
```

3.4 kilograms of beef have been purchased on 3 March 1996.

The final operation of add-list-item is to add the record of the purchase to the instance of **<shopping-list>** supplied as a parameter. This is done by calling **add-shopping-item**; this method is called twice, once from each branch of a conditional which tests whether a brand name is present (if so, it adds the brand name to the record).

The final method in this section takes a shopping list in external list format and converts it into an instance of **<shopping-list>**. It extracts the shop and date information first and then creates an instance of **<shopping-list>**, supplying the first collection of slot fillers. Then the method iterates over the input list, **li**, converting each record into the type and format required by **<shopping-list>**. The newly created instance of **<shopping-list>** is returned by the method.

```
define method convert-shopping-list (li :: <list>)
        let shop :: <string> = list-shopname(li);
        let date :: <list> = list-date(li);
        let purchases :: <list> = list-purchases(li);
        let shopping-list :: <shopping-list>
               = make(<shopping-list>,
                      shop-name: shop,
                      shopping-date:
                         make-purchase-date(head(date),
```

```
                    head(tail(date)),
                    head(tail(tail(date)))));
    for (item in purchases)
        add-list-item(shopping-list,item)
    end for;
    shopping-list
end method convert-shopping-list;
```

## 3.9 Main

Every Dylan program must have a method called **main**. This method is the first one called by the operating system and is the method from which all computation starts. In mindy-1.3, method **main** always takes parameters which allow extraction of the **argv** and **argc** information passed by the Unix operating system to running programs.

Before defining the **main** program (which is a user-defined method added to the **main** generic function) for the shopping database, we define our shopping list, declare a variable, ***database***, and initialise it to the database; we also define a global variable called ***shlist*** to hold the shopping list in its internal form (an instance of **<shopping-list>**). These items of data are required to run the program. We are avoiding the use of I/O routines as explained above; were we to use I/O, the list form of the shopping list (stored in ***shopping***, and intended to be the form most easily readable by people) would be held on disk.

```
define variable *shopping* =
    #("tesco", #(7, #"november", 1995),
    #(#"beef", #(#"kg", 2500), #(5,45), #"fresh"),
    #(#"trout",#(#"num",2), #(2, 99), #"frozen-food"),
    #(#"potatoes",#(#"kg",1500), #(0,82),#"fresh"),
    #(#"milk",#(#"ltr",1250), #(1,44),#"fresh"));

define variable *shlist* = #();
define variable *database* = make(<shopping-info>);
```

With these definitions out of the way, we can now define the **main** routine. This routine is specific to mindy, so the parameters are not discussed.

The **main** method converts the shopping list from list form to an instance of **<shopping-list>** by calling **convert-shopping-list**. It then adds the name of the shop (Tesco) to the database and stores the purchases in the database. The **for** loop which follows is used to print the contents of the database to check that all is correctly stored.

```
define method main (arg, #rest ignore)
    *shlist* := convert-shopping-list(*shopping*);
    add-shopname!("tesco",*database*);
```

```
        store-shopping-list(*shlist*,*database*);
        for (purchases in every-purchase(*database*))
            if (instance?(head(purchases),<string>))
               print(purchases)
            else
               for (purchase in purchases)
                   show(purchase)
               end for
            end if
        end for;
        print("tra")
end method main;
```

When testing the program, we input long shopping lists and performed queries. We have not reproduced the code because it is long and tedious. The reader might care to extend the above method, adding a query facility and an interface to disk files.

# Chapter 4

# Basic Types

## 4.1 Introduction

The purpose of this chapter is to introduce and describe a number of types which are indispensable to programming. Without these types, real programming is impossible. These types are referred to as 'basic' for this reason. Some of the types have atomic values; such values cannot be broken down. For example, a boolean value cannot be broken down into anything simpler; similarly, an integer cannot be decomposed into simpler entities (it could be represented as a bit string, but this is a change of representation and can be viewed as a change of type). Vectors, strings and lists, on the other hand, contain component values of other types; sometimes the components are of the same type (e.g. a list of lists), sometimes not (e.g. a vector of integers).

The purpose of the current chapter is to introduce the reader to a range of types which are frequently used in programming. The types will be familiar from other programming languages, and are:

1. boolean (truth-values)
2. character
3. strings
4. symbol
5. numbers (including integer, floating point, rational, ratio, complex)
6. vectors
7. lists.

At the end of the chapter, comparison operators such as less-than, greater-than equality, are discussed in some detail. Although they can be grouped together with the booleans, they appear in their own section at the end because they rely upon knowledge of the other types.

With the exception of structures (or records), these types are the most convenient for general programming (as well as being the most commonly encountered). Dylan uses the class concept to provide a facility similar to structure. There is no concept of a pointer in Dylan. With this set of basic types, most programs can be written with greater or lesser ease.

The reader might question the inclusion of the symbol type in this list, for symbols appear in 'AI languages' like Lisp, Prolog or Pop-11, but not in 'conventional' languages like C, Pascal, FORTRAN or Ada[1]. Symbols are, however, an extremely convenient representation for some kinds of entity, and the inclusion of this type makes the construction of some kinds of program more convenient than would otherwise be the case. Symbols will be considered in more detail in Section 4.5.

List, vector and string types have internal structure which is represented in Dylan itself; they are Dylan classes (hence extensible types). Furthermore, there is a relationship between the various numeric types; this will be discussed below (Section 4.6), but this relationship depends on the concept of a class for its full exposition.

The organisation of this chapter presents the types appearing in the above list and that same order as in that list. For each type, its values are first described, and the operations defined over the type are then outlined. Relationships between values of the type are also discussed where appropriate. Dylan, like LISP, is equipped with an extensive library of functions for manipulating its various data types; a good part of Dylan programming (like LISP programming) consists of the application of library functions, so an adequate knowledge of the language's built-in functions is required in order to write programs. For this reason, the present chapter somewhat tediously describes a number of the built-in functions associated with the types dealt with below.

## 4.2 Booleans

The boolean type is conceptually the simplest. It is usually defined as having two values: true and false. Dylan represents these two values as `#t` and `#f`, where:

1. `#t` is the canonical representation of the value true;

2. `#f` is the canonical representation of the value false.

The usual operations are defined in Dylan over boolean values. The negation operator (not) is represented by the symbol ~ and has the usual interpretation:

1. `~#t` ⇒ `#f`

2. `~#f` ⇒ `#t`

[1] Ada is a registered trademark of the US Department of Defense.

(the symbol ⇒ will be used throughout this book to denote the evaluation function; in each case, the left-hand side of the arrow evaluates to the right-hand side). In a similar fashion, Dylan provides conjunction (and) and disjunction (or) of boolean values. The Dylan symbol for 'and' is `&`; that for 'or' is |. These operations are defined as follows, where *form1* and *form2* are Dylan forms (expressions) which can be composed of other expressions, as well as constants and variables.

*form1* `&` *form2* evaluates the expressions forms from left to right. If *form1* returns `#f` as its value, `#f` is returned as the value of the conjunction, and in this case *form2* is not evaluated. If *form1* does not evaluate to `#f`, *forms2* is evaluated and its result is returned as the value of the entire expression. This is the so-called 'short-cut' rule for the evaluation of and.

*form1* | *form2* evaluates forms from left to right. If *form1* evaluates to `#f`, *form2* is evaluated and its value is returned as the value of the expression. If, *form1* does not evaluate to `#f`, its value is returned instead. This is the so-called 'short-cut' rule for the evaluation of the or function.

A slightly unusual property of Dylan's treatment of booleans needs to be addressed. In Dylan, any value other than `#f` counts as true. The symbol `#t` represents only thecanonical value 'true.' The symbol `#t` can be used in code to make the meaning clearer, but any value at all that is not equal or identical to `#f` can be used to denote truth. The object represented by `#f`, on the other hand, is the unique representation for falsity; no other value can stand for 'false'. As a consequence, the following are legal Dylan forms (expressions) which evaluate to boolean values (the result of evaluating the expression is shown in brackets–integers have their usual interpretation in Dylan):

```
#f & 22 (⇒ #f)
1 & 2 (⇒ 2)
7 & #f (⇒ #f)
#t & 7 (⇒ 7)
2 | 22 (⇒ 2)
22 | #f (⇒ 22)
#f | 27 (⇒ 27)
~1 (⇒ #f)
~#t (⇒ #f)
~#f (⇒ #t)
```

(Note that the last case employs the canonical representation for the value 'true'.) The examples show how the value returned by either the first or the second form can be returned as the value of the entire expression. The effect of allowing any value to represent truth has a simplifying effect on code. It does, of course, require both programmer and reader to remember the rule. This is seen as a minor penalty for the increased clarity and perspicuity of representation. In addition to the logical operations just described, Dylan also provides comparison operations of the familiar kind. Although these operations are discussed in more detail below (Section 4.9), they are mentioned here because they return boolean values. Thus, for example, when the expression:

$$1 = 1$$

is evaluated, Dylan returns a non-`#f` value (in fact, it will return the value 1, here).

When an equality fails, it returns the value `#f`. The interpretation of comparison operators is entirely consistent with their normal interpretation (i.e., their intuitive interpretation), given the Dylan convention for the representation of the value 'true.'

Dylan provides an identity operator, written `==`, and an equality. Identity is strict and if two objects are identical, they are the same object. When two objects are equal, they have the same value. Equality is written `=`.

Dylan also includes an operation written `~=`. This is the 'not equal' operation, and is defined in terms of `=`. The `~=` operation can be used to determine when two objects are not identical because anything which is `==` is also `=`. Because `~=` is defined on `=`, it is general. Thus:

1 ~= 2 (⇒ `#t`)
`#f` ~= `#t` (⇒ `#t`)
1 ~= 1 (⇒ `#f`)
`#f` ~= `#f` (⇒ `#f`)

For arbitrary types, however, the user must define `~=` as a method based on `=`.

Because Dylan considers anything that is not `#f` to be true, it is not really possible to define a class that represents the boolean values. Dylan considers anything that can be represented as a class to represent a type, so it cannot really be said that booleans constitute a type. (The Mindy implementation of Dylan defines a boolean class, so, in that case, the booleans constitute a type.)

## 4.3 Characters

Characters are objects (instances) of the class `<character>`. This class is a subclass of `<object>`. Instances of class `<character>` represent characters taken from the underlying character set. Character constants are written as ordinary characters enclosed within single quotes. Thus:

```
'a', 'z', 'A', 'M', '0', '7', '&', '*'
```

are valid characters and instances of class `<character>`.

Characters can be compared using `==`, `~=`, and any of the other comparison operators. In addition, the following operations are defined over this class:

- **as-uppercase***character* converts character to uppercase. If character is already in upper case, or else does not exist in an uppercase form, character is returned unchanged.
- **as-lowercase***character* converts character to lowercase. If character is already in lower case, or else does not have a lowercase representation, character is returned unchanged.
- **as <integer>***character* returns the integer equivalent of character. The integer returned is implementation-specific and depends upon the character set chosen for the implementation. This function is not necessarily portable.
- **as <character>***integer* returns the character equivalent of integer in the character set chosen for the implementation. This function is implementation-dependent; it is not necessarily portable.

## 4.4 Strings

Strings are linear sequences of characters. A string can contain any character from the implementation'ss character set. Within strings, the character '\' (backslash) is used as the escape character. Backslash has to be escaped when it appears in a string as itself, thus the string "\\" is printed as a single backslash. Escaping is used to represent the standard carriage control characters, so:

- \" is the double quote character
- \n is the new line character
- \t is the tab character

You should consult your local manual for further information on escaped characters.

Strings can be altered in various ways; there are predefined Dylan functions for their manipulation. In addition, strings can be compared using the < relation and tested for equality using =. The functions over strings provided by Dylan include the following.

- **as-lowercase***string* converts all non-lowercase characters in a string to lowercase. If any character is already in lowercase or does not have a lowercase representation, as-lowercase is equivalent to identity. This function copies the string (produces a completely new string).
- **as-lowercase!***string* converts all non-lowercase characters in a string to lowercase. If any character is already in lowercase or does not have a lowercase representation, as-lowercase is equivalent to identity. This function destructively modifies string.

- **as-uppercase***string* converts all non-uppercase characters in a string to lowercase. If any character is already in uppercase or does not have an uppercase representation, as-uppercase is equivalent to identity. This function copies the original string.

- **as-uppercase!** *string* converts all non-uppercase characters in a string to lowercase. If any character is already in uppercase or does not have an uppercase representation, as-uppercase! is equivalent to identity. This function destructively modifies string.

In addition, there are Dylan functions that extract characters from strings, and that set the value at a given position in a string. These functions are the equivalent of subscripting on the right- and left-hand sides of the assignment operator, respectively. They are directly analogous to the subscripting operations defined for vectors. Indeed, Dylan allows the subscripting operations to be written in a form that will be familiar to many readers. If **str** is a string, then:

```
str[n] := 'a'
```

assigns the character 'a' to the nth element of **str** (the symbol := as in the Algol family of languages, represents assignment), while

```
str[n]
```

retrieves the nth character from **str**.

## 4.5 Symbols

Symbols are instances of the class **<symbol>**. This class is a subclass of **<object>**. Class **<symbol>** provides a dictionary that associates a string with a unique immutable object. Since the object related to the string is immutable, it can be compared using ==. Comparison using string-comparison routines is also possible, but is much slower than ==.

Symbol literals (i.e. literal symbol constants) have the form:

```
\#"characters"
```

where characters is a list of any printing characters (the set of characters that can legally appear in a symbol is not restricted to that for identifiers). Thus:

```
\#"Foo"
\#"foo"
\#"^%&{}"
\#"joe987"
```

are all legal symbols.

The as function, **as(<symbol>,***string***)** converts a string to a symbol (adds it to the dictionary if it is not already present). Its inverse, **as(<string>,** *symbol***)** returns the string that names symbol.

The detailed behaviour of **as(<symbol>,***string***)** is as follows. It creates a new symbol with the name string, if that symbol does not already exist. The function (a method on **as**) always returns the same symbol for strings composed of the same characters, regardless of alphabetic case. So we have:

```
as(<symbol>,"foo") ⇒ #"foo"
as(<symbol>,"f*987sa") ⇒ #"f*987sa"
```

Note that:

```
\#"Foo" == as(<symbol>,"Foo")
```

The inverse of **as(<symbol>,***string***)** is **as(<string>,***symbol***)**. For example: **as(<string>,#"fido75") ⇒ "fido75"**.

## 4.6 Numbers

Programming would not be possible without numbers. Dylan provides the user with a rich collection of numeric types. Dylan programmers can either ignore the details of the numeric types they manipulate, and let the implementation take care of the details, or they can specify the precise type of number they want to use. In the former case, numeric data can be treated as if it were instances of the general **<number>** class; in the latter, the programmer employs instances of the more specific types, for instance the classes **<integer>**, **<complex>** or **<ratio>**. Dylan also provides a number of floating point types, each with a different precision. If the programmer merely wants to manipulate numbers with a fractional and a whole part, the type **<real>** can be used; otherwise, one of the more specific floating point types can be employed. The most general numeric class is **<number>**; it is the superclass for all numeric types, whether discrete or continuous. In addition, the user can define special-purpose numeric types as and when the need arises. The type hierarchy for number classes is shown in Fig. 4.1.

The subtypes of **<float>**, i.e., **<single-float>**, **<double-float>** and **<extended-float>**, are intended to implement the IEEE standard floating point formats, with the exception that comparison operations do not conform to the standard for NaNs (see Section 4.9, below).

Conversions between numeric types are permitted, and are automatic in most cases. The conversion rules for Dylan are the same as those for Common LISP [18]. In particular, floating-point contagion (with rational contagion for comparisons) and rational canonicalisation are as for Common LISP. Individual type classes provide methods for automatic coercions.

The operations defined over the number classes can be divided into two sets: those which test properties, and those which perform arithmetic.

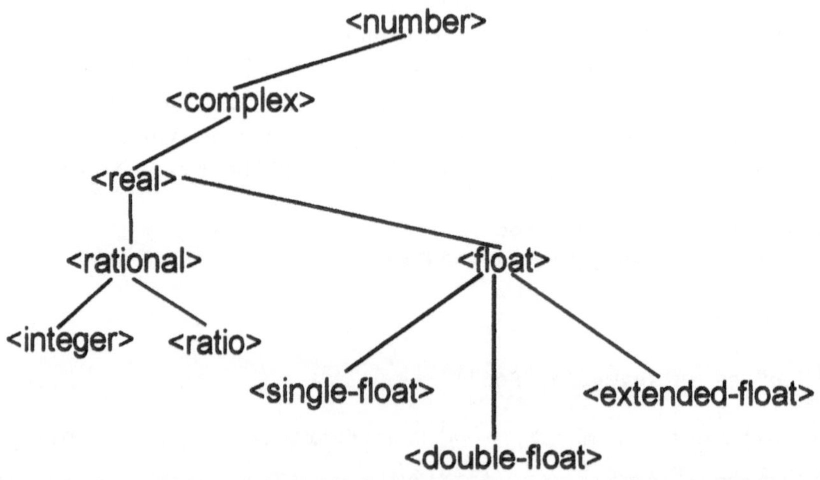


Figure 4.1: *The Dylan number class hierarchy*

Trigonometric and other functions are provided by libraries; they are not defined in [6].

### 4.6.1 Properties

The following functions test the properties of numbers.

- **odd?** *integer* ⇒ is true if its argument is odd
- **even?** *integer* ⇒ is true if its argument is even
- **zero?** *number* ⇒ is true if its argument (any number, note) is equal to zero
- **positive?** *real* ⇒ is true if its argument has a positive value
- **negative?** *real* ⇒ is true if its argument has a negative value
- **integral?** *number* ⇒ is true if its argument (any number, note) has an integral value

Note that **positive?** and **negative?** are defined in class ¡real¿ and are inherited by that class's subclasses. Consequently, positive? and negative? can be applied, inter alia, to instances of **<integer>**, **<ratio>** and **<double-float>**.

### 4.6.2 Arithmetic Functions

Dylan provides the usual arithmetic functions. The four usual functions: +, * , - and / have their usual interpretation (addition, multiplication, subtraction and division). Division by zero causes the run-time system to signal an error. Dylan also provides, inter alia:

- **abs** *negative number* ⇒ *number* returns *number* but with the opposite sign (+4 ⇒ −4; −1 ⇒ +1, i.e.).
- **abs***number* ⇒ *number* changes the sign of number if it is negative; the identity otherwise.

Functions to manipulate integers as bit strings are also provided; these functions include:

- **logxor #rest** *integers* ⇒ *integer* returns the logical (bitwise) or of the arguments. The arguments are treated as bit strings.
- **logand #rest** *integers* ⇒ *integer* returns the logical (bitwise) and of the arguments. The arguments are treated as bit strings.
- **lognot** *integer* ⇒ *integer* returns the bitwise negation of the argument.
- **logbit?** *index integer* ⇒ *boolean* tests the bit indexed by *index* in *integer* to see if it is on (equal to one).

General-purpose functions are included:

- **lcm** *integer1 integer2* ⇒ *integer* returns the lowest common multiple of *integer1* and *integer2*.
- **gcd** *integer1 integer2* ⇒ *integer* returns the greatest common divisor of *integer1* and *integer2*.
- **min** *real* **#rest more-reals** ⇒ *real* returns the minimum of the arguments; if there is only one argument, return it unchanged. (Note the use of **#rest** to allow a variable number of arguments.)
- **max** *real* **#rest more-reals** ⇒ *real* returns the maximum of the arguments; if there is only one argument, return it unchanged. (Note the use of #rest to allow a variable number of arguments.)

In addition to these functions, Dylan provides a number of others for performing functions such as **floor**, **ceiling**, truncation and rounding. The precise definition of these functions is the same as in Common LISP [18].

## 4.7 Vectors

Vectors are one-dimensional linear sequences of values; the component values can be of any type. A vector may contain values (elements) of different types; for example, a vector can simultaneously contain integer, symbol, and boolean types. This extreme polymorphism (which, in a language like ML [13] or

Haskell [9], cannot properly be employed, unless implemented using a sum type) is permitted because all Dylan types are subtypes (subclasses) of the root type **<object>**. Thus, because of the rule which states that subtypes (subclasses) of a given class are counted as subclasses of all types of which the class is a subclass, vectors may contain elements of any type derived from **<object>**. The vectors that we consider in this section have fixed length (variable—or stretchy—vectors are also possible and are defined in terms of class operations).

Instances of the Dylan class **<simple-object-vector>** are fixed-length vectors. The class **<simple-object-vector>** is a subclass of a more general type called **<vector>**. The properties of **<simple-object-vector>** and its operations are the focus of this section because they will seem familiar to most readers. They correspond closely to those found in other languages.

Vectors are typically used when the number of elements in a collection is known *a priori*, and is also known to remain constant. Vectors can be accessed in constant time and are, therefore, to be preferred over lists in this respect. Equally, vectors typically require less space than lists, and are preferred in this respect also. If an element of a vector must be found via search, the choice is more difficult; for both vectors and lists, the time taken to search for an arbitrary element is on average proportional to one half of the length of the list or vector. When the number of elements is not known, or is known to be variable, lists are probably the best initial choice for a representation; an alternative can always be implemented if the resulting code is sufficiently modular.

A literal vector constant can be written as:

**#[***elements***]**

where *elements* is a comma separated sequence of literal values. For example, the vector composed of the first four natural numbers is written as:

```
#[1,2,3,4]
```

The literal vector composed of two positive integers, a symbol and a list of three numbers is written as:

```
#[1,#"foo",2,#(101,27,34)]
```

The empty literal vector is written as:

```
#[ ]
```

The following are the operations defined over this class are the following.

- **vector #rest arguments** ⇒ *vector* creates a new vector. This function (like list) takes an arbitrary number of arguments (indicated by the **#rest** keyword) and creates a vector from them. It evaluates its arguments (like list). It is also possible to create an instance of **<simple-object-vector>** by calling the **make** function (see Section 7.4).

- **dimensions** *vector* ⇒ *sequence* returns a sequence (typically a list) whose single element is the length of the vector.
- **element** *simple-object-vector index***#key***default* ⇒ *element* returns the value that is stored in the vector at element *index*. If there is no such value and a default is specified, the default value is returned; otherwise, the function should signal an error. For vectors of class **<simple-object-vector>**, element provides constant time access to the instance's elements.
- **element-setter***new-element simple-object-vector index* ⇒ *new-element* updates the instance of **<simple-object-vector>** with new-element at the element referenced by *index*. If the index is out of bounds, the function should signal an error.

The following are example uses of the above functions (the literal form is used to represent results or other vectors):

```
vector(1,2,4+5) ⇒ #[1,2,9]
vector(pair(1,#(2,3)),4,5,6+7) ⇒ #[#(1,2,3),4,5,13]
dimensions(vector(pair(1,#(2,3)),4,5,6+7)) ⇒ #(4)
dimensions(#[1,2]) ⇒ 2
dimensions(#[]) ⇒ 0
```

Given the vector:

```
#[1,2,3]
```

the following are valid applications of the element and element-setter functions:

```
element(#[1,2,3],0) ⇒ 1
element(#[1,2,3],2) ⇒ 3
element(#[1,2,3],4,#key #()) ⇒ #()
element-setter(22, #[1,2,3], 1) ⇒ #[1,22,3]
element-setter(101, #[1,2,3], 0) ⇒ #[101,2,3]
```

These function applications can also be written in more familiar notation as follows (the vector `#[1,2,3]` is assumed to have been assigned to variable vec):

```
vec[0] ⇒ 1
vec[2] ⇒ 3
vec[1] := 22 (⇒ #[1,22,3])
vec[0] := 101 (⇒ #[101,2,3])
```

These are as would be expected in a language such as Pascal, Ada or C. Note that the form `element(#[1,2,3],4,#key #())` cannot be written in terms of subscripting and assignment.

## 4.8 Lists

Lists are sequences of values. Elements can be added to and removed from a list at any time (provided the list has at least one value). The class of lists is `<list>`. It is partitioned into two subclasses `<pair>` and `<empty-list>`. It is impossible to create new subclasses of `<list>` (it is 'sealed'—see Section 7.8).

Lists usually come in three flavours: empty lists, proper lists and improper lists. An empty list in Dylan is represented by `#()`, and is the unique object of type `<empty-list>`. A proper list is a sequence of values of any type whatsoever, terminated by the empty list. An improper list is one that is terminated by a value other than `#()`; alternatively, an improper list is a list that is circular (i.e. one in which the last element points back to the head of the list).

In Dylan, lists are similar to LISP lists; they are, in fact, trees. This is achieved by permitting the elements of lists to be lists. In most other languages, for example ML, it is permitted for a list to have elements of a single type; for example, ML allows lists of characters and lists of integers. ML allows lists of lists to be constructed, but the component lists can only be of a single type. Thus, ML allows a list of lists of integer. In Dylan, LISP and Prolog, lists can have elements of any type whatsoever—including lists. A list of lists is one way to represent a tree with an arbitrary branching factor.

Lists are composed of elements, each of which has a head and a tail. Literal lists have the general form:

```
#(head, tail)
```

where `head` is an object of any type (including `<list>` and `<empty-list>`), and `tail` is either a list, the empty list, or an object of any other type whatsoever (in the latter case, the list is improper). Thus:

```
#(1 , 2)
```

is a proper list whose elements are 1, 2 and the empty list (this is indicated by the comma). However:

```
#(1, 2 .  3)
```

is an improper list whose head is 1, and whose tail is the list `#(2 .  3)`. Here, the period '.' denotes the fact that the tail is not terminated by the empty list; in fact, the tail of:

```
#(2 .  3)
```

is 3 (which is neither a list nor `#()`). A list of the form `#(x .  y)` is called a *dotted pair*. Dotted pairs are the data type underlying the list type in most implementations (the concept of the dotted pair is described in detail in most books on LISP—see, for example, [1].

Most lists are proper lists, so the concept of the dotted pair can be ignored by the reader until greater familiarity with lists is obtained. However, it is worth noting that some built-in Dylan functions are not guaranteed to terminate on improper lists (for example, printing a circular list can be considered an infinitely long computation). Some implementations, therefore, test lists and either fail to return, return the expected and correct result, or else signal a `<type-error>`, depending upon the implementer's beliefs about improper lists. The functions to which this warning applies are those Dylan methods (functions) defined over collections and sequences. The reader is advised to check the implementation manual in all cases.

The empty list, `#()`, is often called *nil.*

There are many functions that can be applied to lists. Only a few are described.

- `pair`*head tail* creates a new pair whose head and tail are as indicated. For example:

  `pair(1,2)` ⇒ `#(1 . 2)` (a dotted pair—an improper list, note)
  `pair(1, #(2,3))` ⇒ `#(1,2,3)`
  `pair(1,#())` ⇒ `#(1)` (proper list construction)
  `pair(#(1,2),#(3))` ⇒ `#(#(1,2),3)`
  `pair(#(1,2),3)` ⇒ `#(#(1,2) . 3)` (an improper list)
  `pair(#(1,#(1,1))` ⇒ `#(1,1,1)`

- `list #rest`*args* ⇒ *list.* This function takes an arbitrary number of arguments and returns the (proper) list composed of them in the order specified. For example:

  `list(1,2,3)` ⇒ `#(1,2,3)`
  `list(1)` ⇒ `#(1)`
  `list(3+4,5+6)` ⇒ `#(7,11)` (list evaluates its arguments.)
  `list(2,3,#(4,5),#(5,6))` ⇒ #(2,3,#(4,5),#(5,6))
  (arguments can be lists)
  `list(1,1,2)` ⇒ `#(1,1,2)` (duplicate arguments are permitted)
  `head list` ⇒ returns the first element of the list.
  `head(#(1,2))` ⇒ `1`
  `head(#(1,2,3))` ⇒ `1`
  `head(#())` ⇒ `#()` (the head of the empty list is the empty list)
  `head(#(#(1,2),3)` ⇒ `#(1,2)`

- `tail`*list* ⇒ *object* returns the tail of the list (i.e., the list with the head removed). The tail need not be a proper list.

  `tail(#(1,2,3))` ⇒ `#(2,3)`
  `tail(#(1))` ⇒ #()
  (the empty list is always the last element of a proper list.)
  `tail(#(1 . 2))` ⇒ `2` (Improper list.)
  `tail(#(1 , 2))` ⇒ `#(2)` (because `#(2) == #(2,#())`)

```
tail(#()) ⇒ #()
tail(#(1,#(2,3)) ⇒ #(#(2,3))
```

- **size***list* ⇒ *integer* or **#f** returns the number of elements in *list*, or **#f** if *list* is circular. For example:

```
size(#(1,2)) ⇒ 2
size(#()) ⇒ 0
```

- *list1*=*list2* ⇒ *boolean.* Returns true if the two lists are composed of the same number of elements, in the same order: every successive head is equal to the corresponding successive head in the other list (so heads can be lists), and the final tails are also equal.

The above functions are non-destructive in the sense that they do not alter the structure of a list in memory. There are operations defined over **<list>** which alter the structure by manipulating pointers. These are relatively dangerous operations and should be used only when the reader has had considerable experience with list manipulation.

## 4.9 Comparison Operations

As stated in Section 4.2, Dylan provides a number of operations for the comparison of values. The object-oriented nature of Dylan implies that every value is an instance of (at least) one class, so comparison operations apply to what would normally be considered to be simple, atomic or scalar types as well as to complex types such as strings, vectors, lists and arrays.

In Dylan, there are two predefined equality relations: equality and identity. There is also a pre-defined relation for not equal. These relations are written as =, == and ~=, respectively. In addition, there are the less-than, greater-than, less-than-or-equal and greater-than-or-equal operations, written, <, >, <= and >=, respectively. Although most of these operations have their usual interpretation, identity, equality and not equal need special care. In Dylan, two objects are identical if and only if they are computationally equivalent (indistinguishable). At the implementation level, identity is interpreted in terms of storage locations. Two objects that are identical are pointers to the same storage locations; alternatively, two identical objects can be characters or numbers. Typically, symbols are implemented as pointers. When a symbol is constructed, its name (a string) is stored in a table by Dylan, and is always referrred to by the pointer to the record in the table. Since identity is a matter of pointer comparison, symbols can be compared for identity. Characters and numbers cannot be changed, so they can be tested for identity (the concept of change here should not be confused with that of transformation: 1 + 1 transforms the number 1; it does not change it).

Equality is a less stringent condition; it merely depends upon being the 'same' in some sense. Two lists:

$l_1$: `#(1,2,3)`

and

$l_2$: `#(1,2,3)`

are equal (=) because they have the same elements, and their elements appear in the same order. If the lists occupy the same storage locations, they are also identical (==). (The empty list is unique, so it is always the case that `#() == #()`.)

Two identical objects are always equal; the converse is not true (since the objects might not occupy the same storage, or be the same number, character, or symbol).

Now, the operator denoted by `~=` is that of inequality. It tests the difference in 'sameness'. For any two objects, `o1` and `o2`, `~=` could be defined as `~(o1 = o2)`; it is defined in terms of equality and not identity.

Whenever a new Dylan class is defined, it is possible to define comparison operations for it; this is done by specialising the predefined ones. It is not often possible to define == for arbitrary objects. The = relation can always be defined. For example, the velocity of an aircraft can be defined in terms of the pair:

(speed,direction)

In their Dylan representation, two velocities, **v1** and **v2**, are equal (=) if and only if:

**v1.speed = v2.speed**, and
**v1.direction = v2.direction**

I.e., if both components are equal. This can be used as the definition of equality for the velocity class for aircraft.

Just as identity cannot be directly defined for an arbitrary class, inequality cannot be directly defined. Instead, the definition of = must be specialised for the new class and inequality defined in terms of the specialisation.

In some circumstances, = and `~=` do not return. In particular, when circular or infinite structures are involved, these relations do not terminate.

It is only possible, of course, to define >, <, <= and >= if there is some way of ordering instances of a class. When defining comparisons for a new class, it is possible only to specialise < (the other operators are defined in terms of it in the obvious ways for each class). The comparison implemented by < is as follows:

- Built-in real numbers are compared by mathematical value;
- Characters are compared by the ordinal value of the underlying character set; case is significant;

- Strings are compared lexicographically by applying ¡ to corresponding elements; if one string is a strict prefix of the other, the shorter string is considered the 'smaller'.

Because of the interpretation of non-`#f` in Dylan, booleans can always be compared by =; the application of == to arguments of appropriate types does not always yield anything useful or meaningful.

Programs can extend the behaviour of the primitive = and < methods by defining specialised methods appropriate for newly defined classes. For this protocol to work, all methods specialising = and ¡ must preserve the following properties:

> If `(a == b)`, `(a = b)` [Identity] If `(a < b)` and `(b < c)`, `(a < c)` [Transitivity] Exactly one of `(a < b)`, `(a = b)`, or `(b > a)` holds. [Trichotomy]

Note that trichotomy also implies antisymmetry:

> If `(a < b)`, `~(b < a)`

antireflexivity:

> If `(a == b)`, `~(a < b)`

and commutativity for =:

> If `(a = b)`, `(b = a)`.

The trichotomy property implies that the way in which Dylan represents floating-point numbers is not IEEE-compliant. IEEE requires that all comparison operations return false if one operand is NaN; the generic Dylan equality and magnitude comparisons are not, therefore, IEEE-compliant.

# Chapter 5

# Expressions and Assignment

## 5.1 Introduction

The purpose of this chapter is to introduce the various expression types provided by Dylan. Expressions in Dylan are forms including what, in other programming languages, are considered to be control statements such as the conditional and various forms of iteration. In Dylan, however, every form returns a value. Hence, it is possible to talk of the 'while expression' rather than the 'while statement', even though side effects are permitted in Dylan.

When looking for control statements, the reader always needs to remember that everything in Dylan returns a value (unless specificially directed not to); Dylan programs are composed entirely of expressions. Dylan is called an expression language. As an expression language, Dylan contains no constructs which resemble statements in other languages. Thus, when looking for the description of the 'if statement', it is necessary to look for 'if expression'. It is quite possible to ignore the result returned by a control expression and, in this way, to mimic the effects of control statements in other languages. Thus, a control expression can be used for its effect and its result can be ignored.

If control constructs were presented as statements, i.e. constructs which do not return values (as 'impure' continuations ), but which alter the state of the computation and return a 'pure' continuation, the semantics of the Dylan language would not be correctly represented. It is for this reason that control structures are referred to, and described in terms of expressions. As noted above, the programmer is free to treat this kind of expression in various ways, according to habit, need or convention. Dylan does not have a goto construct.

Before it is possible to discuss control, it is necessary to discuss the concept of the variable. In Dylan, variables are always typed. However, types are not necessarily statically assigned to variables as they are in Pascal or Ada; these languages are said to be statically typed. Instead, the type of a variable can be assigned when a value is first bound to it; this is referred to as dynamic typing. Dylan is designed to allow both static and dynamic typing of variables. Dynamic typing has the property that the type of a variable can change during the execution of a program.

## 5.2 Types and Variables

### 5.2.1 Types

In Dylan, variables can be explicitly associated with a type. Variables in parameter lists of functions, in binding statements like **`let`** and **`define variable`**, in **`for`** loop clauses, and in other places, also allow the programmer to make such an association. In Dylan, the process of associating a type with a variable is called specialisation. When a variable is assigned a type, it is said to be specialised to that type. Once a variable has been specialised, it cannot be reassigned a type—it cannot be re-specialised. If a variable is not specialised, its type is assumed to be **`<object>`**.

A variable is specialised using the syntax:

*variable-name* :: *type*

where type is any valid Dylan type (that is, an instance of **`<type>`**). In particular, all classes are valid types; they are all instances of **`<type>`**. When a variable is not specialised, it can take values from any type; when it is specialised, its range of bindings is restricted. In particular, if a variable is specialised to type $\tau$, it can only be bound to objects of type $\tau$ or to objects whose type is a subtype of $\tau$ (i.e. to objects which are subclasses of $\tau$). Assignment of an object of a supertype of $\tau$ to a variable specialised to type $\tau$ is an error.

The type of a variable is evaluated in the same environment as its initialising expression (see below, and also see Section 5.6), but before the initialising expression is evaluated.

If a variable is not explicitly assigned a type by the programmer, that variable is not typeless. Typeless programming languages do not make much sense and have paradoxes associated with them. Instead, it can be assumed that a variable that is not associated with an explicit typing, or type specialisation, has the type **`<object>`**. That is, without further information, a variable is assumed to have the most general type possible. An unspecialised variable can hold a value of any type whatsoever. This is a useful feature when programs are exploratory or experimental, or when the programmer is unsure as to the types of object to which a variable will be bound. During the execution of a program, an unspecialised variable may be bound at different times to values of different types; this is perfectly legal. In this case, the variable is said to be dynamically typed. (Smalltalk, BASIC and LISP are very often described as being dynamically typed for this reason.) If a variable is always associated with a specific type, it is said to be statically typed. (Pascal, Ada, C, and FORTRAN are statically typed.) Dylan allows both kinds of variable.

Dynamic typing brings with it the problem of determining the type of the object to which a variable is bound at any point in a computation in which that variable is used. The reason for this is that the type of the binding determines which the permitted operations are. For example, if a variable is currently bound to a boolean value, it cannot be added to an integer; if a variable is bound to a window in the user interface, taking its logical-or makes little sense (unless this is construed as or-ing every pixel in the window, which is not what was intended). If either of these variables is re-bound to a value of the appropriate type (number or bit string/integer), the desired operations become possible; but they cause errors given the bindings initially described. When the current type of a variable is known, the operation to be performed can be verified.

Dylan performs such dynamic type checks automatically and as necessary.

### 5.2.2 Variables

Dylan provides two kinds of variable: module and lexical variables . Variables can be thought of as places where data is stored for the purposes of the computational process. Dylan is based upon a storage model. Lexical variables have scopes (see Section 5.6 for discussion) which are considerably more restricted than module variables. It is usual for a Dylan program to be composed of one or more modules. Each module defines a namespace or environment. A namespace is set of variables and their associated values; it is available to a specific part of a program. Module variables are similar to global variables in Pascal programs; their scope extends throughout the module in which they are defined. Lexical variables tend to have a scope extending for only a few expressions or the body of a function.

Dylan also considers that functions and classes are bound to variables. In the case of generics (a form of function) and methods, the language permits multiple simultaneous bindings of different values (a binding is an association of a variable with a value). In all other cases, a variable can be bound to one and only one object at any time. Generics, methods and classes will be considered in due course. Here, the emphasis is on variables, in particular module variables, and simple data objects. A module variable can be referenced and updated from any point in a module. It is, in effect, global to the module in which it is defined.

The definition of a module variable has the form:

**define variable** *bindings* = *init*

The execution of this form creates one or more module variables in the current module. A given module variable can be defined only once. In a define variable expression, bindings are the variables to be created. It can have the form:

*variable*

or the form:

( {*variable*}* [ **#rest** *rest-variable-name* ] )

where *variable* is either a legal variable name, or else is of the form *variable-name*:: **type** (this is the specialisation of a variable to a type—otherwise known as the assignment of type to variable variable-name).

An example variable definition is:

```
define variable v1 = 1;
```

and also:

```
define variable v2 = 3.14159;
```

When these forms are evaluated, the variables are defined and can be employed in computation. The first definition is of a variable **v1** whose initial value is 1; the second is of a variable **v2** whose initial value is $\pi$.

The following is now possible:

```
define variable foo = 10;
foo : = foo + 1;
```

Now **foo** has the value 11. Assignment is possible to module variables only after they have been defined.

The second form of definition specialises (or assigns) the type of the variable being defined. If there is no type specification, **<object>** is assumed. If the type is specified, and if the value of *init* is not of that type, or one of that type's subtypes, an error is signalled. For example:

```
define variable foo :: <integer> = 1;
```

is legal.

```
define variable foo :: <real> = 1;
```

is also legal. However:

```
define variable foo :: <integer> = #t
```

is illegal because it is ill-typed (boolean is not a subtype of integer).

Definitions of the form:

```
define variable (x,y,z) = init
```

and:

```
define variable (x,y,z, #rest foo) = init
```

concern multiple values and are described in Section 5.7.

Finally, there is the form:

```
define constant bindings = init
```

This has exactly the same effect as **define variable**, but the variable that is created is read-only ; any attempt to modify its value (write to it) will cause an error to be signalled. The alternative forms for bindings are exactly as in **define variable**; a constant can be declared from a multiple value binding.

Examples of define constant are:

```
define constant c = 1;
```

and:

```
define constant pi = 3.14159;
```

A type could be associated with each constant symbol, for example:

```
define constant pi :: <real> = 3.14159;
define constant ten :: <integer> = 10;
```

If the value returned by *init* is not of the same type as that specified for the constant, or is not a subtype of the specified type, an error is signalled (the same rule as for define variable).

## 5.3 Assignment Expressions

Variables denote places where values are held. The model which underpins Dylan is one in which there is a store containing locations that can be modified by definition or by assignment. Assignment is the most common way to alter the content of the store; assignment destructively updates a location in the store. The Dylan assignment special form is :=. Its interpretation is similar to that in the Algol languages; it is used to set variables to new values. The form of an assignment is:

*place* := *new-value* ⇒ *new-value*

Like any other expression, assignment returns a value. The value returned by an assignment is the value of its right-hand side. The object *place* is usually a variable name. Extended forms are also possible in Dylan (see later in this section). If place is not a variable name or an extended form, an error is signalled.

If place is a variable name, *new-value* is stored in the corresponding variable. There is no restriction on the kind of variable, for it can be a module variable or a lexical variable. If no variable of any kind corresponds to place, an error is signalled. If place corresponds to a read-only variable (a constant), an error is signalled. If place corresponds to a variable whose type is not the same type as new-value, or is not a super-type of type of the type of new-value, an error is also signalled.

An example of assignment is:

```
define variable x = 100;
x := x + 100;
```

The variable **x** is referenced on the right-hand side as part of the assignment. This referencing process is the same as in other languages; the contents of the location named by **x** are fetched and used in the right-hand expression (the contents are not affected by fetching them). At the end of this sequence, x has the value 200.

A second example is:

```
define variable x = 1;
x := 201;
```

The variable **x** has the value 201 at the end of this code segment; the original value assigned to it has been overwritten by the assignment expression.

Other examples of assignment will be found throughout this chapter. The reader should consult Section 5.6 for examples of assignments to local (lexical) variables. The semantics of assignment in Dylan is similar to that in many other languages. However, the fact that assignment returns a value can be important in some places (in this respect, assignment is similar to assignment in Algol-68, **setq** in LISP, and to = in C).

The extended form of assignment requires place to be a call to a function whose value is a location in which to store something. For example, assignment to an element of a vector **foo** can be written as:

```
foo[i] := 22;
```

It can also be written as:

```
element(foo,i) := 22;
```

The function element is the function which retrieves vector elements; on the left-hand side, it can be thought of as evaluating to the location of the ith element of **foo**.

In fact, **element** is a retrieval function ; it only retrieves values. The vector type has associated with it a setter function, a function which sets the value of vector elements. The full name of this function is **element-setter** (see Section 3.X). The following are all equivalent expressions in Dylan:

```
foo[i] := 22;
element(foo,i) := 22;
element-setter(22,foo,i)
```

In general, for any sequence, **seq**, of $n$ dimensions, assignment can be written as:

```
seq[i1,i2, ..., in] := v
```

and access can be written as:

```
v := seq[i1,i2, ..., in]
```

Assignments to the slots of a class will be described in detail in Section 7.3, after the relevant concepts have been introduced.

## 5.4 Conditional Expressions

### 5.4.1 If

The most common conditional is the **if** expression. It has the following syntax:

```
if ( test ) consequent
   [elseif ( elseif-test ) elseif-consequent]*
   [ else alternative]
end [ if] ⇒ values
```

The optional parts of the **if** expression are the **elseif** and **else** branches, as well as the final **if** (the **if** appearing after the final **end**). It is permitted to repeat the elseif part as many times as necessary (it is often better to use case whenever there are many **elseif** branches).

The **if** expression is evaluated as follows. First *test* is evaluated. If *test* evaluates to a non-**#f** value (true), *consequent* is evaluated and the results of evaluating *consequent* become the results of the entire if expression. Once *consequent* has been evaluated, control exits the entire expression. If *test* evaluates to **#f**, and there there are no **else** or **elseif** clauses, control passes out of the entire **if** expression; the **if** expression returns the value **#f** in this case.

For example, the following expression returns 1 if its test is true:

```
if (even?(n))
   1
end if;
```

When n = 2, 4, 6, ..., the expression returns 0, otherwise it returns **#f** (false). Another example is the following. Assume that there is a test that evaluates to true if its argument represents Saturday or Sunday. The following **if** expression tests for a weekend:

```
if (weekend?(day))
   print("Hoorah:  the weekend!");
   1
end if;
```

Here, **day** is a variable that is bound to the name of a day of the week. If **day** represents a Saturday or Sunday, the message is printed and the value 1 is returned by the expression as a whole. If **day** is bound to a working day, no message is printed and the value **#f** is returned. This example shows how a consequent can be an implicit block (see Section 5.8).

If the **if** expression has an **else**, a sequence of **elseif** alternatives, or both, its evaluation scheme will differ from the simple one just outlined. The description continues with the case of the **else** alternative.

**if** ( *test* ) *consequent*
**else** *alternative*
**end if;**

If the expression has this form, and *test* evaluates to **#f**, the **else** part is evaluated. That is, when *test* evaluates to **#f**, *alternative* is evaluated. The values returned by *alternative* are returned by the if expression as a whole. Once *alternative* has been evaluated, control passes out of the **if** expression. The alternative is an implicit block; it can be composed of an arbitrary number of expressions separated by semicolons.

The first examples are derived from those given for the simple conditional case.

```
if (even?(n))
   1
else
   0
end if;
```

In this case, when n = 2, 4, 6, ..., 1 is returned as the value of the whole if expression; when **n** is odd, 0 is returned as the **if** expression's value. This is an expression which returns the parity of an integer.

With the second example, greater expression is possible:

```
if (weekend?  (day))
   print("Hoorah:  the weekend!");
   1
else
   print("Boo:  working day!");
   0
end if;
```

This example also prints a kind of parity (1 is returned if **day** is bound to a Saturday or Sunday, otherwise the value returned is zero). This example merely shows where blocks are permitted. If printing the messages were all that was wanted, the expression would be:

```
if (weekend?  (day))
   print("Hoorah:  the weekend!")
else
   print("Boo:  working day!")
end if;
```

This second version is used for its effect and not its value; it will return whatever value **print** returns (probably something useless). It is possible to use an if expression for its effects as well as for its value.

Next, we show an expression which computes the maximum of two numbers (Dylan provides a built-in function, **max**, but it is ignored here). The numbers are assumed to be bound to variables **n** and **m**:

```
if (n <= m)
   m
else
   n
end if;
```

The result of the if expression is $max(n, m)$. It is possible to assign this result to a variable; thus:

```
maxval := if (n <= m) m else n end if;
```

where **maxval** is a variable of some numeric type. It is possible to rewrite this so that the **if** expression is used for effect and not for value:

```
if (n < m)
   maxval := m
else
   maxval := n
end if;
```

Finally, there is the case in which the **if** expression contains at least one **elseif** branch. There can be an unlimited number of **elseifs** in an **if** expression. Such an expression has the general form:

**if** ( *test* )
    *consequent*
**elseif** ( *elseif-test*$_1$ )
    *elseif-consequent*$_1$
**elseif** ( *elseif-test*$_2$ )
    *elseif-consequent*$_2$
    ...
**elseif** (*elseif-test*$_k$ )
    *elseif-consequent*$_k$
**else** *alternative*
**end if;**

The expression has been shown with an **else** alternative.

The evaluation rule for an **if** expression is as follows. If test evaluates to non-**#f**, *consequent* is evaluated and control passes out of the **if** expression (as described above). If *test* evaluates to **#f**, each *elseif-test* is evaluated in succession; should any *elseif-test*, say *elseif-test*$_i$, evaluate to non-**#f**, the corresponding consequent, *elseif-consequent*$_i$ is evaluated. Each *elseif-consequent*, like *consequent* and *alternative*, is an implicit block and can be composed of an arbitrary number of expressions. The value of an *elseif-consequent* is the value returned by its last expression. Once an *elseif-consequent* has been evaluated, control passes out of the entire **if** expression, the value of which is the value returned by the *elseif-consequent* just executed.

If an **if** expression contains *elseif* branches, but does not contain an else alternative, and if none of the *elseif-tests* evaluates to non-**#f**, control passes out of the entire if expression; the value of the **if** expression as a whole is then **#f** (Dylan's default value).

The following example is of an **if** expression that converts marks (in terms of percentages) into degree classes. In UK universities, and in many universities in the British Commonwealth, a system of degree classification is employed. Typically, the classes awarded by an institution are first, upper and lower second, third, pass and fail. There can be variations on this, but this is the most common. The class which is awarded to a student depends upon their overall mark (in the UK, there is typically no transcript, and only the final overall mark counts). The following **if** expression assigns a class depending upon the overall mark. The class is assigned to the variable **degree_class**, and the input **mark** is in the variable **overall_mark** (which is assumed to have been assigned by some piece of code that is not shown here). The variable **degree_class** is assumed to be a string; **overall_mark** is assumed to be a percentage (a floating- or fixed-point number). Thus:

```
if (70.0 <= overall_mark)
   degree_class := "first class"
elseif (60.0 <= overall_mark)
   degree_class := "upper second"
elseif (50.0 <= overall_mark)
   degree_class := "lower second"
elseif (40.0 <= overall_mark)
   degree_class := "third class"
elseif (30.0 <= overall_mark)
   degree_class := "pass"
else
   degree_class := "fail"
end if;
```

### 5.4.2 Unless

The **unless** expression is a simpler form of the if expression. It has the form:

**unless** ( *test* )
        *body*
**end** [**unless**] ⇒*values*

To evaluate an **unless** expression, the *test* is first evaluated. If *test* evaluates to a non-**#f** value, *body* is skipped (not evaluated). If the test evaluates to **#f**, the body is evaluated, and the values returned by the last expression in *body* are returned as the values of the entire unless expression. If *body* contains no expressions, **#f** is returned. The **unless** expression can be defined in terms of **if** as follows:

```
unless (c)
      e
end unless;
```

and can be defined as:

```
if (~c)
   e
end if;
```

The body of an **unless** expression is an implicit body; it can be composed of an arbitrary number of expressions.

The conditional which prints a message when it is a working day can be written as:

```
unless (weekend?(day))
       print("Boo:  working day!")
end unless;
```

Notice how the message is different. It is assumed that a day which is not at the weekend is a working day.

### 5.4.3 Case

The **case** expression is a way of testing for many conditions. It can be considered as a multi-way conditional (like if expressions with elseifs), and is similar to the 'McCarthy conditional' found in LISP. The form of the case expression is:

```
case
     test₁ => body₁ ;
     ...
     testₙ => bodyₙ ;
     [otherwise => otherwise-body] [; bf]
end [case] ⇒ values
```

The expression evaluates the $test_i$ in order. When some test, $test_j$, evaluates to non-**#f**, the corresponding body, $body_j$, is evaluated. The value of the last expression in the body is returned as the value of the entire **case** expression.

If there is no body expression for a successful test, the (first) value of the test is returned. Subsequent tests are not evaluated.

If none of the tests evaluates to true, the entire case expression evaluates to **#f**.

It is possible to include a default case, denoted by the keyword **otherwise**. The **otherwise** keyword is considered as a test that always succeeds in the case in which there are no other successful tests. That is, if none of the *testi* evaluates to true (non-**#f**), the otherwise-body is evaluated. The result of otherwise-body is returned as the value of the **case** expression.

The degree class example can be written as a case expression:

```
case
     70.0 <= overall_mark
```

```
                => degree_class := "first class";
      60.0 <= overall_mark
                => degree_class := "upper second";
      50.0 <= overall_mark
                => degree_class := "lower second";
      40.0 <= overall_mark
                => degree_class := "third class";
      30.0 <= overall_mark
                => degree_class := "pass";
otherwise
      => degree_class := "fail";
end case;
```

The maximum example can also be written as a case expression:

```
case
      n < m
        => m;
      m < n
        => n;
      m = n
        => m;
end case;
```

Note that every case is considered; the expression could have been written with an **otherwise** branch, but it is considered clearer always to enumerate as many cases as possible.

### 5.4.4 Select

The **select** expression is more akin to the case statement of Pascal and Ada, and, to a lesser extent, to the switch statement in C. However, as will be seen, select generalises the conventional case statement. It must remembered that select is an expression.

**select** ( *target-form* [ **by** *test* ] )
        $match_{1a}$ , ... , $match_{1n}$ => $body_1$;
        ...
        $match_{ma}$ , ... , $matchm_n$ => $body_m$ ;
        [**otherwise** => *otherwise-body*] ;
**end** [**select**] ⇒ *values*

When the evaluation of a **select** expression begins, *target-form* is evaluated to produce a target-value. This value is matched against successive match lists. A match list is composed of a sequence of expressions, $match_{jk}$, separated by commas (they appear on the left-hand side of the symbol => above). If no match list matches the target value, and an otherwise is present, the *otherwise-body* is evaluated and provides the result value of the entire select expression. The bodies of the match lists are implicit bodies—they can contain an arbitrary number of expressions and always return the value returned by their last expression.

The matching process is as follows. The clauses are tested in order. Thus the clause $match_{1a}$ , ... , $match_{1n}$ is tested first. Each clause is composed of one or more matches.

The rules for evaluating a match are:

- Each match is evaluated to produce an object. The matches in a clause are evaluated in sequential order.

- If a match is a test function, it is used to compare the target object with the match objects. If no test function is supplied, matches and target object are compared using identity (==).

- If a match is found, the corresponding body is evaluated. The values of the last expression of the body form are returned as the values of the **select** expression. If there is no body in the matching clause, the value **#f** is returned (the Dylan default value).

- Once a match has been found, subsequent matches are not performed. All match clauses which are between the successful one and the end of the select expression are ignored; they are not tested, and, consequently, their bodies cannot be evaluated. Once a match has been found and a body executed, control passes directly out of the select expression. If there is no matching clause and there is no **otherwise** clause, the evaluator signals an error.

If a match list fails, the next match list is evaluated; this continues until all match lists have been exhausted.

When a **select** expression contains an **otherwise** clause, and when no match is found, the body part of the otherwise clause, *otherwise-body*, is evaluated. As a consequence, in the case in which a select contains an **otherwise** it cannot signal an error because of failure to match the target-value.

Testing of matches stops when a match has been found. It is thus immaterial whether the test function would have returned true for some later match. An example of select is:

```
let x = 2;
    select (x)
           1 => x := 0;
           2 => x := 1
    end select;
```

The select expression tests the value of **x** and compares it with 1. This match fails, so **x** is next matched with 2. This match succeeds and **x** is assigned to the value 1. If **x** had been bound, say to 3, control would, in this case, have passed out of the **select** expression. If the value of **x** cannot be anything other than 1 or 2, the **otherwise** clause can be employed. The **otherwise** clause serves as a catch-all and matches any value that is not otherwise specified by a select expression. The **select** expression which follows uses an otherwise clause to detect erroneous input.

If the target value is computed using **by** and **instance?**, select is equivalent to Common LISP's **typecase**. The reader will recall an example of **select** by **instance?** from the example program in Chapter 3. That expression is reproduced below as an example of this kind of expression.

```
select (quantity(si) by instance?)
       <number-quantity> =>
        if (branded?)
           item := make(<counted-branded-foodstuff>);
           brandname(item) := brandname(si)
        else
           tt item := make(¡counted-foodstuff¿)
        end if;
        number(item) := quantity(si);
       <mass-quantity> =>
        if (branded?)
           item := make(<branded-foodstuff-with-mass>);
           brandname(item) := brandname(si)
        else
           item := make(<foodstuff-with-mass>)
        end if;
        mass(item) := quantity(si);
       <volume-quantity> =>
        if (branded?)
           item := make(<branded-foodstuff-with-volume>);
           brandname(item) := brandname(si)
        else
           item := make(<foodstuff-with-volume>)
        end if;
        volume(item) := quantity(si);
       otherwise =>
            error("Cannot recognise quantity
                   -- shopping-item-to-purchase.  %=")
end select;
```

The built-in function **instance?** returns true if its first argument is an instance of the class named by its second argument. Thus:

```
instance?(n,<integer>)
```

is true exactly when **n** is an instance of the **<integer>** class. In the case of the **select** expression above, the use of **by instance?** applies **instance?** to the first argument in order to return its class. It is the class of the argument that is matched during the evaluation of the **select** expression. The **by** extension can be used to transform the value of the argument to select.

## 5.5 Iteration

### 5.5.1 While

The **while** loop has the following form:

**while** ( *test* )
    *body* **end** [**while**] ⇒ **#f**

The **while** loop is composed of a test and a body. The loop executes the body until the test returns **#f**. On each iteration, the test is evaluated. If the test evaluates to a value other than **#f** (recall that any value other than **#f** is counted as true in Dylan), the body is executed. The body is a sequence of expressions whose values are thrown away; any expression is permitted in the body of a loop. When the body has been executed, the test is evaluated again. The pattern of test evaluation, body execution is continued until the test evaluates to false.

There are three things to note about the while loop. The first is that the test is enclosed in parentheses; the second is that, after the terminating end, the token while may appear as documentation. Finally, the value returned by a while loop is always **#f**. Some examples of the while loop are:

```
i := 0;
n := 2;
while (i < 4)
      i := i + 1;
      n := n + n
end while;
```

This loop computes $2^3$ (= 16). Note that the semicolon acts as an expression separator. The value of the entire loop is **#f**; the value computed by the loop is held in n.

A more general version is:

```
i := 0;
n := 2;
while (i < limit)
      i := i + 1;
      n := n + n
end while;
```

This computes the value of **2n**. Note that a value for limit must be specified elsewhere, otherwise the system will signal an unbound variable error.

The next example is that of searching for an element of a vector. The vector is denoted by **vec**, and its size (length) is recorded in the variable **vecsize**. The integer-valued variable i indexes the vector. The loop searches for a vector element that is equal to the contents of the variable **goal**; it can be assumed that goal is set before control reaches the code that appears below. Finally, a boolean is needed as a flag to signal to the loop that the current vector element is equal to goal. The code is then:

```
vecsize := size(vec);
i := 0;
found := #f;
while ((i < vecsize) & ~found)
      if (vec[i] = goal)
         found := #t;
      else
         i := i + 1;
      end if
end while;
```

After the loop terminates, if **found** is non-**#f**, i indexes the element of **vec** which is equal to **goal**. Note that it is possible for there to be no element of **vec** matching **goal**. When the loop index, **i**, is equal to the length of **vec**, the loop will terminate (found will be false).

It is necessary to note that vector indexing is zero-based; i.e., the first element of a vector, **vec**, is **vec[0]**. Given a vector of length $k$, its elements are indexed by $0 \ldots (k-1)$. Hence, when the index is equal to $k$, all elements of the vector have been indexed.

The size of a vector (in fact, any subclass of **<array>**) can be obtained by applying the function size to the vector. In the case of vectors, size returns the number of elements.

The while loop:

```
while (#t)
      body
end while;
```

is an infinite loop (it never terminates) whereas the loop

```
while (#f)
      body
end while;
```

is a no-operation.

### 5.5.2 Until

The **until** loop has the following form:

```
until ( test )
      body
end [until] ⇒ #f
```

The **until** loop repeatedly evaluates the expressions in the body until the test returns true.

Execution of the loop begins with evaluation of the test. If the test evaluates to **#f**, the expressions forming *body* are evaluated, and control then returns to the top of the loop where the test is evaluated again. If the test evaluates to a value which is non-**#f**, the loop terminates.

The following example uses an **until** loop to calculate the sum of the elements of a vector (the vector is assumed to hold only numbers). The sum is held in the variable **total** (which is initialised to zero before the loop begins). The vector is called **vec**, and the number of elements in the vector is stored in the variable **vecsize** (the function **size** is again used to compute the vector's length). The vector is indexed by the variable **i**, which is initialised to 0 before the loop begins. The loop terminates when the value of **i** is equal to the length of the vector. Given a vector of length $k$, its elements are indexed by $0 \ldots (k-1)$ because indexing is zero-based; hence, when the index is equal to $k$, all elements of the vector have been indexed.

```
vecsize := size(vec);
i := 0;
total := 0;
until (i = vecsize)
      total := total + vec[i];
      i := i + 1
end until;
```

The result of executing an **until** loop is **#f**. The result of the above computation is to be found in **total**. When the loop terminates, **i** will be equal to **vecsize** (the number of elements in the vector **vec**).

For comparison purposes, the code to search a vector for a goal element is repeated here. The reader should compare this version with the one using a while loop.

```
vecsize := size(vec);
i := 0;
found := #f; until ( (i = vecsize) | found )
                   if (vec[i] = goal)
                      found := ~found;
                   else
                      i := i + 1;
                   end if
end until;
```

(Note that the expression **found := #t** has been replaced by the assignment **found := ~found**; this change has been made to show that boolean operations can be performed like ordinary operations—they are not restricted to tests.) The reader should also compare the tests in this and the previous version of the loop; the relationship between them is quite general.

The relationship between `while` and `until` loops is as follows. `While` loops execute their body as long as their test is true; they terminate when the test becomes false. `Until` loops, on the other hand, execute their body as long as their test is false; they terminate when the test becomes true. The choice between them is usually arbitrary, and can often depend upon the form of the test. Programs must be read by others, so finding the clearest form of test is always worthwhile; sometimes a test expressing a negation is more natural than one expressing a positive proposition. In some cases, for example, when summing the elements of a vector or searching for an element of a vector, the choice is arbitrary. The loop:

```
until (#f)
      body
end until;
```

is an infinite loop (it never terminates), whereas:

```
until ( #t)
      body
end until;
```

is a no-operation.

### 5.5.3 For

The `for` loop is the most complicated of the loops encountered so far. Its syntax is as follows:

```
for ( clauses
      [ { until | while} end-test] )
    body
    [finally result-body]
end [for] ⇒ value
```

The clauses control each control one iteration variable throughout the entire iteration. For each clause in clauses there is an iteration variable whose behaviour (in terms of the values to which it is bound during iteration) is regulated by the kind of clause in which it is defined.

An 'interation variable' is a variable which is used to control the iteration of a loop. For example, in a simple for loop of the form:

```
for (i to 10)
    ...
end for
```

| | *increment* >= 0 | *increment* < 0 |
|---|---|---|
| **to** | **variable > bound** | **variable < bound** |
| **above** | **variable <= bound** | **variable <= bound** |
| **below** | **variable >= bound** | **variable >= bound** |

Table 5.1: *Exhaustion conditions for numeric clauses*

the variable **i** is an iteration variable; it controls the number of times the loop is executed. In the other forms of the for loop, variables are used to control the behaviour in exactly the same way, although they do not necessarily count the number of times the loop has been executed.

The clauses which are permitted include explicit step clauses, collection clauses (see [6] for more details on this advanced topic), and numeric clauses. These options make for a complex yet powerful iteration construct. The syntax of these three kinds of clause are as follows.

Explicit step clauses are as follows:

{*variable* | *variable* :: *type* } = *init-value* **then** *next-value*

Collection clauses, when used with any collection class (such as **<list>**, **<string>** or **<vector>**), are as follows:

{*variable* | *variable* :: *type* } **in** *collection*

Numeric clauses, controlling iteration using numeric-valued variables, are as follows:

{*variable* | *variable* :: *type* }
    **from** *start*
    [{**to** | **above** | **below**}*bound*]
    [**by** *increment*]

In order to assist the reader, the metasyntactic conventions are as follows. Items enclosed within braces and separated by vertical bars are alternatives. Thus {*variable* | *variable* :: *type* } denotes a choice between an occurrence of an untyped variable or an explicitly typed variable; one of these must appear in the program text.

The optional *end-test* does not control any iteration variables. Instead, it controls whether the iteration should continue. The interpretation of *end-tests* depends upon the immediately preceeding keyword in the for loop's clauses.

The evaluation of a **for** loop is somewhat complicated. The following description will, therefore, be fairly close to that in the [6], p. 33-34.

The evaluation of a for loop takes place in nine steps.

1. The expressions in *clauses* which are evaluated exactly once are evaluated in left-to-right order as they appear in the text of the for loop. The following subcases must be handled:

- For explicit step clauses, the expressions evaluated exactly once are *type* and *init-value.*
- For collection clauses, the expressions evaluated exactly once are the *type* and *collection.* If the value of collection is not a collection (that is, is not an instance of a collection class), an error is signalled.
- For numeric clauses, the expressions evaluated exactly once are *type* and *start.* The *bound*, if it is supplied, and the *increment*, if it is supplied, are also evaluated precisely once. The value of *increment*, if it is not supplied, defaults to one.

2. The iteration variables of explicit step and numeric clauses are bound. There are two cases:

   - For each explicit step clause, variable is bound to *init-value.* If *type* is supplied and the value to which *init-value* evaluates is not of the specified type, an error is signalled.
   - For each numeric clause, variable is bound to *start.* If *type* is supplied and *start* evaluates to a value not of the specified type, an error is signalled.

3. Numeric and collection clauses are checked for exhaustion (i.e. they are tested to see that none remain). If a clause is exhausted, go to step 9. Otherwise, there are the following two cases:

   - A collection clause is exhausted if its collection has no next element (is empty, in other words).
   - A numeric clause cannot be exhausted if *bound* is not supplied. If *bound* is supplied, Table 5.1 states the exhaustion conditions.

4. The iteration variables of the collection clauses are next to be bound. Fresh bindings are created for each iteration of the loop.

   - For each collection clause, *variable* is bound to the next element of the collection for that clause. If *type* is supplied, and if the next element of the collection is not of that type, an error is signalled.

5. If *end-test* is supplied, it is evaluated. The termination conditions depend on the symbol used to introduce *end-test* in the for loop. There are three cases:

   - If the value of *end-test* is `#f` and the symbol is `while`, go to step 9.
   - If the value of *end-test* is non-`#f` and the symbol is `until`, go to step 9.
   - Otherwise, continue with step 6.

6. Execute the expressions in *body* in the same sequence as they appear in the program text. The expressions in *body* are employed to produce side-effects.

7. Obtain the next values for explicit *step* and numeric clauses. Values are obtained in left-to-right order in the environment which results from step 6. That is, the values are produced given the variable bindings which are created in step 6. There are two cases to consider:

   - For each explicit *step* clause, evaluate *next-value*.
   - For each numeric clause, add the values of *variable* and *increment* to obtain the next value.

8. Bind the iteration variables of explicit *step* and numeric clauses to the values obtained in step 7. For each kind of clause, if *type* is supplied and the next value for the clause is not of that type, an error is signalled. Fresh bindings are created for the iteration variables on each iteration. When fresh variables are bound, the evaluation process continues from step 3 (exhaustion checks).

9. Finally, evaluate the expressions in *result-body* in the same order in which they appear in the program text. Bindings created in steps 2 and 8 remain visible during the execution of *result-body*. Bindings created in step 4 (iteration variables of collection clauses) are not visible during the execution of *result-body*. The values of the last expression in *result-body* are returned as the values of the for loop. If there are no *result-body* expressions, `for` returns `#f`.

Some examples of the for loop are the following. It cannot be hoped to cover all possible instances of the for loop. Instead, some relatively common patterns are presented; the interesting features of each loop are discussed.

The first example shows how iteration over a collection can be performed using a `for` loop. In this case, the collection is a list of integers. In order to compute the sum, a variable called `total` keeps a record of the running total. The form of `for` loop uses the collection clause.

```
total := 0;
l := #(1,2,3,4);
for (e in l)
    total := total + e end for;
```

The code begins by initialising the `total` variable to zero so that it can record the running total (the partial sum). The list, `l`, is also initialised. The for loop has a body in which the current element of the list, `e`, is added to the running total. In this and the next example, the variable `e` refers to the current element of the collection (here a list, below a vector). The loop can be thought of as running along the collection binding each successive element to `e`. Note that the choice of identifier—here `e`—is arbitrary; it could have any name whatsoever. After the above code fragment has executed, total is bound to 10.

The following is similar, but is adjusted to show how iteration over a vector can be performed without use of indexing variables.

```
total := 0;
v := #[1,2,3,4];
for (el in v)
    total := total + v
end for;
```

Note that the name of the iteration variable has been changed from **e** to **el**.

If the sum is not to be returned in total, the finally clause can be used to assign the final value to another variable:

```
total := 0;
v := #[1,2,3,4];
for (el in v)
    total := total + v;
    finally
        vecsum := total
end for;
```

In this last example, the value of the sum is assigned to **vecsum** when the loop terminates. This is performed by the **finally** clause, which is evaluated immediately after the termination of the loop, and before control is passed to the next expression. When the **finally** clause is evaluated, total has the value 10; it has built this value during the iterations that have been performed. When the elements of the vector, **v**, have been exhausted (after four iterations of the loop), the **finally** clause is evaluated to assign **total** to the variable that will be used to transmit the result to other parts of the code.

Traditionally, iteration over a vector is performed in terms of an index into the vector's elements. This index is incremented by one each time round the loop and is used to access (either read or write) the vector. The next fragment is, again, one that computes the sum of a vector; but this time, iteration is controlled by an index. This index must always remain in bounds (i.e. must always remain a valid index into the vector). As in the other examples, some initialisation code precedes the **for** loop:

```
total := 0;
v := #[1,2,3,4];
for (i :: <integer> from 0 to (size(v) - 1) by 1)
    total := total + v[i]
end for;
```

It is not necessary to include an increment when the value to be added to the loop variable is 1. The loop could also be written as:

```
for (i ::  <integer> from 0 to (size(v) - 1))
    total := total + v[i]
end for;
```

Similarly, the type can be omitted from the declaration of the integer loop variable, i:

```
for (i from 0 to (size(v) - 1))
    total :  = total + element(v,i)
end for;
```

Here, the vector reference has been written in terms of the primitive **element** function which extracts the ith element of the collection (vector) **v**. The element function is the underlying function which accesses vectors (and other sequences). This last loop can be used in conjunction with a **finally** clause in exactly the same way as in the previous example.

The final example of a **for** loop is that of searching for a particular element in a vector. As in the above examples, the length of the vector is not known a priori, so the **size** function must be used to determine this value. The loop binds the variable **position** to the position of the element matching the goal element; the loop also binds a variable called **found** which it uses to control iteration, and which is also used to determine whether **position** is bound to the position of the goal element (in other words, **found** is true if and only if the goal has been found in the vector). It is assumed that **goal**, the variable containing the object to be sought in the vector, is bound elsewhere.

```
v := ...; // Some initialisation of the vector.
goal := ...; // The element to be sought is set up.
    ...
position := 0;
found := #f;
for (i from 0 to (size(v) - 1) until found)
    position := position + 1;
    found := (goal = element(v,i))
end for;
```

This loop terminates either when the control variable **i** has the value **size(v)** (i.e. when **i** indexes beyond the end of **v**—vectors are zero-based, so the last element is always **size(v) - 1)**—*or* when found is true (in which case **i** can have any value between 0 and **size(v) - 1)**. The variable found is set on the second line of the loop. Notice that instead of a conditional:

```
if (goal = element(v,i))
   found := #t
end if;
```

the boolean expression:

```
goal = element(v,i)
```

is used to produce the next value for `found`. The expression returns a boolean, which is the type required for found. The use of a boolean expression is better style.

On termination, if found is non-`#f` (if found is true), `position` will index the goal object in the vector. If found is `#f`, the value of position is immaterial (its actual value is `size(v)`) because `found`, which is in scope outside the loop, indicates whether goal has been found.

## 5.6 Local Bindings

Above, the define variable construct was introduced. This construct introduces and initialises a new variable. Unfortunately, use of this construct is very awkward. In particular, it only introduces module variables. All variables defined using define variable have the same scope. Variables declared using define variable are dynamic variables; they have dynamic scope.

When dynamic scoping is used, the value of a procedure's free variables are taken from the environment which is current when the procedure is called, not when it is defined. This contrasts with static scoping, in which the value of a free variable depends upon where it was defined and the values of the constants, procedures and other variables which were in scope when it was defined. The value associated with a statically scoped free variable can be read from the text of the program. The value associated with a dynamically scoped variable can only be determined by executing the program.

It is often necessary to introduce a new variable, but to restrict its scope. The let expression does this. The `let` expression introduces new statically scoped variables. The `let` expression declares and initialises a new lexical variable. That is, it declares and initialises a variable with lexical scope. Variables with lexical scope can only be referenced in a limited region of program text; they correspond to local variables in other languages.

The form of a `let` is:

`let` *bindings* = *init*

The `let` form creates one or more lexical variables within the smallest enclosing implicit body containing the `let`. Outside of that implicit body, the variables introduced by `let` are not visible. The bindings are the variable(s) to be created. They have one of the following forms:

*variable*

or:

( {*variable*}* [ `#rest` *rest-variable-name* ] )

where *variable* can be a variable name or else *variable*::*type* (a typed variable). *variable* and *rest-variable-name* must have the syntax of variable names; they are not evaluated. The values returned by *init* provide initial values for the variable(s) specified by bindings.

The simplest form of **let** is one in which *bindings* is a single variable and *init* returns a single value; that value is used to initialise the single variable. For example:

```
let v = 10;
```

creates a new variable, v, and initialises it to 10. In the next case:

```
let l :: <list> = #(1,2,3);
```

creates a new variable, l, whose type is **<list>**, and which is initialised to the list #(1, 2, 3). If the initialising expression, init, does not return a value of the same type as that specified when a variable is declared, an error is signalled. Thus:

```
let v :: <integer> = #[1,2,3];
```

creates a new integer variable which is then initialised with a vector; an error is signalled.

The value to which a lexical variable is initialised can be changed in the body which surrounds the let. For example:

```
let n = 1;
n := 200;
```

and

```
let n := 1;
n := n + 1;
```

are both perfectly legal.

It is possible for lets to be nested within **lets**, as in:

```
let n = 1;
let m = 2;
    m + n
```

To show how **let** interacts with other contexts, consider the following examples. Lexical variables override all other variables with the same name. For example:

```
define variable v = 100;
begin
      let v = 20;
      let v = 40;
          v + v
end;
```

returns 80. The reason for this is that the innermost (bottom-most) `let` declares a variable which overrides the two previously declared ones with the same name. For the same reason:

```
define variable v = 100;
begin
        let v = 20
             v + v
end
```

returns 40.

To show the scoping of lexical variables, consider:

```
begin/* block 1 */
      let x = 1;
      ...
      begin /* block 2 */
             let y = 2;
             ...
             E(x,y);
             ...
             end /* block 2 */
end; /* block 1 */
```

The scope of the variable `x` extends from the `let` where it is declared to the end of block 1; that of variable `y` extends from the `let` where it was declared to the end of block 2. Variable `x` is in scope throughout block 2, so the expression `E(x,y)` is perfectly legal. Any expression involving `y` in block 1, where the occurrence of `y` is intended to refer to that declared in block 2, is an error and causes an error to be signalled.

## 5.7 Multiple Values

A Dylan expression can return no values, one value or more than one value (in a way explained in Section 5.7.1). The ability to return more than one value is referred to as returning multiple values. Above, it has often been stated that a control expression returns the values of its last enclosed expression; if that last expression returns more than one value, so will the enclosing expression.

### 5.7.1 Returning Multiple Values

Multiple values are returned using the function values. This function has the form:

**values #rest** *the-values* ⇒ *the-values*

It returns the values passed to it. Note that because values takes a **#rest** parameter, it can accept zero or more arguments. The following are, therefore, valid calls to values:

```
values()
values(1)
values(1,2,3)
```

Each of the above expressions returns its arguments in the order in which they are passed to values. In the case of **values()**, the result is as if nothing had been passed to the function. Calls to **values()** are useful in ensuring that functions and expressions return no value. For example:

```
if (i < size(seq))
   total := total + element(seq,i);
   i := i + 1;
   values()
end if;
```

ensures that the conditional returns no useful value.

### 5.7.2 Binding Multiple Values

If multiple values can be returned from an expression, it must also be possible to bind them. The bindings part of many constructs, such as **let**, **define variable** and **define constant**, can have the following optional form:

( {*variable*}*[ **#rest** *rest-variable-name*] )

This form is used to bind multiple variables. The **#rest** variable is used to hold any values that are left over after the variables named on the left are bound. There are, as is to be expected, checks performed on multiple bindings. The checks are as follows.

1. If the number of values is the same as the number of variables, the variables are initialised to the corresponding values.

   ```
   begin
   let (x,y) = values(2,3);
       list(x,y)
   end
   ```

   evaluates to the list #(2,3).

2. If there are more variables than values returned by the initialising expression, the remaining variables are initialised to **#f**. (If a variable has been specialised to a type—assigned a type—and is made to default by this rule, and if the variable's type does not admit **#f** as a value, an error is signalled.)

```
begin
let (x,y,z) = values(1,2);
    list(x,y,z)
end
```

evaluates to the list `#(1,2, #f)` (on the assumption that `z`'ss type accepts `#f` as a value).

3. If there are more values returned by the initialisation expression than there are variables, the excess values are placed in a sequence which is used for the initial value of the rest-variable. If no rest-variable is specified, any such excess values are discarded.

   ```
   begin
   let (x,y, #rest restvals) = values(1,2,3,4,5);
       list(x,y,restvals)
   end
   ```

   evaluates to the list `#(1,2,#(3,4,5))`.

4. If there is a rest-variable, but there are no excess values, the rest-variable is initialised to the empty sequence.

   ```
   begin
   let (x,y,#rest restvals) = values(1,2)
       list(x,y,restvals)
   end
   ```

   evaluates to the list `#(1,2,#())`.

An example of multiple value binding using let is the following:

```
let (x, y) = values(10.0, 15.6);
```

which lexically binds 10.0 to `x` and 15.6 to `y`. The scope rules for variables declared by `let` apply to multiple values.

Multiple values can be used to perform parallel binding:

```
begin
let x = 10;
let y = 5;
let (x,y) = values(y,x);
    list(x,y)
end
```

returns the list #(5,10).

# 5.8 Blocks and Exits

Blocks are sequences of expressions. They have already been seen in expressions such as **if**, **while**, **until** and **for** in the form of implicit blocks Here, they areconsidered more formally. The concept of an explicit block, of the form **begin** ... **end**, is first considered, and then a more complex form that allows remedial processing and non-local exits.

## 5.8.1 Begin-End Blocks

The simplest possible form of sequence is the **begin** block. It has the form:

**begin**
    *body*
**end** ⇒ *values*

where *body* is a sequence of zero or more expressions (it is, in fact, an implicit block!).

The expressions that compose *body* are separated by semicolons. The values returned by the last expression in *body* are the values of the entire block.

Because of the syntax of Dylan programs, **begin** blocks are only needed to restrict the scope of lexical variables (variables introduced by **let**), or to evaluate multiple expressions where the syntax requires a single expression. The principal example of the latter is an argument to a function call: arguments are intended to be single expressions.

There is no need to use a **begin** block where an implicit block is permitted by the syntax.

## 5.8.2 Blocks

The **block** construct is somewhat more complex. It combines the functionality of non-local exits, protected forms and exception handling. It has the following form:

**block** ([*exit-var*] )
    *body*
    [**cleanup** *cleanup-clause* | **exception** *exception-clause*]*
**end** [**block**] ⇒ *values*

The block contains an arbitrary number of expressions in *body* (an implicit block). These expressions are executed when control enters the expression. After *body* has been executed, the optional *cleanup-clauses* are executed. There can be any number of *cleanup-clauses*, and they can be arbitrarily interleaved with *exception-clauses* (see Chapter 8 for information on exceptions). Normally, the values returned by the last expression of body are returned as the values of the entire block; if *body* contains no expressions, **#f** is returned as the value of **block**.

If *exit-var* is provided—note that it is optional—it is bound to an exit procedure during the execution of *body* and of the various clauses. At any point before the last clause returns, it is possible to call the exit procedure. The effect of calling the exit procedure is that of immediately terminating the evaluation of *body*. The exit procedure can take an arbitrary number of arguments; the values passed to the exit procedure are also returned by it unaltered, and, in this case, they represent the return values of block. Calling an exit procedure is referred to as performing a non-local exit (because it immediately exits to a region of code that is not within—not local to—the block).

It is generally guaranteed that the *cleanup-clauses* will be executed. If an expression in *body* is composed of, or is terminated by, a call to the exit procedure (performs a non-local exit, in other words) and thereby exits the block, the *cleanup-clauses* are executed before the non-local exit completes.

If, on the other hand, one of the *cleanup-clauses* is terminated by a non-local exit from the block, no *cleanup-clauses* within the same block are executed.

An example of the use of **block** with a non-local exit is that of a segment of code that searches for a value in a sequence:

```
block(found_item)
    let indx = 0;
    let found = #f;
        while ((indx < size(seq)) & ~found)
            if (element(seq,indx) = goal_item)
              found_item(indx)
            else
              indx := indx = 1
            end if
        end while;
        #f
end block;
```

The most important lines of this example are the consequent of the conditional and the last line of the block's body. The consequent consists of a call:

```
found_item(indx)
```

to the exit procedure. The index into the sequence is passed to the exit procedure as its argument. If the exit procedure is called, the index will be returned as the value of the entire block. The last line of the block consists of the constant **#f** to indicate that **goal_item** has not been found in the sequence. This block, then, returns either a number or **#f**; the former when the search has been successful, the latter when it has not.

A typical use of **block** is to open some files and operate on them. The cleanup clauses can be used to cause automatic closing of files when the block exits. It is also possible to have the files closed when an error occurs.

A **block** can be nested within another block. There are restrictions on non-local exits, as will now be discussed.

### 5.8.3 Restrictions on Non-Local Exits

The block in which an exit procedure is established (the one in which its name first appears) is not the only one in which it can appear. However, it is an error to invoke an exit procedure after its establishing block has returned or after the execution of its establishing block has been terminated by a non-local exit. Thus, even though an exit procedure can be passed to another block, it can only be called within the block in which it was established.

There are three cases to consider. An example for each should clarify matters.

```
block (return)
      ...
end block
```

Here, there is a **block** which establishes an exit procedure called **return**. It is legal for **return** to be called at any point within the block.

The following case is more complex and is intended to show how errors can be caused.

```
block
      A1
      block (inner-return)
            B
      end block;
      A2
end block;
```

There are two blocks, each establishing its own exit procedure. The outer block establishes no exit procedure; the inner block, however, establishes exit procedure **inner-return**. It is legal to call the exit procedure **inner-return** from inside the inner block; that is, it can be legally called from the region of code labelled with B. The exit procedure, **inner-return**, defined in **B** can be passed out of **B** via function calls or assignments; this makes it accessible in **A1** and **A2**. However, **inner-return** cannot be called from the region **A1**; the procedure can only be manipulated as data in that region.

Equally, **inner-return** cannot be called from region **A2**, and can only be treated in the way described above. A call to the exit procedure in region **A1** or region **A2** would violate the condition stated above.

The final case is exemplified by the following example.

```
block (outer-return)
      A1
      block
```

```
        B
    end block;
    A2
end block;
```

In this case, the outer **block** establishes an exit procedure which is called **outer-return**. For simplicity, the inner **block** does not establish an exit procedure. Exit procedure **outer-return** is in scope throughout the outer block (in regions A1 and A2) and inside the inner block; the exit procedure **outer-return** can be called from anywhere in A1, A2, and in B. The exit procedure is in scope throughout B, but not in A1 and A2. The exit procedure can legally be called from any of these regions.

If the exit procedure is called from within the inner block, it will initiate a non- local exit from its establishing block (the outer block). Before the non-local exit can complete, the cleanup clauses of all of the *intervening blocks* (blocks that have been entered but not left) are executed; this process starts at the most recently entered intervening block. Once the cleanup clauses of an intervening block have been executed, an error is signalled if the exit procedure established by the intervening block is invoked. When all intervening blocks have had their cleanup clauses executed, the cleanup clauses of the establishing block are called; if any of them call the exit procedure, that call is ignored. The values passed to the exit procedure at the point of call are returned as the values of the sequence of nested blocks. If, during the execution of any cleanup procedure in an intervening block, any valid exit procedure is invoked (e.g. error is called), the exit procedure interrupts the non-local exit.

In the above example, if **outer-return** is called from inside region B, the cleanup clauses of the inner block (if any) are executed, and control passes from that block back into the outer block. The cleanup clauses of the outer block (if any) are executed, and control then passes out of the block. The value of the block is the value of **outer-return**; that is, the values passed to **outer-return** from the code in region B. Another way of describing the order of execution of cleanup procedures is that they are executed in the reverse order to that in which their establishing blocks were entered.

# Chapter 6

# Methods and Generic Functions

## 6.1 Introduction

Dylan has a single concept for what, in other languages would be two separate constructs; procedures (or subroutines) and functions. This concept in Dylan is called a 'method'. Because of its expression-oriented nature, all Dylan functions return a result—the default is `#f`. More usually, the user defines methods to accept and return values of particular types (it is possible for a method to return one or more objects of different types). Even when a method is used solely for its effect, as is the case with procedures in Pascal and Ada, and **void** functions in C, Dylan ensures that the method returns `#f` as a default value. Although all methods return values, it is not necessary for the programmer to take that returned value into account; in other words, the value returned by a method can be thrown away (this kind of use will be familiar to LISP and Scheme programmers). Unlike C, where the value returned by a function must always be assigned to a variable, in Dylan the returned value can be simply ignored.

A method is a single function whose input and output types are known. A method implements a particular algorithm using and producing those types. A generic function, on the other hand, specifies the number and kind of parameter (required, keyword, rest parameters), but does not specify their types. A generic function, in effect, relates a name to a set of parameters. Generic functions must be instantiated by the definition of invidual methods. Without defined methods, generic functions only serve as interface definitions. A generic function definition serves to state that there is a function of a particular kind; this function is then defined over various types.

Generic functions are inherently polymorphic in the sense that their implementing methods can be (and typically are) applied to objects of different types, but perform the 'same' operation over these different types. (Here, 'same' means that the relationship between input and output types is similar, modulo structural differences.) A generic function can be applied to objects of different types. To do this, a method must be defined for those types and included in the generic function. Generic functions are one of the principal means for introducing polymorphism into a Dylan program.

## 6.2 The Reason for Using Methods

Functions, or methods, they are really the same, are a primary way of constructing *abstractions* in programs. A method is a named sequence of operations. As such, it stands for some complex or composite operation that is meaningful as far as the program is concerned. For example, the push operation on a stack is meaningful, and will be implemented as a method named something like 'push' or 'push-stack'.

A method abstracts from the expressions implementing it by providing a 'black box' which renders the implementing expressions invisible to clients (those parts of the program which call the method). Rather than deal with the sequence of expressions which implement the method, it is possible to think of the operation which those expressions implement as an entity in its own right.

Once a meaningful operation has been identified, it can be coded and named. Thereafter, whenever that operation is required, it can be referred to or invoked using its name.

Once a method has been defined, it is tested. Once it works, it can be assumed to continue to work unless the representations upon which it depends (the data structures it uses) are redefined or otherwise altered. If any of the assumptions upon which a method depends alters, the method must be retested and again shown to work.

Because the operation implemented by a method is treated like a black box, it need be tested only once. Whenever the method is called within a program, provided that the method has been shown correct, its call can be assumed correct. Thus, if an error occurs, the method cannot, itself, be responsible; perhaps the data supplied as arguments to the method is of the wrong form, or wrong value, or even of the wrong type. (Sometimes, of course, a method call will demonstrate the incorrectness of the assumptions on which the method's definition was based.)

The above reasons are all fairly standard; they can be found in any book on programming or software engineering. Within the context of a language like Dylan, the most important reason for using methods is that a method represents an *abstraction*, or an abstract operation over some type(s).

In Dylan, as noted above, methods are often associated with classes. As will be seen in the next chapter, classes form abstractions over data. The association of operations (methods) with abstractions over data makes for very powerful abstractions which can be used to construct programs. The process of abstraction also leads, if the program is constructed with care or, more particularly, using a methodology like formal specification techniques, to programs of high reliability. Furthermore, abstractions can, at least in theory, be used across programs; that is, they can be *reused*, thus reducing programming effort.

In this chapter, the emphasis is on the active component of Dylan abstractions. Once methods (functions) are understood, it becomes possible to examine the concept of the Dylan class.

## 6.3 Named Methods

When constructing a program, it is usual to write one or more named methods (functions with names). This allows operations of greater or lesser complexity to be referred to by name. Repeated use of the same operation then requires only the method to be called. Furthermore, named functions (methods) can be called recursively. In this section, the named method is considered. Bare methods (anonymous functions) are considered in the next section; they are substantially the same as named ones, but cannot be called recursively. In addition, bare methods have an existence that is more fleeting than named ones; they can be applied to arguments, passed as parameters, and returned as results, but they cannot be handled in any other way.

### 6.3.1 Syntax

There are two issues to consider when dealing with method syntax: method definition, and method application (calling). The syntax of method definitions will be considered first. Before the syntax of method calls can be considered, it is necessary to understand a little about parameters and about the semantics of method names. The syntax of method definitions is as follows:

**define** [ *adjectives* ] method *name parameter-list*<br>
        *implicit-body*<br>
end [ method [ *name* ]

where *name* is the user-supplied name of the method, *parameter-list* is a list of formal parameters to the method (see Section 6.3.2, for more details), and where *implicit-body* is the body of the method (a sequence of expressions implementing the algorithm the method represents).

The *name* of the method has the same syntax as a Dylan variable name.

The *adjectives* relate to the level of dynamism of the named method (actually, its generic function—Section 6.7). The *adjectives* are words separated by spaces. The words are **open** and **sealed**. Because issues related to dynamism have not yet been encountered, further discussion of adjectives will be deferred until Section 7.8.

The parameters (formal parameters) of the method are defined by the elements of *parameter-list*. The method can only be called with arguments (actual parameters) which match the parameters in ways described later.

When the method is invoked (called, or applied), the *implicit-body* of the method is executed. This amounts to the execution of each of the *implicit-body*'s expressions in order; that is, the expressions are evaluated in the same order as they appear in the method's source code. The algorithm defined by the method is executed by executing or evaluating the method *implicit-body*'s expressions. The *implicit-body* can be executed in order to cause side-effects (updating variables, changing data structures) or to compute some value; both of these are legal purposes for a method, as, incidentally, is the combination of the two—that is, a method can be called for side-effects and to compute a value (the value often being computed as a consequence of the side-effects caused by the body). A method body can (and almost invariably does) contain calls to other methods, as well as to primitives.

Before executing the body of a method, the method's parameters must be bound. That is, the values supplied as arguments (actual parameters) must be bound to the (formal) parameters of the procedure. In Dylan, like other languages of the LISP family, this is done by associating the parameters and their values in a structure called the environment; the process of association is called *binding*. The process of binding is exactly analogous to that performed when executing a let expression.

Every method (named or bare) has an associated environment. The environment maps names to values (actually, to be strictly correct, the Dylan environment maps names to locations where values are stored). When a method is called, it has an environment in which its parameters are already named but are not bound to values (they are *unbound*). The call provides the values to be bound to the parameters. Similarly, every `let` expression has an environment in which the variable introduced by the let appears unbound. Execution of the init expression causes a value to be bound to the let's variable.

An attempt to access unbound variables causes an error to be signalled.

The binding process just discussed should not be confused with lexical and dynamic binding. The process just described is one of associating a value with a variable. Lexical and dynamic binding deal with the origins of values and where to look them up (alternatively, lexical and dynamic refer to ways in which the environment is manipulated).

Instead of referring to a method's body or the implicit-body of a method, the body of a method will be referred to simply as the method. Thus, the last sentence of the last paragraph will be rephrased as:

> 'A method can (and almost invariably does) contain calls to other methods, as well as to primitives.'

If a method contains a call to itself, it is said to be *recursive*. If a method, $M_1$, contains a call to a method, $M_2$, which contains a call to $M_1$, $M_1$ and $M_2$ are said to be *mutually recursive*. (Warning: mutual recursion is very often extremely prone to error unless the algorithm is supported by a rigorous argument. Mutual recursion is, in any case, hard to understand and should be removed where possible; it can be somewhat demanding in terms of resources and time.)

When a method is called, all occurrences of the method's parameters in the body are bound to the corresponding argument. Parameters are bound as *lexical variables* over the scope of the *implicit-body*. Thus, each parameter is treated as a lexically-scoped variable within the body of a method. Among other things, this allows assignment to parameters within the body of a method. Because parameters are lexical variables, their scope is that of the method body; they can be hidden by the definition of lexical variables with the same name within the body.

The value returned by the last expression executed when executing the body of a method is the value returned by the method. The last expression evaluated in the body of a method is not necessarily the last expression in the body.

The end of the form deserves a little attention. A method can be terminated by:

```
end;
```

(the word 'end' followed by a semicolon), by:

```
end method;
```

(a closing bracket composed of the words 'end' and 'method' followed by a semicolon). Alternatively, it can be terminated by:

```
end method name;
```

where *name* is the user-supplied name of the method. These three forms are, in effect, alternative forms of a closing bracket, the particular form adopted depending upon the programmer's choice. However, it is recommended that the third form, the longest of the three, be adopted as a standard for it affords the greatest documentation; it explicitly names the method which is being ended (this can be useful if the programmer must resort to very long method definitions).

When a method is defined, something rather more than the definition of a function occurs. In particular, when the definition of a method (named or not) is elaborated that method is added to a *generic function* with the same name as the method. Generic functions are intimately related to the Dylan type system and are closely related to the language's classes. Further discussion of generic functions is deferred until later in this chapter (Section 6.7).

Use of **define method** ensures that the name of the method is in scope throughout the module in which it is defined. Method definitions are considered to be elaborated in parallel at the top level of the module within which they are defined (similarly, module variables and constants are also simultaneously elaborated). As a consequence, every method in a module defined in this way is in scope as far as every other method is concerned. The order in which method definitions appear in a module's text has no effect on the methods' visibility (this is in contrast to languages such as Pascal which require routines to be defined before they can be called or passed to or returned from routines).

### 6.3.2 Methods—Examples

With these formal issues out of the way, it is now possible to turn to some examples. The examples show each of the points in the formal definition given above. Given that method definition requires the definition of parameters, it will be necessary to anticipate the next subsection just a little. Furthermore, because methods must be called in order for them to perform their computations, and because method invocation forms a natural part of the definition of a function, it is necessary to explain how methods are called (this account will be incomplete because a full treatment requires knowledge of the full Dylan parameter-passing mechanism).

Before giving the examples, it is necessary to issue a warning. The examples that follow are all relatively simple. Furthermore, the reader is asked to forgive the fact that the examples are small and relatively abstract; they are intended to exemplify particular points made above.

The first example is of extreme simplicity. It is given because it only shows how to define a Dylan method. The method is particularly useless (and rather silly):

```
define method one ()
      1
end method one;
```

This method defines the 'one function', the function which always returns the value one. The method's name is `one` and the name is followed by a pair of round brackets. The round brackets delimit the method'ss parameter list. This method has no parameters. The body of the method is simply the digit `1`. The body contains only one expression (the digit `1` in this case—a number is a perfectly valid expression, as is a character, a truth value, a string, a list, a symbol, or any other value). It is the last expression which is evaluated when the body is executed (it is the first *and* the last), so the method will always return the value 1.

The next method definition is almost the same as the last one:

```
define method one (n)
      1
end method one;
```

The difference between this definition and the last one should be clear. Within the round brackets there is the letter `n`. This definition of the `one` method has been provided with a parameter which is thrown away; the body of the method is the same as before. This example shows how to define a method with one parameter (for the time being, all methods will have one parameter).

The next example is more useless than the other two:

```
define method one (n)
       n + n;
       1
end method one;
```

The method again takes one parameter. The body now contains two expressions. The first expression, `n + n`, is followed by the expression `1`. The method again returns one as its result, but it has another (previous) expression in its body. The execution of the body is performed as follows. First, the arguments (actual parameters) are evaluated and bound to n. n now has a value (prior to argument binding, method parameters do not usually have values—there are exceptions, as will be shown in the next subsection). Once the parameters have been bound to their actual values, the body of the method is evaluated (executed). First, the expression `n+n` is evaluated. The result of this computation is then thrown away; it is not assigned or bound to a variable, nor is it returned from the method because it is not the last expression in the body of the method. Next, and finally, the expression `1` is evaluated; the result of this (the number denoted by the digit '1') is returned as the value of the method because it is the last expression in the method.

The next example is similar to the above:

```
define method addup (n)
       1;
       n+n
end method addup;
```

What has happened is that the body has been reversed (the method's name has also been changed). The expression `n+n` is now the last in the method body. The expression `1` is the first expression. The evaluation of the method is similar to that just described, but now the expression `1` is thrown away and the value of `n+n` is returned as the value (result) of the method.

At this point, it is possible (and meaningful) to give the first example of how a method is invoked (called). For example:

```
addup(2)
```

returns the value `2`. The call is composed of the name of the method name followed by an open bracket, followed by the actual parameters (the arguments), followed by a closing bracket (a final semicolon might be necessary, depending upon context).

An example of a method call involving a variable is:

```
let x = 2;
addup(x);
```

Here, **let** binds the variable **x** to **2**. The variable is then passed as an argument to the method **addup**. When **addup** is called, the value bound to **x** is passed to the method and is bound to the method's parameter **n**. As a gross simplification, this is similar to, but not identical to:

```
let x = 2;
    let n = x;
        <body of addup>
```

This shows how the initial value bound to **x** is then bound to **n**.

A similar effect would be had if the example were:

```
define variable x = 2;
addup(x);
```

which could be rewritten as:

```
define variable x = 2;
n := x;
<body of addup>
```

These two examples should not be taken as indicative of how Dylan actually performs the binding of arguments to parameters (the process is somewhat more complex). It is only intended as a hint of how things work in terms of those concepts already covered in this book.

The next example is as simple as those given above. Its purpose is to introduce a feature of parameters. The method is:

```
define method times-two (n)
    n * 2
end method times-two;
```

The method takes a parameter whose value it doubles. This definition is only marginally different from those given above. However, there is a problem with the times-two method as it stands. The problem is this: the method expects a number as its argument. (In fact, it expects an *integer* value unless automatic coercion rules such as widening are being used.) If a value of another type is supplied as the method's argument, the function will signal an error. It is not possible to multiply a string by 2; any attempt at this leads to an error being signalled. As the method stands, it is quite possible to call it thus:

```
times-two("programming in Dylan")
```

This is not prevented by the language. A call such as this will lead to an error (a type error) which will only be detected at run-time; it would be far better to trap the error at compile-time or when the declaration is elaborated by the interpreter. It would be far better if the type of the parameter could be specified.

Type specification is possible in Dylan. Sometimes it is necessary to specify types in order to make Dylan do what is wanted. Sometimes type specification is optional; sometimes the type of an object is not known until run-time.

Returning to the current **times-two** example, the parameter can be restricted to integers by providing a *parameter specialiser*. The specialiser is a specification of the parameter's type. The term 'specialiser' is used in Dylan where 'type specification' or 'variable-type association' is employed in other languages—the reason is that variables without specified types are assumed in Dylan to have the most general type possible (this type is called **<object>**), and the process of associating a variable with a type is the specialisation of its type ('specialisation' is a term from object-oriented process which denotes the operation of defining a subclass of a given class and the production of methods for that subclass).

The **times-two** method with parameter specialisation is:

```
define method times-two (n ::  <integer>)
      n * 2
end method times-two;
```

The difference between this definition and the previous one is that the parameter list of the method is somewhat more complex. Instead of the name **n**, the parameter has the form:

```
n :: <integer>
```

This is treated as a single parameter. The symbol :: is used to indicate that specialisation is being performed. The type is specified as **<integer>** (a convention in Dylan is that all classes and types have their names enclosed in angle brackets). The parameter now specifies the name of the parameter variable as well as its type; the parameter has the name **n** and type **<integer>**—**n** can only be bound to values which are integers.

As a consequence, the call:

```
times-two(3)
```

is legal and returns the value **6**, but the call:

```
times-two(3.14)
```

is now illegal (ill-typed) and causes an error. The error should be detected at compile-time, or when the interpreter processes the call, and be signalled as a type mismatch error.

It must be noted that if the call to a method involves a variable as an argument, for example:

```
times-two(v)
```

It might not be possible for the compiler or interpreter to detect type errors until run-time. The reason for this is that, although every literal, or manifest, constant (such as 2, "foo", 'a', #"bar") is implicitly typed in the sense that the value directly determines the constant's type, it is possible, in a dynamic language like Dylan, for a variable to be bound to values of *different* types at *different* times. When a variable is declared as having a type (as in the **let**, **for** and **define variable** constructs), the specified variable can only ever be bound to variables of that type. When a variable is not declared as having a specific type, it can be bound to objects of any type whatsoever (its inferred type is **<object>**). In the latter case, run-time type checks must be performed because the value bound to a variable can only be determined at run-time. In Section 7.6, the concept of type in Dylan will be discussed in detail.

The next example represents an increase in complexity as well as a case in which a specialised parameter is used. The method, called **sumlist**, takes a list of numbers as input and returns the sum of the list'sys elements. One way of writing it is:

```
define method sumlist (lst ::  <list>)
       let total = 0;
           let l = lst;
               while (l ~= #())
                     total := total + head(l);
                     l := tail(l)
               end while;
       total
end method sumlist;
```

Here, the method's argument, **lst**, must be of type **<list>**. That is, it must be a list. If sumlist is called with an argument which is not a list, for example an element of type **<vector>**, or one of type **<string>**, or one of type **<integer>**, the compiler or interpreter should signal a type mis-match error. (A summation function will be defined for vectors below.) The following is a valid call to **sumlist**:

```
sumlist( \#(1,2,3))
```

(it returns **6** as its value).

It does not matter if the argument to sumlist is the empty list because its type (**<empty-list>**) is a subtype of **<list>**. In any case, the algorithm in the body of sumlist takes the empty list into account as a valid case.

Method **sumlist** is also an example of a method with a body that is more complex than a couple of simple expressions. Its body contains two nested **lets** and a **while** loop; the last expression in the method's body is a reference to a variable introduced in one of the **let** expressions. It would have been possible to write the body using either **for** or **until** as the main loop; the while loop was a relatively arbitrary choice. As an illustration of this, the following method adds the elements of a vector (it will be seen how similar the two methods are, although some additions have been made):

```
define method sumvec (v :: <vector>)
       let total :: <integer> = 0;
           for (indx :: <integer> = 0 to (size(v) - 1))
               total := total + element(v,indx)
           end for;
       total
end method sumvec;
```

The most important difference is that the **while** loop has been replaced by a **for** loop whose variable, **indx**, is used to index the vector **v**. The index variable is declared as being of type **<integer>**. This has been done in the interests of clarity, but it also allows the Dylan compiler to produce more appropriate and faster code (it will generate integer-specific instructions and not general-purpose numeric instructions which must test the actual types of their arguments each time they are called). The index variable ranges from the least index into the vector (zero) to the index of the last element.

Vector sizes are given by the **size** function (note: this is the first example of a function call within a method body) which returns the number of elements in the argument (error if the argument is not some form of sequence). **size** is zero-based. Thus, the last element of a vector **v** is indexed by **size(v) - 1**.

The body of the for loop is simpler than in the case of the while **loop**. Instead of having to extract the element from a list, the **sumvec** method uses indexing to obtain elements of the vector. Vector elements are extracted using the element built-in function. The call to this function could have been written **v[indx]**, but the primitive form has been used here to exemplify function calls within method bodies (the form **v[indx]** is, in any case, expanded as a macro into **element(v,indx)**). The vector element is added to the running total in the usual way.

The running total is given an explicit type in the body of the **sumvec** method. This is to exemplify variable typing in **let** expressions. Type specialisation is not really necessary, but it does serve as good documentation. The reason why the specialisation is not really necessary is that, although the vector is supposed to be composed of elements which are all of type **<integer>**, within **sumvec** there is no way of explicitly stating this constraint; it is not possible to specialise the parameter **v** to something like **<vector>(<integer>)**, which would state that **v** is a parameter of type vector of integers. The reason why this is impossible is that the Dylan type system is not strong enough to support it. It is quite possible to define a vector of integers, but the programmer must explicitly make the effort and define a new type; it is impossible to create the type automatically within the type system provided by the language. This is unfortunate.

For comparison purposes, here is sumlist using a for loop:

```
define method sumlist (l :: <list>)
       let total :: <integer> = 0;
```

```
          for (e in l)
              total := total + e
          end for;
      total
end method sumlist;
```

The process of extracting the element from the list is simpler than in the first definition of **sumlist**, and is even simpler than in **sumvec**. The for loop automatically extracts the next element of the list. This element is then added to the running total in the obvious way. Again, **total**, the running total, has been specialised to type **<integer>**, even though, as has been seen, there is no guarantee that the list **l** is entirely composed of elements of type **<integer>**. One advantage that the specialisation affords, in common with this version of **sumlist** and of **sumvec**, is that any attempt to assign a value which is not of type **<integer>** to **total** will result in an error. Perhaps some will find this small comfort, but it is better than nothing.

It is worth noting that a **for** loop of the form **for (e in v)** could also be used to iterate over a vector. This is possible because vector is a subtype of the sequence type, as is the list type. This form of the for loop was not used because it requires knowledge beyond that covered in this book so far, and because it is useful to see the other forms of the **for** loop in action.

Before moving on to new issues, one final version of sumlist is presented:

```
define method sumlist (l)
      if (l == #())
         0
      else
         head(l) + sumlist(tail(l)) // ***1***
      end if
end method sumlist;
```

This is the method expressed as a *recursive function.* The function works by successively taking the head from the list and adding it to the sum of the remaining elements. By definition, the sum of the elements of the empty list is zero (because $x + 0 = x$). The recursive call to **sumlist**, marked with the comment *****1*****, is where the sum of the remainder of the list is computed.

The recursive method for sumlist can be written in a slightly different form:

```
define method sumlist1 (l , total)
      if (l == #())
         total
      else
         sumlist1(tail(l),total + head(l))
      end if
end method sumlist1;
```

This definition is tail-recursive. As such, it computes the function in linear time and consumes no additional stack space. Tail-recursive functions can be compiled down to parameter passing plus jumps; this makes recursive calls both fast and inexpensive. The Dylan language requires that this implementation (tail recursion optimisation) always be adopted.

The definition called **sumlist1** shows how methods with more than one parameter are defined. Each parameter is separated from the following one by a comma. If the method **foo** has four parameters, its parameter list would be something like:

```
foo(a, b, c, d)
```

If the parameters to **sumlist1** were specialised to the obvious types, the parameter list would be:

```
sumlist1(l :: <list>, total :: <integer>)
```

A parameter followed by a specialisation is considered to comprise a single parameter, so the entire declaration is separated from the following specification by a comma. Thus:

```
l :: <list>
```

is considered as a unit as in **total :: <integer>**.

It should be noted that it is not required that all parameters to a method be specialised if one of them is. For example:

```
sumlist1(l, total :: <integer>)
```

is valid, as is:

```
sumlist1(l :: <list>,total)
```

The following is also valid:

```
foo(a, b , c :: <symbol>, d)
```

as is:

```
foo(a, b, c, d :: <string>)
```

It should be noted that specialisers should be given whenever a unique type can be assigned to a parameter. Parameter specialisers are good documentation and can lead to the detection of programming errors. When polymorphism is considered, it can be seen that type specification can be used to avoid making tests within methods and for selecting the correct method among a number of potentially applicable ones.

The next point is that it is possible to specialise a parameter to a particular value. This is called a *singleton* specialiser. For example, if a function is to be called with its third parameter equal to zero, its parameter list could be defined as:

```
foo(a :: <integer>, b, c :: singleton(0))
```

or as:

```
foo(a :: <integer>, b, c == 0)
```

the two forms being equivalent.

The method **foo** is declared to have its first argument specialised to **<integer>**, its second argument can be bound to values of any type (i.e. is implicitly of type **<object>**), but its third argument, **c**, must be bound to the value zero. If the value passed to **foo** at call time is not equal to zero, or if a variable which is to be bound to **c** as an argument is not bound to zero, or if an expression is evaluated in order to produce a non-zero value to be bound to **c**, an error is signalled.

The method to compute the maximum of two numbers is predefined in Dylan. If it were not, and a definition were required, the following would suffice:

```
define method max (m ::  <number>,
                   n ::  <number> => i ::  <number>)
      if (m < n)
         n
      else
         m
      end if
end method max;
```

The body of the method should be obvious.

The first two elements of the method's parameter list should be familiar. What is new is the sequence of symbols:

```
=> i :: <number>
```

This is called a *value declaration.* It specifies the type returned by the function.

This is a specification of a result type; it states that the method max returns an object of type **<number>**. A result type declaration is called a **value declaration**. If an attempt is made to return a value of another type, a type error will be detected. Furthermore, if the method is used to supply a value which will be bound to a variable or parameter, there must be type congruence between the method and the variable or parameter. As an over-simplification, the method cannot be used to supply a value to a variable or parameter of type other than **<number>** (the real case is slightly more complex).

More precisely, *parameter-lists* can include value declarations. The value declarations must come at the end of the parameter list, and must be separated from the other parameters by **=>**. Note that more than one value declaration is possible, so the types returned by a method returning multiple values can be specified.

A value declaration can take the form:

*variable-name* :: *type-expression*

(as in the above example), or can just take the form:

*variable-name*

if *type-expression* is **<object>**. The result of evaluating *type-expression* at the time the method is defined is a type, called a 'value type'. The *variable-name* never comes into scope, and is there purely for documentation and for syntactic consistency with other parameters. It is valid for the same name to be used for a parameter and for a value declaration.

The last value returned can be preceded by **#rest** to indicate that a variable number of values is to be returned. A value declaration preceded by **#rest** is called a 'rest value declaration'. A value declaration not preceded by **#rest** is called a 'required value declaration'. The value type in a rest value declaration is the type of each of the remaining individual values, and not the type of a conceptual sequence of multiple values.

If a *parameter-list* does not contain =>, it defaults to:

```
#rest x :: <object>
```

which indicates that the function can return any number of values of any type.

A function must always return the number and types of values declared in its *parameter-list*. The rules are as follows:

- Each value returned by a function must be an instance of the corresponding value type, or else a **<type-error>** is signalled.

- If fewer values are returned by the function's body than the number of required value declarations in the function's *parameter-list* (or by an applicable method if the function is a generic—see below Section 6.7), the missing values default to **#f** and these values are returned. If **#f** is not an instance of the corresponding value type, a **<type-error>** is signalled.

- If a function does not have a rest value declaration, and more values are returned by the function's *body* than the number of required value declarations in the function's *parameter-list* (or by the applicable method if the function is a generic function), the extra values are discarded and not returned.

The next method defined searches for the maximum element of a vector. The parameter types are specified, as is the return type:

```
define method vec-max (v :: <vector> => i :: <number>)
      let len = size(v);
      let maxel = 0;
```

```
      let indx = 0;
          while (indx < len)
                let e = element(v,indx);
                    if (e > maxel)
                       maxel := e
                    end if;
                indx := indx + 1
          end while;
      max
end method vec-max;
```

There is little to be said about the method except for the body which requires a note. Within the **while** loop, the current element of the vector is bound to **e**. It is then compared with **maxel**. The variable **maxel** contains (represents) the current maximum value (it is initialised to zero when defined; there is an *implicit assumption* that all elements of the vector are non-negative). If the element is greater than the current maximum, it becomes the new current maximum (by assigning the current vector element to **maxel**). If the element is not the current maximum, the value of **maxel** remains the same. A local variable is used to hold the vector element in order to reduce the number of vector accesses. Without the local binding, the body of the while would be:

```
if (element(v,indx) > maxel)
   maxel := element(v,indx)
end if;
```

which is clearly suboptimal, requiring twice as many vector accesses as in the method definition. It would be better to have:

```
let indx = 0;
let e = 0;
    while (indx < len)
          e := element(v,indx);
          ...
    end while;
```

The next method is one that will be considered again when local definitions are investigated. The reason for this is that the interface to the method as defined below requires knowledge of the method's functioning. The method continues the maxima theme, and searches for the maximum element of a list. It is a recursive function:

```
define method lmax (l ::  <list>, maxelem ::  <integer>)
      if (l == #())
         max
      else
         let hd = head(l);
             if (hd > maxelem)
```

```
                    lmax(tail(l),hd)
                 else
                    lmax(tail(l),maxelem)
                 end if
      end if
end method;
```

This function is not the best because the user must specify a value for **maxelem**. The value to be supplied should always be zero, but the unwary user might supply another value, with the consequence that the method will not necessarily return the correct value. A value *must* be supplied to **maxelem** because the method is recursive and needs to keep a record of the running maximum (it could be written in terms of a global variable, but this would be distasteful). A singleton (Section 7.5.2) is not practical because the value of the **maxelem** parameter must vary with each call; a singleton remains constant.

Above, it was stated that the parameters of a method constitute lexical variables whose scope is that of the body of the method. Thus, parameters can be treated as if they were variables introduced by let expressions. Because parameters have the same status as any other locally defined variables, it is possible to assign to them and to hide them by means of inner **let** expressions. For example, it is possible to write the **sumlist1** method as follows:

```
define method sumlist (l)
      let sum = 0;
          until(l == #())
               sum := sum + head(l);
               l := tail(l)
          end until;
      sum
end define sumlist;
```

Inside the body of the **until** loop, there is the assignment expression **l :=** **tail(l)**. That is, the input list is assigned to successive tails of the list **l**; on each iteration of the loop, **l** is rebound to its current tail. This leads to more compact code, but it can also be slightly misleading unless some thought is given to this technique. For these reasons, it is suggested that it is avoided until the following points are fully understood.

Parameters to methods are new lexical variables. Their scope is that of the entire implicit block which defines the method's body. When a value is bound to a lexical variable, it is visible throughout the scope defined by its binding construct, but not outside that scope. Thus:

```
X;
let xx = e1;
<scope of let>
```

The variable **xx** is in scope throughout the region of program text denoted by '<*scope of let*>'. Within that scope, it is possible to access the contents of **xx** and to assign to it. Thus, the scope can contain within it expressions such as:

```
xx := xx + 1
```

or:

```
yy := xx
```

(provided **yy** is in scope, of course).

Reading and writing a lexical variable is only possible within that variable's scope, not outside it. As a consequence, it is not possible to refer to (read or write) **xx** within the region denoted by **X** above. The reason for this is that the particular **xx** created and bound in the **let** is not in scope; that particular **xx** does not come into existence, so to speak, until its defining **let** expression is evaluated. As a consequence, the following is not permitted unless the identifier **xx** refers to an instance of a variable other than that defined by the **let** expression:

```
X1;
xx := e0;
X2;
let xx = e1;
    <scope of let>
```

Unless there is a variable defined in **X1** with name **xx**, the assignment of **e0** to **xx** will cause an undeclared variable error. Even if **X1** defines an **xx**, within the scope of the **let**, the variable named **xx** will start off with value **e1** and any access to variable **xx** will refer to the variable defined by the let following **X2**. The variable **xx** defined in the **let** overrides any variable with that name which is defined in outer, enclosing scopes (**X1**, **X2**, or any scope enclosing the entire example).

The above relates to method parameters in the following way. Consider a method with two parameters, **p1** and **p2**. Parameters are placeholders; they 'stand for' values which will be supplied when the method is called. Assume that when the method is called, **a1** and **a2** are supplied as arguments. When **p1** and **p2** are bound, something akin to:

```
let p1 = a1;
let p2 = a2;
    <method body>
```

occurs (this is a simplification, but it is close to what actually does happen). Outside of the method body, **p1** and **p2** have no significance. When the method is called, **p1** and **p2** have a significance (as they do when the method is defined) *and* they have values.

The parameters are lexical variables whose scope is the method body. Before the point at which a parameter is bound, the parameter has no meaning; its meaning is restricted to the body of its method. Consequently, anything that is done to a parameter within its scope can have no effect on anything outside. In particular, and still assuming the binding process just shown, and if the program does something like the following:

```
define variable x = 99;
/* Call method and bind arguments to parameters:  */
let p1 = x;
let p2 = <some expression>
    /* body of method:  */
    p1 := x + 217;
    <expressions>
/* end of method body */
```

The assignment of `x + 217` to `p1` can have no effect whatsoever on the `x` defined at the start of the example (the actual parameter, in other words). This is an immediate consequence of the fact that parameters are considered local *lexical* variables.

Another example is the following:

```
x // case 1
define method foo (x)
        ...
        x // case 2
end method foo;
x // case3
```

We will assume that all three variables named `x` refer to the parameter `x` of method `foo`. In case 1, `x` is out of scope because it is not inside the body of method `foo`; the `x` appearing as `foo`'s parameter cannot be referenced because it is not in scope. In case 3, variable `x` is, again, outside method `foo`; variable `x` cannot refer to parameter `x` of method `foo`. In case 2, variable `x` refers to parameter `x`; variable `x` is in scope.

Dylan parameters are treated differently from parameters in some versions of Lisp (not Common LISP), and they differ from Pascal **var** parameters, C pointer parameters, and from Ada **in out** parameters. In each of these cases, a pointer to the actual argument is passed to the function. Assignment to one of these parameters within the body of a procedure in Pascal, C or Ada, side-effects the corresponding argument. Thus, if `x` is a Pascal **var** parameter which is bound to `v`, and `x := x + 1` occurs in the body of `x`'s procedure, `v` will have a value greater by one on exit from the procedure than it had when the procedure was called (identical things happen in C and Ada). In Dylan (and Common LISP and other lexically scoped LISPs), assignment to a parameter *within* a method leaves the argument (actual parameter) unchanged.

An example should make matters clearer. Consider:

```
define method seventy-seven(x)
        x := 77
end method seventy-seven;
```

Now consider the call:

```
let a = 10;
```

```
    E1;
    seventy-seven(a);
    E2;
```

where **E1** and **E2** are arbitrary expressions; assume that **E1** does not change the value of **a**. The call to the method seventy-seven returns the value 77. Within **E1**, a has the value 10 (if it is referenced). Immediately after the call to **seventy-seven**, a still has the value 10. The assignment of 10 to **x** within the method has no effect on **a** for the reason that **x** is a lexical variable local to the body of the **seventy-seven** method.

When an argument is a complex structure (a pointer), matters seem different, but, in fact, the same principle obtains. Consider the method:

```
define method set1 (v)
        v[1] := 77
end method set1;
```

which sets the second element of a vector to 77.

Now consider a call of the following form:

```
let vv = #[1,2,3,4];
    set1(vv);
    E2;
```

Here, the vector **vv** is passed to method **set1** as its argument. Method **set1** returns the value 77 (assignment always returns the value of its right-hand side). Immediately after **set1** returns, **vv** is bound to the value to which it was bound immediately prior to the call. However, after the call to **set1**, the second *element* of **vv** will now be 77. The vector element is different but the value bound to the variable **vv** remains: it is the vector to which **vv** was originally bound.

Now consider the following:

```
let v = #[1,2,3,4];
    let vv = v;
        set1(vv);
```

Here, the vector bound to **vv** is side-effected (its second element is now 77), but **v** remains untouched; this is exactly as would be expected from the definition of lexical binding.

Because parameters are just lexical variables whose scope is the body of their method, they can be hidden by means of inner definitions. For example, in the method:

```
define method foo (x)
        E1;
        let x = e1;
            E2 end method foo;
```

the parameter x is hidden by the variable x which is defined by the let in the middle of the body. Inside E2, any reference to x will yield the value of e1 (unless assignments have been made to x in the meanwhile), and not to any value which was supplied as an argument to foo in a call to the method. More concretely, let:

```
define method foo (x)
       let y = 10;
       let x = y * 2;
           x
end method foo;
```

and let a call to foo be:

```
foo(396)
```

The value returned by the call will be 20 and not 396. The reason is that the x defined in the body overrides the x defined as the parameter of foo; a lexical variable *lv* becomes hidden whenever a variable of the same name is defined (by let, local or as a method parameter) within an inner scope of the variable *lv*.

Consideration of the Dylan method started with the example of a method which returns the value 1 under all circumstances. The definition of this method was:

```
define method one ()
       1
end method one;
```

This is a method in no arguments, and is called by:

```
one();
```

Note that an empty argument list *must* be specified (as is the case with C). It is not legal Dylan to write:

```
one;
```

and expect that the method named by one is called. The reason for this is that the name of a method stands for the method in its entirety. The value returned by:

```
one;
```

will be something like:

```
{Method: no. of arguments = 0; return type = <object>}
```

A method's name is a variable bound to the internal representation of the method (this is usually called the method's *closure*). What is returned is just the value to which the name (variable) is bound. In order to call a method, the method name is specified together with a list of actual parameters (arguments); if the method has no parameters, its call must specify the empty sequence of arguments. Otherwise, the name of a method just represents a value of a particular (esoteric) type. Methods, as will be seen are first-class in the sense that they can be passed to and returned from other methods (including themselves).

### 6.3.3 Parameters

Dylan's parameters appear at first sight to be rather complex. They are more complex than those of C, Pascal or Ada, but less so than Common LISP. Dylan supports more than one type of parameter. It supports the following kinds of parameter:

- required parameters
- rest parameters
- keyword parameters
- next-method parameters
- return type declarations

Required parameters are those which will be familiar from other languages. As their name suggests, they must be supplied when calling a method. All the other kinds of parameter are optional. One, the return type declaration, really serves only to document the method in which it appears.

The methods defined in the last section all had required parameters. One or two had return type declarations. The concepts underpinning these two kinds of parameter should, at this point, be clear; familiarity with other languages will also aid in their understanding. The purpose of this section is to deal with the rest and keyword parameter types; discussion of the next-method parameter will be deferred until the next chapter because its explanation requires concepts from the object-oriented component of Dylan.

Before moving on, it is to be noted that any required parameter can be specialised to a given type; this has already been observed in the last section. It does not, in general, make sense for key and rest parameters to be specialised. However, there are default values which can be assigned to key parameters, and rest parameters default to the empty sequence (see below), so their types are implicitly specified, although at call-time they can be bound to objects of a different type.

The interpretations of rest and key parameters are as follows.

A rest parameter allows a method to accept an unlimited number of arguments (in fact, the implementation can place an arbitrary limit on the number of arguments which may legally be passed to a method). After the required arguments have been supplied, all other arguments are collected as a sequence and passed to the method.

Let the method plus be defined as:

```
define method plus (n1 :: <number>, n2 :: <number>,
                    #rest nums)
      <body of plus>
end method plus;
```

This method has two required parameters, **n1** and **n2**. It also accepts a rest parameter. The rest parameter is called nums; the fact that it is a rest parameter is signalled by the **#rest** which appears before the name **nums**. The method **plus** accepts at least two arguments. The method returns the sum of all of the arguments supplied.

The following are all legal calls to **plus** (**n** and **m** are arbitrary variables):

```
plus(1,2);
plus(1,n,m)
plus(1,2,3,4,5)
```

In the first case, only the two required parameters are bound. The method returns the value 3. In this case, nums, the rest parameter, is bound to the empty sequence. This leads to part of the specification of plus:

$$n + m + () = n + m + 0 = n + m$$

(i.e. the empty sequence—here written as ()—is equivalent to zero). In the second case, **plus** returns **1 + n + m**. The argument **m** is in the last argument position, so it is included in the sequence bound to **nums**; **nums** is, in this case, bound to a sequence of length one. In the last case, **nums** is bound to the sequence **(3,4,5)**, and the value computed by plus is:

$$1 + 2 + (3 + 4 + 5)$$

In other words, if the sequence bound to **nums** is $N$, and $N$ is of length $\lambda$, then plus returns:

$$n_1 + n_2 + \sum_{i=1}^{\lambda} N_i$$

This is, in fact, the specification of **plus**:

```
define method plus (n1 :: <integer>, n2 :: <integer>,
                    #rest nums)
      let sum = n1 + n2;
          for (n in nums)
              sum := sum + n
          end for;
      sum
end method plus;
```

If **nums** is bound to the empty sequence, the **for** loop will not be executed, so **sum** will not be incremented. The point of the **for** loop is to iterate over the sequence bound to **nums**, computing its sum.

The rule for checking methods with rest parameters is that they must be called with arguments for all their required parameters plus zero or more additional parameters. The first example call above was:

```
plus(1,2)
```

an example of a call with only required parameters. A call of the form:

```
plus(1)
```

is not legal because arguments have not been supplied for all required parameters.

The definition of a method which only accepts a rest parameter is permitted. In LISP, the **times** function can take an arbitrary number of arguments; it computes the product of its arguments. If **times** is called with no arguments, it returns one (the identity for multiplication). If an analogue of the LISP times function were required, it could be defined as:

```
define method times (#rest nums)
      let prod = 1;
          for (n in nums)
              prod := prod * n
          end for;
      prod
end method times;
```

The times function as just defined can be called by:

```
times()
```

which returns 1; it can be called by:

```
times(1,2,3)
```

which returns 3! (= 6); it can be called by:

```
times(1,2,3,5)
```

which returns 30. It can even be called by:

```
times(1,2,3,4,5,6,7,19.67,86.523)
```

which returns 8577613.3464.

Note that, because times accepts a **#rest** parameter, a call to it with no arguments is quite valid.

It does not make much sense for there to be more than one rest parameter in a parameter list. On *extremely rare* occasions, more than one rest parameter can be specified.

Keyword parameters correspond to optional parameters and can be given in any order as arguments. Each keyword parameter is named by a symbol—these are called the 'keywords'. The keywords used to name parameters guide the matching of arguments and parameters. Keyword arguments can be presented in any order. Keyword parameters can only appear *after all* required parameters have been supplied to a call. Keywords are used in calls to the function *as well as* in its definition.

Because keyword parameters can be treated as optional parameters, they are often associated with default values. If a method's keyword is not given a value in the call to that method, a default value is associated with the parameter.

The basic form of keyword parameter definition will be discussed first, and then the issue of alternative syntax and defaults will be considered.

The following is part of the definition of a method which specifies keyword parameters:

```
foo(a, b, #key c, d)
```

Here, the method takes two required parameters (`a` and `b`) and two keyword parameters (`c` and `d`). The start of the list of keyword parameters is signalled by the token #key. Those parameters following **#key** are *keyword* parameters. Here, the keyword parameters are `c` and `d`.

Another example is the following:

```
bar(#key a, b, c, d)
```

Here, the method accepts only keyword parameters. Another way of viewing this is that method **bar** requires all of its arguments to be named at call-time.

The definition of a keyword parameter can be as simple as that shown above, but it can also be more complex. Not only are there different syntactic forms that a keyword parameter's definition can take, there is the issue of associating a default value with a keyword to be taken into account. The syntax of a keyword parameter is as follows:

*name*
*name ( default )*
*keyword parameter*
*keyword parameter ( default )*

In the first two forms, *name* is used to denote both the keyword and the parameter. In the last two forms, *keyword* is not the same as *parameter*. The keyword is used when calling a method, and the parameter is used to refer to the value bound to the keyword inside the body of the method.

Discussion will begin with the first and third forms given above (the simpler ones). The second and fourth forms, the forms which involve default values, are considered.

To make the default-free use of keyword parameters clearer, consider the following definition:

```
define method Euclidean-distance (#key x1:  x-coord1,
                                       y1:  y-coord1,
                                       x2:  x-coord2,
                                       y2:  y-coord2)
      let x-diff = x-coord1 - x-coord2;
      let y-diff = y-coord1 - y-coord2;
          sqrt(abs(x-diff^2 - y-diff^2));
end method Euclidean-distance;
```

Here, the method defines the keywords **x1:**, **y1:**, **x2:**, and **y2:**. A eywords has the form of a colon-terminated symbol. Within the body of the method, as can be seen, the identifiers in the parameter list which follow the keyword parameters are used in the body of the definition. That is, instead of **x1:** and **x2:** being used to compute **x-diff**, **x-coord1** and **x-coord2** are used instead.

To call **Euclidean-distance**, **x1:**, **x2:**, **y1:** and **y2:** are used, thus:

```
Euclidean-distance(x1: 2.0, y1: 1.5, x2: 4.5, y2: 5.2)
```

In the call, each keyword is associated with a value. That value is bound to the corresponding parameter. Consequently, the argument named by **x1:** (the value 2.0) will be bound to the parameter **x-coord1**; the argument named by **x2:** (the value 4.5) will be bound to **x-coord2**, and so on.

The **Euclidean-distance** function could equally have been defined using the first form of keyword parameter. Here is the definition which results:

```
define method Euclidean-distance(#key x1, y1, x2, y2)
      let x-diff = x1 - x2;
      let y-diff = y1 - y2;
          sqrt(abs(x-diff^2 - y-diff^2))
end method Euclidean-distance;
```

The difference between this definition and the previous one is that the keywords and the parameters they name are the same tokens. In the body of the method, the keywords themselves are used to refer to the method's parameters. Hence, **x-diff** is computed in terms of **x1** and **y1**. Within a method, keywords are used without the trailing colon.

A call to Euclidean-distance using this second definition takes the following form:

```
Euclidean-distance(x1: 2.0, y1: 1.5, x2: 4.5, y2: 5.2)
```

The parameters are named as before; each parameter is named by a keyword whose name is terminated by a semicolon.

It is possible to present the arguments in an order different from that given in the method definition. The order in which keyword-value pairs occur in a call is immaterial. For example:

```
Euclidean-distance(x1: 2.0, x2: 4.5, y1: 1.5, y2: 5.2)
```

The following is also possible (although a little bizarre):

```
Euclidean-distance(y2: 5.2, x1: 2.0,  y1: 1.5, x2: 4.5)
```

The method will still compute the same result, namely **2.728** (rounded). The reason for this is that the arguments actually provided in the call (here numeric values) are paired with the keywords. The keywords are then directly used in the method body or are used to provide values to bind to the method'ss parameters. Because each argument is given a name, and because the names are used to bind parameters, the association between argument and parameter is performed correctly.

As long as the keyword-argument association is correctly made, position is irrelevant to keyword parameters (as the last two examples have shown). All keyword parameter lists must have an even length.

Keyword parameters are optional, so the question must be asked as to what happens if a keyword is omitted from a call. The second and fourth forms of keyword syntax allow default values to be associated with keyword parameters. Thus:

*name ( default )*
*keyword parameter ( default )*

allow the programmer to associate a default value with a parameter. The default value is an expression which is evaluated each time the method is called, provided that a value is not explicitly associated with a keyword parameter in a call to a method.

To show the use of defaults, consider the following example. Certain systems maintain databases of structured objects. The objects are composed of lists of **<key, datum>** pairs called the object's slots. These objects are typically referred to by name. Whenever the system needs to retrieve an object, it typically does so by name (some operations do not use names, but use of the name as a key is the norm). When creating an object, the user can supply a name or can leave the system to define one for itself (sometimes users want to have objects named in ways that make sense to people; sometimes such names are not necessary, so the system can supply names itself). The operation to define one of these objects could be defined in Dylan as:

```
define method create-object (slots, #key name (make-name()))
      ...
      let object = ...  ;
          store-in-database(name, object);
          ...
end method create-object;
```

The second form of keyword parameter is used, but now the keyword, **name**, is supplied with a default expression which appears between brackets and immediately follows the parameter. The expression used to supply the default behaviour is a call to the method **make-name** which is assumed to generate object names. In the body of the method, the name of the object is referred to as **name** (it is assumed that the call **store-in-database** stores the object indexed by its name in some database).

A call to **create-object** can take one of two forms (note that the first parameter is required and must, therefore, be specified):

```
create-object(actual-slots, name: user-supplied-name)
```

or:

```
create-object(actual-slots)
```

In the first case, the user supplies the name of the object to be created, and the name is supplied in the variable **user-supplied-name**. In the second case, there is no argument corresponding to the name parameter; only the slots are provided by the user of the method. In this second case, the method employs the default value for **name** which is provided by the expression in brackets after the keyword parameter's name.

The second form of default specification is the one which corresponds to a keyword parameter definition in which the parameter and keyword are distinct. This is shown below:

```
define method create-object
          (slots, #key name:  object-id (make-name()))
     ...
     let object = ...  ;
         store-in-database(object-id, object);
         ...
end method create-object;
```

Here, the keyword is still **name**, but the parameter's name is **object-id** inside the method. Following the keyword and parameter name specification comes the default expression, again enclosed in brackets. Once again, the default expression is a call to the method which generates names for objects. This method can be called as:

```
create-object(actual-slots, name: user-supplied-name)
```

or:

```
create-object(actual-slots)
```

Again, an argument must be supplied for slots; the slots parameter is still required. The token **name:** is used outside the method body to refer to the parameter which is known internally as **object-id**. In the second case, the name of the object is the default value computed by **make-name()**.

If a keyword parameter is omitted from a call, the question of the default value when none is explicitly given arises. That is, for cases:

*name*
*keyword parameter*

of the definition of keyword parameters, there is no specification of a default. In this case, whenever a parameter is omitted from a call, its default value is **#f**. This can clearly lead to problems. If, for example, one of the keyword parameters were omitted from a call to **Euclidean-distance**, an error would result because arithmetic operations cannot be performed on **#f**. In general, it is better to supply a default value for a keyword parameter whenever **#f** is not a permitted operand of any of the operations in a method.

It is possible (permitted) for a method to have only keyword parameters. The following is permitted in Dylan:

```
define method create-object
                (#key system-defined, slots (#()),
                                      name (make-name()))
     ...
end method create-object;
```

This method takes three keyword parameters, **system-defined**, **slots** and **name**, respectively. Parameters **slots** and **name** are provided with explicit defaults. If the user does not supply any slots, the empty list is assumed as a default; if the user does not supply a name, the function **make-name** is called to compute one. If the user does not specify a value for **system-defined**, the default value is **#f**. In this case, it can be seen that default values can act sometimes as flags.

A variety of different calls are possible for this function. Among others, there are:

```
create-object()
```

in which each parameter's default value is used;

```
create-object(system-defined: #t)
```

in which defaults are used for **slots** (the empty list) and **name** (the result of calling **make-name**), but the resulting object is declared not to be system defined;

```
create-object(slots: user-supplied-slots)
```

in which the name is generated by a call to **make-name**, and in which the value of **system-defined** defaults to **#f** (the object is not system defined);

```
create-object(slots:  user-supplied-slots,
              name:  user-supplied-name)
```

in which the parameters **user-supplied-slots** and **user-supplied-name** supply the values of **slots** and **name**.

```
create-object(name: user-supplied-name)
```

in which only **name** is supplied by the user; the other defaults are employed, so that **system-defined** has the value **#f**, and **slots** is bound to the empty list.

Whenever a method is to accept **#rest** and keyword parameters, **#rest** must come first in the parameter list. The rest parameter is then bound to a sequence containing all the keywords and their corresponding values. The programmer must unpack the sequence so that the various values are correctly used.

The following is a legal combination of **#rest** and **#key**:

```
(#rest body, #key header-id, header-val)
```

whereas:

```
(#key x1, y1, #rest other-coordinates)
```

is not.

A method can also specify **#all-keys** in a keyword parameter list. When **#all-keys** is employed, it must follow all other keyword parameter specifications, as in:

```
(#key k1, k2, #all-keys)
```

The **#all-keys** specification indicates that the method is permitted to accept all keyword values. In such a case, it is the responsibility of the programmer to handle them correctly.

There is one more kind of parameter, the **#next** parameter. This is intimately bound up in inheritance.

## 6.4 Bare Methods

So far, every method considered has been associated with a name. The names are used to identify the method and are used to call them. It is equally possible to define methods which do not have names. Their syntax is almost identical to the syntax of named methods:

**method** *parameter-list*
        *implicit-body*
**end** [ **method** ]

Execution of this kind of method causes a nameless (or bare) method to be created; bare methods correspond to anonymous functions. Bare methods accept the arguments passed by *parameter-list* and then execute *implicit-body* to produce a value (the default value returned by the implicit body is still **#f**).

Bare methods can be created and used directly, or can be passed to or returned from another method (see the discussion of higher-order methods in Section 6.6—named methods can also be passed to and returned from methods).

Among other things, bare methods can be used:

- to perform a local calculation
- as a function that does not require class dispatch
- to build up generic programs under programmer control
- to provide methods with function arguments that will only be used once.

Here is the definition of a bare method:

```
method (n1, n2)
       n1 + n2
end method
```

Its form is directly analogous to that of a method created using **define method**, the difference being that bare methods have no names. With this sole exception, the form is identical. The bare method that has just been defined is not of very much use; it is necessary to apply the method to a pair of arguments and produce a result. There are two ways of doing this:

```
(method (n1, n2) n1 + n2 end method)(1,2)
```

and:

```
apply(method(n1,n2) n1 + n2 end method, #(1,2))
```

In the first case, the bare method has to be defined inside round brackets. Immediately after the method definition is a list of arguments to the method; the method is applied to the arguments (the arguments are passed to the method and the method's body is executed), and a result is returned.

In the second case, the **apply** built-in function is used to apply the bare method to its arguments. The form of **apply** is:

```
apply(f, list)
```

where **f** is a function and list is a list of arguments of the form appropriate to **f** (i.e. containing **#rest**, **#key**, etc, parameter lists). When using **apply** with a bare method, the bare method is defined as the first argument to **apply**; the arguments to the method are supplied as a list of values. For example:

```
apply(method(n1,n2) n1 + n2 end method, #(1,2))
```

Bare methods are of some considerable value. For one thing, they help the programmer avoid thinking up names for every method in a program. For another, they allow a function to be defined for a specific once-only use in a program. An example of the utility of bare methods can be seen from the **member?** predicate. This predicate takes the form:

**member?** *value collection* **#key** *test*

and returns a boolean. The predicate returns **#f** is value is not a member of collection, and **#t** if it is. When no test is supplied, **member?** assumes == as default. As will now be seen, the programmer can define a bare method and supply it to **member?** in order to obtain the desired test.

Consider a program which manipulates a list of vectors, each vector being of length 3. Before adding a new vector to a list, it is necessary to determine whether a similar vector is already present. The three-element vector is assumed to hold objects which can be tested for identity using ==.

It would be possible to define a named method to implement the test on the vector. If this test is only performed in one place (in a call to **member?**), this would appear to be an unnecessary cluttering of the namespace. A better solution would then be the following:

```
member?(v, vl, test:  method (ev1, ev2)
      (ev1[0] == ev2[0]) &
      (ev1[1] == ev2[1]) &
      (ev1[2] == ev2[2]) end method)
```

where **v** is the vector being tested, **vl** is the list of vectors, and the test is supplied by the bare method passed as the final argument to **member?**. In this case, **member?** successively applies the bare method to each element of **vl** as one of its arguments, and **v** as its second argument.

If, instead of taking two arguments, the **test:** keyword parameter to **method?** only took one, it is simple to specialise the identity predicate so that one of its arguments is always bound to **v**. The following bare method does this:

```
method (v)
      method (ev)
            (v[0] == ev[0]) &
            (v[1] == ev[1]) &
            (v[2] == ev[2])
      end method
end method;
```

The outer method returns the inner method as its result; this is an example of a higher- order function. The outer method is applied to a particular value and returns a method which tests for identity with this vector; the returned method can be applied to each of the elements of a list until an identical one is found or until the end of the list is encountered.

Functions such as **any?** and **every?** are higher order and require arguments to be handled in this way. Further discussion of higher-order functions will be left until Section 6.6, where a fuller treatment is given.

## 6.5 Local Methods

The syntax of the local method definition is simple:

`local` *method-spec*$_1$ , *method-spec*$_2$ , ... ;

where each *method-spec* is the definition of a named method of the form:

**method** *name parameter-list*
    *implicit-body*
**end** [ **method** ] [*name*]

Note that the method specifications are separated within the list by a comma; the list is terminated with a semicolon. The local construct defines a block which includes the scope of the definitions. For example:

```
local method add1 (n) n + 1 end;
      let x = 2;
          add1(x);
          add1(add1(x))
          x * 2
```

Here, the scope of the `local` construct extends to and includes `x * 2`. The scope of the definitions of the various local definitions will be stated below.

Above, a method was defined for computing the maximum element of a list. The definition given was:

```
define method lmax (l :: <list>, maxelem :: <integer>)
       if (l == #())
          max
       else
          let hd = head(l);
              if (hd > maxelem)
                 lmax(tail(l),hd)
              else
                 lmax(tail(l),maxelem)
              end if
          end if
end method;
```

It was stated that this definition poses problems, particularly interface problems. The user of the method must always call **lmax** with **maxelem** bound to zero. Thus, for a list ll, the following is a call which will result in the computation of the correct maximum value:

```
lmax(ll,0)
```

This is an unfortunate property of the method (indeed, it will also be an unfortunate property of any recursive method that uses a collecting variable).

It would be far better to hide the definition in something which made the interface simpler. In particular, it would be better only to have to supply the list to be searched and not the initial value for the maximum element.

One way to simplify the interface is to define another method, say list-max, as follows:

```
define method list-max (l ::  <list>)
      lmax(l,0)
end method list-max;
```

This is not very satisfactory either because there are now two methods. The user is still able to call **lmax** as before, and, in such a case, still needs to know which value (and of which type) to supply as **lmax**'s second argument.

A second way to simplify the interface is to rewrite lmax so that it is iterative. This gives:

```
define method iter-lmax (l ::  <list>)
      let maxelem = 0;
         for (e in l)
            if (e > maxelem)
              maxelem := e
            end if
         end for;
      maxelem
end define iter-lmax;
```

This is a good solution (note that a **for** loop has been used because it is simple—it is a perfect match with the needs of the problem). It does everything wanted, and, under certain circumstances, it can lead to an implementation which is faster than the original, recursive, definition. There is, though, a reason why rewriting is not a convenient option; in the limit, all code must be rewritten in order to make it better suit current needs. This is clearly not an economic option in most cases. It is also an option that does not sit well with the concept of code reuse that underpins languages such as Dylan. In Dylan, it is to be preferred that previously written code that is appropriate to current needs be reused intact and without modification.

The third approach to the interface problem for **lmax** is one which still requires the code to be rewritten. However, given the constraint that the method must be written as a recursive function, it is one which might well be adopted by the original programmer. Here, the person who first writes the **lmax** method realises that the interface will cause problems and will, therefore, write the method in such a way that this problem is obviated. The solution is to make the method doing the work is hidden within an outer method.

The definition is:

```
define method lmax (l ::  <list>)
      local method lmax-aux (l,maxelem)
```

```
            if (l == #())
               maxelem
            else
               let hd = head(l);
                   if (hd > maxelem)
                      lmax-aux(tail(l),hd)
                   else
                      lmax-aux(tail(l),maxelem)
                   end if
            end if
      end lmax-aux;
      lmax-aux(l,0)
end method lmax;
```

The scope of the local definition (the region in which lmax-aux is in scope) extends from its point of definition the line starting '`local`' where its name first appears, to the end of the body of the method in which the local method is defined. Thus, **`lmax-aux`** can be called at any point between its definition and the end of the body. Because local definitions are of *named* methods, any method defined by means of a local can be recursive; the local function defined above is recursive.

An even better approach is the following:

```
define method lmax (l ::  <list>, #key initial-maxelem (0))
      local method lmax-aux (l, maxelem)
            if (l == #())
               maxelem
            else
               let hd = head(l);
                   lmax-aux(tail(l),
                            if (hd > maxelem)
                               hd
                            else
                               maxelem
                            end if)
            end if
      end lmax-aux;
      lmax-aux(l,initial-maxelem)
end method lmax;
```

The keyword parameter is used to supply a default maximum which is used by the inner method. If no value is supplied for the keyword, the default is employed. The local method is identical to the one above, with the exception that the two calls to **`lmax-aux`** in the previous version have been combined into one, and the if expression is used to select the value of **`lmax-aux`**'s second parameter. This shows how Dylan control constructs can be used as expressions. The local method is now more clearly in tail- recursive form (the compiler would have detected this in the previous case—the current one is more clearly tail-recursive to humans).

The next method returns the minimum and the maximum elements of a vector. It defines two local methods (one to find the minimum, one to find the maximum) and returns two values (minimum and maximum):

```
define method min-max (v ::  <vector>)
      let len = size(v);
          local method vecmin (v)
                let vmax = 0;
                let i = 0;
                    until (i = len)
                          let e = element(v,i);
                          if (e > vmax) vmax := e end if
                    end until;
                    vmax
                end vecmin,
          method vecmax (v)
                let vmin = 0;
                let i = 0;
                    until (i = len)
                          let e = element(v,i);
                          if (e <= vmin) vmin := e end if
                    end until;
                    vmin
                end vecmax;
      let vmin = vecmin (v);
      let vmax = vecmax (v);
      values(vmin,vmax)
end method min-max;
```

This time, two local methods are defined; their definitions are separated by commas and terminated by a semicolon. The scope of the definitions extends from the token local (they are assumed to be elaborated in parallel so that they can refer to each other in a mutually recursive fashion) to the end of the body of method **min-max**. (The solution involving keyword parameters could also be adopted here.)

Note that the values expression need not be fed from the two lets; this was done for clarity. Each let defines a variable which is bound to the value returned by one of the new, locally defined functions. This was adopted because the calls are clearly visible in the body of the outermost method. If this were 'real' code, the following would probably have been written after the definition of the last local method:

```
end vecmax;
    values(vecmin(v), vecmax(v))
end method min-max;
```

For expository purposes, this second version is, perhaps, a little less clear. A final example is of a method to compute the scalar product of a vector. The method accepts a vector and a scalar value; in order to multiply the vector by the scalar (and without using **for**), the length of the vector must be known. The length could be supplied as an additional argument, but it can equally be computed inside the method:

```
define method scalar-product (v ::  <vector>,
                              sc ::  <number>)
      let len = size(v);
          local method prod ()
                let vec = make(<vector>,size:  len);
                    let indx = 0;
                        until (indx == len)
                              vec[indx] := sc * v[indx]
                        end until;
                vec
          end method;
      prod()
end method scalar-product;
```

Note how scope has been used in this example. In particular **len** is defined outside of the **prod** method; this allows the length to be accessed in the local method because it is in scope throughout the method'ss definition.

## 6.6 Higher-Order Methods

As observed above, it is possible for methods to be passed to and returned from Dylan methods. Methods, both named and bare, are therefore *first-class* objects. Dylan treats methods as just the same as any other type; for example, numbers can be passed to and returned from functions, as can lists, vectors, characters, strings, and classes (the last will be considered in the next chapter). The purpose of this section is to make the concept of a higher-order function clearer.

Above, it was seen that **member?** is, in fact, a higher-order function (method). For any type that admits == as its identity test, it is possible, for any value v and any collection (e.g. list, vector, string) v:

```
member?(v,c)
```

will return the expected value (**#t** if v is in c, and **#f** otherwise). Unfortunately, for types for which == is not valid (certain numbers, lists, strings, vectors, user-defined classes), = is sometimes valid as the equality test; but sometimes a user-defined equality is needed. When calling **member?** on v and c, where v is of a type that does not admit ==, but does admit =, the following must be written:

```
member?(v,c,test:  \=)
```

Where \= is the quoted form of =. When passing an operation (for example =, =, <, +) it must be quoted by placing a backslash (') immediately before the operator symbol;. thus: \=, \ =, \<, \+. An operation is a kind of method (and can be specialised so that it applies to new types). In the example of **member?** given above, **member?** takes a third argument (a keyword argument) which is a function (method).

It is possible to define **member?** as follows (the definition is specialised to type **<list>**, but its definition for strings and vectors can easily be produced):

```
define method member?  (v, l ::  <list>,
                              #key test (\==))
      let present = #f;
          until (present \ (l == #()) )
               present := apply(test, list(v, head(l)));
               l := tail(l)
          end until;
      present
end method member?;
```

The body consists of an iteration which is terminated whenever either the flag **present** is true, or when the list **l** is empty. The list **l** is side-effected within the body of the definition (parameters are lexical variables, recall) in order to obtain successive tails. The flag, **present**, is set by calling the test keyword argument to **v** and the current head of the **l**. If **member?** is called without a third argument, test is bound to the default value (which is the identity predicate).

Above, **member?** was called with a special-purpose equality predicate which was defined as a bare method. The call to member? was as follows:

```
member?(v, vl, test:  method (ev1, ev2)
                                 (ev1[0] == ev2[0]) &
                                 (ev1[1] == ev2[1]) &
                                 (ev1[2] == ev2[2])
                            end method)
```

A bare method is directly supplied as the third argument. This is directly analogous to the use of \= above.

Later, the following was defined:

```
method (v)
      method (ev)
            (v[0] == ev[0]) &
            (v[1] == ev[1]) &
            (v[2] == ev[2])
      end method
end method;
```

This function is slightly different (and possibly a little confusing). It contains the definition of a bare method as its body. Since this definition is the last expression in the body of the outer method, it must be the value returned by the outer method (which it is). The outer method, then, returns a method as its value.

*A higher-order function either takes one or more functions as arguments, or returns one or more functions as result; it can do both.*

The last function returns a function (a bare method in this case) as its result. The method returned is one which, when applied to a vector, **ev**, compares its first three arguments with those of some other vector, **v**. The vector v is bound when the inner method is created; that is, it is applied at some time prior to the application of the inner method to **ev**. The inner method contains a reference to **v**; this kind of function is often called a closure.

The next example, the **double** method takes a function and its argument. It is assumed that the function takes only one argument (this is just a convenient simplification made for reasons of presentation). The method applies the functional argument twice. Note that in the definition, a type is supplied:

```
define method double (f :: <function>, args)
      apply(f, list(apply(f, args)))
end method double;
```

The first argument is the function and is declared to be of type **<function>**. In Dylan, methods constitute a subtype of **<function>**. In fact, **<function>** is the parent of all functional types (methods, generics etc.). Given the particular specialisation of the first parameter, it is legal to call it as a function. The second argument is permitted to be of any type.

The body of the method:

```
apply(f, list(apply(f, args)))
```

consists of two uses of the **apply** method. This method, as noted above, takes a function (name or bare method) as its first argument and a list of arguments as its second. It applies its first argument to its second. There can be an arbitrary number of expressions in the list supplied as the second argument (there should be at least as many as the first requires). If desired, **apply** could be defined as:

```
define method apply (f :: <function>, #rest args)
      f(args)
end method apply;
```

The argument **f** should be a closure; all non-local variables must be bound in the function.

To see how **double** works, consider the **add1** method:

```
define method add1 (n)
      n + 1
end method add1;
```

The **add1** method will now be passed to **double** with argument **2**:

```
double(add1,#(2))
```

This expands to:

```
apply(add1, list(apply(add1, #(2)) ))
```

The result of applying **add1** to **2** is **3**, so, by expanding the innermost **apply**, the following is obtained:

```
apply(add1,list(3))
```

which evaluates to **4**.

The definition of **double** is not particularly useful. In particular, it would be pleasant if a function could be created by another function, and the newly created function could then be stored in a variable or data structure. This is one reason why closures are useful.

The next higher-order function is a method which implements a version of **double**. The definition is presented before any discussion:

```
define method mk-doubler (f :: <function>
                                  => g :: <function>)
      method (args)
            apply(f,list(apply(f,args)))
      end method end method mk-doubler;
```

To make things clearer, the outer method has been given input and return types. The outer method takes an object of type **<function>** and returns a value of type **<function>**. The body of **mk-doubler** is a bare method whose body consists of the calls which implement the **double** function. The inner method is an implementation of **double**. The inner method forms **mk-doubler**'s body. The bare method is returned as the value of **mk-doubler**. When the bare method is returned, the value of **f** is bound within it. **f** is a variable which is more global than any other variable in the bare method; when the method is created the variable, **f** and its value form part of the closure's environment.

What makes **mk-doubler** useful is that the following operations can now be performed:

```
define variable add2 = mk-doubler(add1);
define constant add4 = mk-doubler(add2);
```

The result of applying **mk-doubler** to a unary function can be stored in a list or a vector (for example). In all of these cases, the closure created by **mk-doubler** is stored in the variable, constant or data structure.

The original definition of **double** just computed a value which could only be thrown away. The second version, however, returns a functional object (a bare method), some of whose variables are bound upon creation, others of which—in particular, its parameters—are left unbound so that values can later be bound. It is this property of holding only some, among other, values over time that makes closures so useful.

As a final example of a higher-order function, the method **apply-toall** is presented. This is a straightforward method which accepts a function as its first argument and a sequence of values (bound to a **#rest** parameter) as its second. The method applies its first argument to all of the elements in the sequence and returns the result. The function is iterative (higher-order functions do not necessarily have to have recursive definitions):

```
define method apply-to-all (f ::  <function>, #rest args)
      let result = #();
         until (args == #())
              let app-res = apply(f, head(args));
                 result := pair(app-res,result)
         end until;
      reverse(result) end method apply-to-all;
```

Notice that the last expression of the body is a call to **reverse**; the result list is constructed in reverse order—this is a slight cause of inconvenience.

Higher-order functions are an extremely powerful way of constructing programs. Unfortunately, they can be rather hard to understand, particularly if they are not documented properly.

## 6.7 Generic Functions

In Dylan, as in CLOS[17] and Eulisp[15], methods are collected together as *generic functions*. A generic function is a general interface to a family of functions (methods), each method having its parameter list specialised to different types. Using generic functions, it is possible to have methods which perform operations with similar semantics on objects of different type. For example, a generic function might be defined to push an object onto a queue; specific methods will implement the push operation for stacks (LIFO queues), FIFO and DE-queues. The particular method that is actually employed will depend upon the types of its arguments. Generic functions provide not only documentation, but also a powerful way of grouping methods together (and abstracting away from their details). Generic functions allow the specification of a function's interface in a general way; its methods provide a mechanism for implementing that function in a type-safe way.

In Dylan, it is not always necessary explicitly to define a generic function for every method. Whenever a method is defined which is not associated with a (stored in a) generic function, define method automatically creates a generic function.

### 6.7.1 Syntax

The syntax of generic function definition is:

**define** [ *adjectives* ] *generic name parameter-list*

**define generic** creates a new generic function object (which is an instance of a class called **<generic-function>**). *name* is a variable name, and is defined as a read-only variable in the current module. The generic function is assigned to the variable *name*. The adjectives are words separated by spaces. The adjectives permitted for generic functions in [6] (p. 43) are **open** and **sealed**. The adjectives control the level of dynamism of the generic function (for more details, see Section 7.8 on Controlling Dynamism).

The *parameter-list* specifies those arguments which are acceptable to the generic function; the parameters constrain which methods can be added to the generic function. In its simplest form, the *parameter-list* is a list of variable names separated by commas; this form of parameter list specifies only the required parameters of the generic function.

Methods added to a generic function must have parameter lists which are congruent to the generic function's parameter list in ways that are described below in this section. A generic function with no required parameters can contain only a single method. Adding a method has the effect of replacing the previous method.

Methods are added to a generic function either by means of the **define method** construct or by using a protocol involving explicit additions to the generic function. When using **define method**, the method being defined is always added to the generic function of the same name. Thus, if the module contains:

```
define generic push (x, queue);
```

then

```
define method push (x, queue ::  <stack>)
    ...
end method push;
```

defines a method called push which is specialised for the type **<stack>**; the method is added to the generic function push.

### 6.7.2 Parameter List Congruency

A generic function and all of its methods must have congruent parameter lists.

Generic functions and methods (of all kinds) support an argument passing protocol. The protocol is variously described, depending upon the nature of the parameter list.

- It is said to *accept keyword arguments* if is parameter list specifies **#key**. The parameter list could also specify **#rest**.

- For a function which accepts keyword arguments, if its parameter list also specifies **#all-keys**, it is said to accept *all keyword arguments.*

- If a function has a parameter list which specifies **#rest** but does not specify **#key**, the function is said to *accept a variable number of arguments.*

- If a function has a parameter list which specifies neither **#rest** nor **#key**, it is said to *require a fixed number of arguments.*

A method which accepts keyword arguments is said to *recognise* the keywords which are mentioned by its parameter list. (A method is free to mention them in its parameter list and to ignore them in its body.) It is possible for a method to accept keyword arguments in general, but not recognise any particular ones (by specifying **#all-keys**).

A generic function accepting keyword arguments can specify a set of keywords which *must* be recognised by every method added to the generic function. These are the generic function's *mandatory* keywords.

A function accepting keyword arguments is said to *permit* a keyword argument if the function is a method which recognises the keyword, the function is a generic function and the keyword is recognisable by at least one of the applicable methods (for a definition, see Section 7.5.3), or the function accepts all keyword arguments.

If a function accepting keyword arguments is called, it will signal an error if called with a keyword which it does not permit, or if the arguments following the required arguments are not keyword-value pairs.

Before continuing is is necessary to define the concepts of proper and an improper *subset.* A proper *subset*, $S$, of a set $U$, is a set all of whose elements are members of $U$, but such that there are elements of $U$ which are not elements of $S$. A proper subset is wholly contained within its superset. An improper subset, $S$, of $U$, is a set whose elements are all elements of $U$, and whose elements can be all the elements of $U$ (i.e. a proper subset is one which is permitted to be equal to its superset).

Two parameter lists are congruent if they satisfy the following conditions:

1. They have the same number of required parameters.

2. Each of the method's parameter specialisers is a (not necessarily proper) subtype of the corresponding parameter specialiser of the generic function.

3. One of the following holds:

   - both accept keyword arguments
   - both accept a variable number of arguments
   - both require a fixed number of arguments

4. If the generic function accepts keyword arguments, each method must recognise the mandatory keywords of the generic function.
5. If a method accepts all keywords arguments, the generic function must also accept all keyword arguments.
6. Furthermore, value declarations must be congruent in the following sense:
   - If the generic function's parameter list does not contain a rest value declaration:
     - the method's parameter list must not contain a rest value declaration
     - the two parameter lists must contain the same number of required value declarations
     - each value type in the method's parameter list must be a subtype (not necessarily proper) of the corresponding value type in the generic function's parameter list.
7. If the generic function's parameter list does contain a rest value declaration:
   - the method's parameter list is permitted, but is not required, to contain a rest value declaration;
   - the method's parameter list must contain at least as many required value declarations as does the generic function's parameter list;
   - each value type in the method's parameter list must be a (not necessarily proper) subtype of the corresponding value type in the generic function's parameter list. If the method has a rest value type, it corresponds to the generic function's rest value type. If the method has more required value types than does the generic function, the extra ones correspond to the generic function'ss rest value type.

Generic functions can have value declarations in the parameter list used in **define generic**. The values returned by the generic function will be instances of the value types. Rather than adding run-time checking to the generic function **dispatch**, the parameter list congruency rules are augmented to require each method added to the generic function to have congruent value declarations. **add-method**, **define method**, **define class**, etc. signal an error if this requirement is not obeyed.

If a generic function is implicitly defined by **define method** or **define class**, it is not given any value declarations (return type specifications), so it defaults to **=> #rest x** :: **<object>**. Such a definition imposes no restrictions on its methods.

If a method is called by means of a generic function or by means of **next-method** rather than directly, the method itself does not check whether it has received any keyword arguments which it does not recognise. Equally, it does not verify that the arguments following the required ones are keyword-value pairs.

A call to a function is permitted to supply the same keyword argument more than once. Should this be done, the value of the leftmost occurrence is the one used.

Reference has been made above to 'dispatch'. This is the process by which a generic function determines which actual method is to be evaluated, given a set of arguments. The process of method dispatch depends upon the organisation of classes within a program or system.

## 6.8 Operations on Functions

Dylan defines a number of operations on functions. These operations create new functions from old ones or from objects.

`compose` *function*$_1$ `#rest` *more-functions* ⇒ *function*

When called on a single argument, the function returns that argument. When called with two arguments, `compose` returns a function which applies the second function to its arguments and then applies the first function to the (single) result value. With three or more arguments, compose composes pairs of argument functions until a single composite function is produced. As long as the order of application is preserved, the pairings can be performed from left to right or right to left. `double(f)` can be defined as `compose(f,f)` (if and only if the range of `f` is the same as its domain).

`complement` *predicate* ⇒ *function*

`complement` returns a function which applies predicate to its arguments. If predicate returns `#f`, the complement returns `#t`, and vice versa. `odd?` could be defined as `complement(even?)`.

`disjoin` *predicate*$_1$ `#rest` *more-predicates* ⇒ *function*

`disjoin` returns a single function which is the disjunction of its arguments (i.e. the *or* of its arguments). The disjunction accepts a arbitrary number of arguments; it operates by applying the predicates in order to the arguments. If any of the predicates returns true, the remaining predicates (if any) are not applied and the true result is returned; all predicates are applied and `#f` is returned.

`conjoin` *predicate*$_1$ `#rest` *more-predicates* ⇒ *function*

`conjoin` is similar to disjoin, in that it applies a logical operator to its arguments. This time, the function applies conjunction (*and*) to the arguments.

The function accepts an arbitrary number of arguments and operates by applying the predicate in order to those arguments. If any of the predicates returns **#f**, the entire sequence is abandoned and **#f** is returned. Otherwise, all the predicates will be applied, and the value returned by the application of the last predicate is returned as the value of **conjoin**.

**curry** *function* **#rest** *curried-args* ⇒ *new-function*

The **curry** function returns a function which applies function to curried-args plus its own arguments in that order. For example, **curry(\=,"x")** is a predicate which tests for equality with the string **"x"**; **curry(\+,1)** is the function which adds one when applied; **curry(\>,6)** is a predicate which is true for values less than six. The function called **curry** in Dylan is sometimes known as 'partial application'.

**rcurry** *function* **#rest** *curried-args* ⇒ *new-function*

**rcurry** is a contracted form of 'right curry'. This function operates like **curry**, but it allows the rightmost arguments of function to be specified in advance rather than the leftmost. In other words, **curry** partially applies function to its leftmost arguments; **rcurry** partially applies it to its rightmost arguments. For example, **rcurry(\>,6)** is a predicate which is true for values greater than six.

**always** *object* ⇒ *function*

**always** returns a function which can be applied to any number of arguments. The function ignores its arguments and always returns *object*. Thus **always(1)** is the function which always returns the value **1**.

**apply** *function* **#rest** *args* ⇒ *values*

**apply** calls function with *args* as its arguments. The last element of *args* must be a sequence. The elements of the sequence are taken as individual arguments to function. For example, **apply(\+,#(1,2))** returns **3**.

**identity** *object* ⇒ *object*

**identity** always returns *object*.

# Chapter 7

# Classes, Instances and Inheritance

## 7.1 Introduction

An object-oriented programming language is centred on the concepts of class, instance, and inheritance. This chapter describes these concepts in their Dylan interpretations. Dylan provides a rich set of annotations for defining classes and their slots, and it provides a number of ways of creating instances. An instance can be variously initialised by the annotations of its class and by various parameters to the primitives for instance creation. These issues are described.

Dylan provides multiple inheritance. A class can inherit from more than one superclass. Multiple inheritance poses the problem of how to compute the slots of the new class, and it also poses the problem of how to resolve conflicts between slots. If a class C has super classess A and B, and if each of A and B define a slot S, but A defines it as `<integer>`, while B defines it as `<symbol>`, there is a type clash; a slot cannot be specialised to `<symbol>` and `<integer>` at the same time. The multiple inheritance structure of Dylan is designed to avoid such clashes by assigning a priority to each superclass.

Classes can be annotated in various ways. One particularly important annotation is that which declares a class to be concrete or abstract. It will be remembered that an abstract class cannot have direct instances. The annotation serves to enforce this restriction. Although it is not discussed, the concept of an abstract class is more general than being a simple placeholder in the inheritance lattice. A special form of object- oriented program called a framework can be constructed from abstract classes. A framework is an incomplete program which defines the overall structure of the program, but which does not define the particular details. For example, a graphical interface might provide classes for windows of various kinds, but might not provide classes to define the data presented within windows. A grapher program which draws trees, lattices and other graphs might be needed by an application, but not provided by the GUI framework. The application builder has to define the graph-handling classes and then integrate them with the GUI framework. In fact, the framework constrains the grapher's classes in various ways, but it leaves the application builder free to supply application-specific data types and constraints. The abstract class annotation in Dylan makes the construction of frameworks considerably easier than in languages such as C++.

Finally, Dylan provides facilities for introspection. That is, the classes and instances defined by a program can be inspected and altered at run-time and under program control. The introspective facilities provided by Dylan are relatively rudimentary and are designed to be somewhat safer than those provided by CLOS, the LISP object system. Introspection is an interesting addition to any language, but is relatively dangerous; it has been included in this chapter because it is an interesting topic.

## 7.2 A Simple Example

This section, gives a simple example. This is an implementation of some of the familiar queue data types: stack, FIFO, and a version of double-ended queue (Dylan actually provides an implementation as standard, but this is ignored for the purposes of this exercise). The implementations are straightforward and are intended only to show some of the more important and commonly-used features of the Dylan class system and its relationship to methods. The reader should not consider the algorithms employed as being the best possible (indeed, in order to illustrate one point, a particularly hideous and slow algorithm is implemented—Caveat lector!) The example shows Dylan's polymorphism.

The implementation of the queues is entirely object-oriented. There is a basic class (an implementation of the stack data type) and two derived ones. Both derived classes are based only on the stack class, so the inheritance chain is of length one or zero as far as the inheritance of stack objects and methods is concerned. The stack class is fundamental, and is made a subclass of the class `<object>`; this is so that it can inherit the standard operations on classes.

Associated with the stack class are a few operations. These operations are the ones normally associated with queues. For example, there is an operation to add an element to the stack, one to remove the next element, one to test whether the stack is empty, and one to empty the stack. The FIFO queue class inherits all of these operations. The double-ended queue, while inheriting some of them, adds some methods of its own. In most of the cases, the inherited methods have sufficient functionality, but in other cases extensions are required. The double-ended queue type requires the definition of two new methods.

The following convention is adopted for referring to the contents of a queue. The objects which are contained in a queue are referred to as the *elements* of the queue.

The declaration of the class **<stack>** is as follows:

```
define class <stack> (<object>)
      slot queue-elements, init-value:  #();
end class <stack>;
```

The class is a subclass of **<object>**. Every Dylan class should inherit, directly or indirectly, from **<object>**. Unless this is the case, unexpected things can happen. For example, methods can fail to be inherited properly1. The **<stack>** class only has one slot, **queue-elements**, which holds a list of objects of any kind. The slot is initialised to the empty list whenever instances of **<stack>** are created.

The only way the contents of the **queue-elements** slot can be accessed (read or written) is by means of two generic functions. These functions, called the *setter* and the *getter*, are automatically defined by the system when it processes the define class. The setter is used to assign new values to the slot; the getter is used to read the slot's contents. The name of the setter function is **set-queue-elements**, and the name of the getter is **queue-elements** (the same as the slot). It is possible to call **set-queue-elements** on the left-hand side of an assignment, in which case it is simply called **queue-elements**. Thus, if **q** is an instance of **<stack>**, then:

```
queue-elements(q)
```

returns the contents of the queue-elements slot, while:

```
queue-elements(q) := #()
```

sets the slot to the empty list.

Each instance of **<stack>** contains its own separate instance of the slot called **queue-elements**. Thus, whatever is done to one stack does not impact upon any other one. An instance of **<stack>** is created by the call **make(<stack>)**.

Next, the generic functions defined over the stack data type are declared. The generic definitions define the general form (interface) of the methods which will be defined for the various queue types. The parameter lists of the methods are also defined by the generic definitions.

```
define generic empty-queue?(q);
define generic add-element!(q,elem);
define generic get-element!(q);
define generic clear-queue!(q);
```

Four of the standard operations on stacks are thus defined. These operations are explicitly declared as generic functions. Other operations on stacks (e.g. return the top element, swap the top two elements) are not defined; they do not apply, in general to FIFO or de-queues. At this point in the program, there are four generic functions whose parameter lists are defined.

On the basis of the interfaces defined by the generic functions, methods can be defined. The methods which are first defined are specialised to **<stack>**. Thereafter, methods for the other classes are defined. In each case, the reader can verify that the interface presented by each method is the same as that specified by the generic. What makes the methods differ from the generic is that the former specialise their arguments (by specialising their argument types in order to ensure that the appropriate method is called), whereas the latter do not. This is a real example of polymorphism in Dylan. Generic functions are general declarations of functions; methods are specific functions which instantiate generics. Each method is associated with one or more parameter types; the types specialising a method are used in the method dispatch process.

For example:

```
define method empty-queue?  (q ::  <stack> )
      queue-elements(q) == #()
end method empty-queue?;
```

The method **empty-queue?** is a predicate (hence the question mark at the end of the name—a Dylan convention is that predicate names end with '?'). The predicate returns true when there are no elements in the queue (**queue-elements** is empty), and false otherwise. In this case, the queue is empty when it is the empty list.

The next method, **add-element!** (note the '!' at the end of the name), destructively adds an element to the queue. It does this by creating a new list consisting of the object, e, to be added, and the current contents of **queue-elements**; **queue-elements** is replaced by this new list. The method returns **#f** in every case.

```
define method add-element!(q ::  <stack>, e ::  <object>)
      queue-elements(q) := pair(e,queue-elements(q));
      #f
end method add-element!;
```

The last expression of the above method is the constant **#f**. This makes the function return the standard Dylan default value. If it is desired that no value at all is returned from the method, **values()** can be written instead. The interpretation of values() is literal; no values at all are returned.

The next method removes an element from the stack. The method is called **get-element!**, and it works as follows. First, the queue, **q**, is tested (using **empty-queue?**—this is an example of the abstraction to be expected in languages like Dylan) to see if it is empty. If the queue, **queue-elements**, is empty, elements cannot be removed from it, so an error is called using the function **error** (see Section 8.3.5 for more details) which prints a message and causes the program to terminate. If the queue is not empty, the first element is removed and stored temporarily; then the queue in **queue-elements** is updated, and finally the top element is returned.

```
define method get-element!(q ::  <stack> )
      if (empty-queue?(q))
         error("Cannot get element from empty queue.")
      else
      let top = head(queue-elements(q));
         queue-elements(q) := tail(queue-elements(q));
         top
      end if;
end method get-element!;
```

The last method is **clear-queue!**. This method empties the stack. It does so by assigning the empty list to **queue-elements**. Nothing of importance is to be returned, so the method is arranged to return **#f** or **values()**.

```
define method clear-queue!(q ::  <stack>)
      queue-elements(q) := #();
      #f
end method clear-queue!;
```

It should be clear that each of the above methods specialises the corresponding generic function. This is done by specialising the arguments of the methods. In particular, each method specifies a queue and specialises its type as **<stack>**. All of the above methods are specialised to the **<stack>** class. That is, the methods defined above are only applicable to instances of class **<stack>**.

All remaining methods are specialised to their corresponding class.

Next comes the **<fifo>** class. This class is defined as a specialisation of the **<stack>** class. It implements a FIFO (first-in, first-out) queue. Class **<fifo>** is defined as follows:

```
define class <fifo> (<stack>)
end class <fifo>;
```

The new class does not add slots to **<stack>**. As a consequence, **<fifo>** is just a placeholder, defining the name of a new type. There is nothing illegal or otherwise wrong with this. The difference between **<stack>** and **<fifo>** is the way in which the queue'ss elements are accessed, not in any structural differences between the two types of queue. Therefore, the differences between the two types are to be seen in their methods, not in their structure. The class **<fifo>** has to be defined in a way similar to that above because it is necessary (i) to instantiate it (FIFO queues must be instantiated so that instances can be used to store data), and (ii) so that the type is available as a specialisation of **<stack>** so that methods can be defined over it.

Classes are instantiated using the **make** function. When a class is instantiated objects are created that can be manipulated by programs. To create an instance of class **<stack>**, the following call is executed:

```
make(<stack>)
```

If a class's definition specified **init-keywords:** for some of its slots, say **foo:** and **bar:**, a call to **make** would look something like:

```
make(<the-class>,foo: #"foo",bar: #"bar")
```

Issues such as **init-keywords:** are considered in detail below (Section 7.3.2). The first three methods shown for class **<fifo>** are instances of the generic functions defined above. The order of their presentation is slightly different. They are:

```
define method empty-queue?  (q ::  <fifo>)
       next-method()
end method empty-queue?;

define method get-element!(q ::  <fifo>)
       next-method()
end method get-element!;

define method clear-queue!(q ::  <fifo>)
       next-method()
end method clear-queue!;
```

It can be seen that each method is specialised for type **<fifo>**, whereas the previous collection of methods were specialised for type **<stack>**. The new set of methods are called when their argument is of type **<fifo>**, while those given a couple of paragraphs ago will be called when their argument is of type **<stack>**—this is the essence of method dispatch. All three methods have the same name as the method defined for **<stack>**.

The methods just defined for **<fifo>** have one property in common. The body of each method consists of a call to the same function; each function just calls **next-method()** and returns. This does not mean that they all have the same behaviour. On the contrary, what happens when one of these **<fifo>** methods is called is that the corresponding **<stack>** method is called with the same arguments as were passed to the **<fifo>** method. What **next-method** does (see Section 7.5.4 for more defaults) is to call the method with the same name as its caller but which sits immediately above in the inheritance hierarchy. In other words, **next-method()** searches the inheritance lattice for the next applicable method—this is construed as the next method with the same name as the one calling **next-method()** and with argument types that are more general. In the case of the three **<fifo>** methods, they immediately call the method with the same name defined for **<stack>**. For example, if **empty-queue?** is called with an argument of type **<fifo>**, **next-method** will call the method **empty-queue?**, which takes an argument of type **<stack>**. This is legal because every object of type **<fifo>** is also of type **<stack>**, because type **<fifo>** is a subtype of **<stack>**. In the present case, **<fifo>** does not add structure to **<stack>**, so **empty-queue?** (and **clear-queue!** and **get-element!**) can directly apply to **<fifo>**.

The difference between <fifo> and <stack> is, as noted above, of a behavioural nature. This difference is principally exhibited by the method to add elements to the queue. This is implemented by the **add-element!** method:

```
define method add-element!(q :: <fifo>, e :: <object>)
       queue-elements(q) := reverse!(queue-elements(q));
       next-method();
       queue-elements(q) := reverse!(queue-elements(q))
end method add-element!;
```

The method must add a new element to the end of the queue. It first reverses **queue-elements** so that **next-method** can be called to add **e** to the front of the queue. **next-method** returns with **e** now at the front of the list in **queue-elements**. Since this is the wrong place for **e** (which should be at the end), the list is reversed again.

The implementation of this method indicates something about the general approach adopted in this example. The implementation is extremely inefficient. However, the point of the exercise is exposition, so inefficiencies are permitted because they exemplify valid points. The reader is invited to implement the various types in ways different from those given here and which are more time-efficient (the methods given are relatively good as far as space efficiency is concerned).

The final class to be defined is the **<de-queue>** or double-ended queue. In this type of queue, elements can be added to the front or the back of the queue. In some versions, elements can be removed from the front or the back as well. The implementation given below is of the second kind; elements can be added or removed from the front or back of queue-elements. The definition of the class is:

```
define class <de-queue> (<stack>)
end class <de-queue>;
```

The class is again a direct subclass of **<stack>**, so it can inherit methods from **<stack>**, and it adds no structure to **<stack>**. As argued for **<fifo>**, this definition is quite legal and is easily justifiable.

The methods given immediately below should be familiar. They are all instances of the generic functions defined immediately after the definition of class **<stack>**. The methods are collected together for reasons identical to those for the corresponding methods for **<fifo>**. Here, there are differences, however; the differences will be explained after presenting the methods.

```
define method empty-queue? (q :: <de-queue> )
       next-method()
end method empty-queue?;

define method add-element!(q :: <de-queue>, e :: <object>)
       next-method()
```

```
end method add-element!;

define method get-element!(q :: <de-queue> )
      next-method()
end method get-element!;

define method clear-queue!(q :: <de-queue> )
      next-method()
end method clear-queue!;
```

Each of these methods inherits its behaviour from **<stack>**. The clear and empty methods should also be understood in exactly the same way. The addition and removal methods defined for **<stack>** are applicable because they add and remove elements from the *front* of the queue—this is half of the addition/removal protocol for de- queues.

The remainder of the protocol for **<de-queue>** is provided by the methods for adding an element to the back and for removing the last element. The methods are defined as:

```
define method add-to-back! (q :: <de-queue>, e :: <object>)
  if (empty-queue?(q))
     queue-elements(q) := list(e) // or pair(e, #())
  else
     queue-elements (q) :=
          reverse!(pair(e,reverse!(queue-elements(q))))
  end if;
  #f
end method add-to-back!;
```

and

```
define method get-last-element! (q :: <de-queue>)
  if (empty-queue?(q))
     error("Cannot get last element from empty de-queue.")
  else
     queue-elements(q) := reverse!(queue-elements(q));
     let top = head(queue-elements(q));
         queue-elements(q) :=
         reverse!(tail(queue-elements(q)));
         top
  end if
end method get-last-element!;
```

These two methods similar to the **add-element!** method for class **<fifo>**. They both operate on the end of the list stored in the slot **queue-elements**. In a list- based implementation, manipulation of the end typically requires list reversals. In every case, the **reverse!** function has been used; this function reverses a list by destructively manipulating its pointers. The **reverse!**

function takes a time proportional to the length of the list to compute the result; reverse! also directly operates on the list cells, so there is no overhead of calling the storage manager to allocate new cells (by reversing pointers). The alternative would have been to use reverse, a non-destructive version, which could be defined as:

```
define method reverse (l ::  <list>)
       local method revlist (lst, rev)
                    if (lst == #())
                       #()
                    else
                       revlist(tail(l),pair(head(l),rev))
                    end if
       end method;
       revlist(l, #())
end method reverse;
```

(The local definition is used so that a collecting variable can be used in conjunction with tail recursion to improve performance.) The definition of **reverse** is simple, almost disarmingly so. Unfortunately, it has a poor time-space performance. The input list, **l**, is copied, so the storage manager must be called for every list element (the call to **pair** calls the storage manager to allocate a new list cell). Furthermore, recursive definition also implies the consumption of storage on each recursive call to itself (this is where tail recursion is important).

With the definition of **add-to-back!** and **get-last-element!**, the example is complete. Protocols have been defined for all three types: **<stack>**, **<fifo>** and **<de-queue>**. The following have been shown about Dylan classes and methods:

- How to define a simple class, whether a class inheriting from **<object>** or from some other class.
- How to define generic functions (and, indirectly, how to define a protocol for a class).
- How to define methods specialised for a class and which correspond to the specification provided by a collection of generic functions (albeit with simple parameter lists).
- How methods are related to classes.
- The inheritance and call of methods using the **next-method** function.

These are all very important concepts in object-oriented programming. It is often worth using method parameter specialisation in order to associate types with parameters. This makes for safer programming (because of type checking) and also serves to document the program text better. The author has found this a valuable approach, even though it appears to cost more keyboard time, and also invokes the generic method dispatch mechanisms when they would appear unwanted—when the program has been tested satisfactorily, the type specifiers can be removed to make the program run faster.

## 7.3 Class Definitions

### 7.3.1 Class Definition: Basics

Before a class can be used, it must be defined. The syntax of a class definition is as follows:

**define** [ *adjectives* ] **class** *class-name* ( *superclasses* )
        *slot-spec*$_1$ ;
        *slot-spec*$_2$
        ...
**end** [ **class** ] [ *class-name* ]

Where *class-name* is the name of the class being defined; the *slot-specs* are slot specifications and are considered below. The *superclasses* is a list of comma-separated expressions, each of which should evaluate to (the name of) a class. The *superclasses* list should have at least one expression. A class must have at least one superclass. The adjectives are used to control dynamism (see section 7.8). They can be omitted if so desired.

When defining a class hierarchy or lattice, there is the need to define one or more classes which do not have superclasses in the user-defined organisation. These classes are called 'root' classes. In Dylan, root classes must have `<object>` as their sole superclass; this permits the correct inheritance of a number of system-defined operations whose absence would cause problems.

The **define class** construct creates a new class. **define class** defines the module variable *class-name* and creates the class which is stored in that variable. The variable *class-name* is read-only (so is a constant).

The new class inherits from the *superclasses*. The *superclasses* list cannot contain duplicates. The class hierarchy cannot be circular. A class cannot inherit from itself (alternatively, it cannot be, directly or indirectly, its own superclass).

Class definitions occur at top level in a module.

In addition to inheriting slots from its superclasses, a newly defined class is assigned a slot for each of the *slot-specs* in its definition. The simplest form of slot-spec is:

**slot** *variable-name*

For each slot, a generic function (see Section 6.7) is defined with name *variable-name*. Two methods defined on the generic function; one sets values into the slot (writes to it), and the other returns the contents of the slot (reads from it). The former method is called a *setter* function, and the latter a *getter* function. The name of the setter function for a slot named name is *name*-**setter**, while the name of the getter function for that slot is simply *name*.

For example, the following definition creates a new class and stores it in the module variable **<x-y-point>**. The superclass of the new class is **<object>**. The new class has two slots: **x-coord** and **y-coord**. The class definition is:

```
define class <x-y-point> (<object>)
        slot x-coord;
        slot y-coord
end class <x-y-point>;
```

(Note that the name of the class is included at the end of the definition; this is good documentation.)

The two slots have a getter and a setter defined on them. If **p** is an instance of **<x-y-point>**, then:

```
x-coord(p)
```

returns the $x$-coordinate of instance **p** (the value stored in the slot **x-coord** of **p**), while

```
x-coord(p) := 2.15
```

sets the value of its $x$-coordinate (by setting the **x-coord** slot of **p** to the 2.15). The setter and getter for **y-coord** (the $y$-coordinate) work in an identical fashion. The form of the slot-setting expression can vary. The intuitively clear form has just been given. An alternative form is:

```
x-coord-setter(p,2.15)
```

This alternative form is similar to **element-setter**.

Slot definitions can be much more complicated than those just given. The full form will be considered once issues relating to slot uniqueness have been covered.

There are conditions of uniqueness on the slots of a class. The conditions deal with slot access (getter and setter) functions, and with the inheritance of slots from superclasses, in particular when a class uses multiple inheritance.

The first condition is on slot access functions. The collection of all getter and setter functions for slots specified in a class or inherited from its superclasses must not contain duplicates. This implies that an inherited slot *cannot be overridden* by a definition lower down in the inheritance hierarchy.

The overriding of slots can cause severe problems with the status of classes. In particular, it allows the definition of an object represented by a class to be modified by a class inheriting from it. If overriding were permitted, one class could alter the composition of another class; this would interact with the autonomy of classes and would violate the conditions of modularity and abstraction imposed on classes. A class is an abstraction unit; its internals cannot be changed by any other class. If a class could be redefined by overriding by some class lower in the inheritance hierarchy, it would be possible for a class to alter the contents of its superclasses on a purely local basis. Classes between the one doing the overriding and the one being overridden see the original version of the overridden class. This is a clear case of inconsistency. Slot overriding is not, therefore, permitted in Dylan.

The second case deals with inheritance. If a superclass is inherited through multiple paths, its slots are only counted once. If class A has as its direct superclasses (superclasses which are named in the *superclasses* list in its definition) classes B and C, and if both B and C have class D as a direct superclass, class A then simultaneously inherits the slots of D through both B and C. Class D's slots are only counted once; otherwise, multiple inheritance would lead to multiple copies, a result which is not desired. Thus, D's slots appear only once in the collection of slots which will eventually comprise the slots of class A. As a side-effect, the multiple inheritance of class D does not cause the duplication of the accessor functions for D's slots.

If two classes each specify a slot and if each slot has the same accessor functions, the defining classes are considered to be *disjoint*. It is not permitted for the two classes to have a common subclass, so no object can ever be an instance of both classes. If, rather than having identical accessor functions, the two classes are defined such that one slot's getter function is the other slot's setter function, the classes are considered disjoint (the reason is that such an identification would cause a parameter list congruency error).

## 7.3.2 Slot Definitions: Details

In this section, the three kinds of *slot-spec* allowed in class definitions are described. They are:

- slot specifications
- initialisation argument specifications
- inherited slot specifications

They are considered in turn.

### Slot Specifications

A slot specification describes a slot. The syntax of this description has the form:

[ *adjectives*] [ *allocation* ] **slot***getter-name*
    [ :: *type* ] **#key** *setter*
    *init-keyword required-init-keyword init-value init-function*

The components in italics are interpreted as follows:

- *getter-name* is the name of the slot. It is also the name given to the slot's getter function. The *getter-name* must be a variable.
- The *adjectives* are words separated by spaces. The adjectives allowed in [6] are **open** and **sealed**. The adjectives are used to control the level of dynamism of the getter, and, if specified, the setter for the slot. (Section 7.7 gives the details.)
- The *setter* option names the function to be used in setting this function.
- The *init-value* option is used to supply a keyword which is used when initialising the slot, and can supply a value used to initialise the slot. The value of this slot is used when creating an instance of the class. This option cannot be used when allocation is **virtual**.
- The *init-function* is used to provide an initialisation function which is called to initialise the slot when an instance of the class is created. This option cannot be used when allocation is **virtual**.
- The *init-keyword* option is used to provide a keyword for slot initialisation. This will be considered below.

If there is an *init-keyword* which is specified as using **init-keyword:** or **required-init-keyword:**, the slot is said to be keyword *initialisable*.

The following is an example class definition. The class has two slots which are keyword initialisable:

```
define class <xy-point> (<object>)
       slot x-coord, init-keyword:  init-x-coord:;
       slot y-coord, init-keyword:  init-y-coord:;
end class <xy-point>;
```

The accessor functions are **x-coord** and **y-coord**. When creating an instance of this class using the **make** function, the call:

```
make(<xy-point>, init-x-coord: 1.0, init-y-coord: 5.1)
```

will create an instance of **<xy-point>** with **x-coord** initialised to 1.0, and **y-coord** initialised to 5.1. A call to make of the form:

```
make(<xy-point>)
```

will create an instance of the class, but will assign no values to the two slots. The following will lead to an error:

```
let p = make(<xy-point>);
    x-coord(p);
```

The error is signalled because the call to **make** did not initialise the slots in the instance.

In the following example, an error will not be signalled:

```
let p = make(<xy-point>);
    x-coord(p) := 7.1;
    y-coord(p) := 2.4;
    x-coord(p);
```

The reason why this is error-free is that the setter functions are immediately used to install values into the instance's slots. Hence, they are bound to values. It is the fact that the slots are unbound that causes the error.

The *allocation* of a slot determines how the storage for the slot will be allocated. The possible values for *allocation* are as follows: **instance**, **class**, **each-subclass**, or **constant**. Additional implementation-dependent values are also permitted by the Dylan language definition; the above are standard. The argument supplied to allocation is not evaluated; the argument cannot, therefore, be an expression that requires evaluation (it must already be fully evaluated).

The interpretation of the possible values are as follows.

**instance** This indicates that space should be allocated for the slot in each instance of the class. This is the default. class This indicates that only one location should be allocated. This location is used by all instances of the class, whether they be direct or indirect. All instances share a single value for the slot. If the value is changed in one instance of the class, all instances will see the new value.

**each-subclass** This indicates that the class gets one storage location for the slot. This location is to be used by all *direct* instances of the class. In addition, every subclass of the class is assigned a location for the slot; this location is used by the direct instances of the subclass. And so on.

**constant** This indicates that the slot has a constant value. No setter method can be defined for such a slot (otherwise an error results). The value of the slot must be specified as an *init-value*.

**virtual** This indicates that no storage will automatically be allocated for the slot. If allocation is **virtual**, it is the programmer's responsibility to define methods on the setter and getter generic functions to retrieve and store the value of the slot. Dylan ensures the existence of generic functions for any specified getter and setter, but will not add any methods to them in this case.

The values of virtual slots are not automatically initialised when a new instance is created. It is the programmer's responsibility to perform all necessary initialisation which would normally be done by a method defined on the generic function initialise. Because the values of virtual slots are often computed from other values at run-time, many virtual slots do not require explicit initialisation.

In order to support the **slot-initialised?** protocol in a virtual slot, programmers have to define a method for **slot-initialised?** which shares a protocol with the getter method for the slot.

The keywords which are in slots are now described.

Each keyword can be specified at most once. Each keyword must be followed by a value. The following list is the minimum required by the Dylan language; more keywords can be added by implementations. The minimum list of keywords is:

**setter:** The value supplied for this keyword must be the name of the module variable to which the setter method should be added. (Setter functions are methods in generic functions and are stored in a variable local to the module in which the class is being defined.) If no setter method is to be defined, the value **#f** must be supplied. The argument is not evaluated, so expressions which evaluate to a variable name cannot be supplied. If no value is supplied, a default value which is a symbol whose name is the concatenation of *getter-name* and **-setter** is used. If the allocation is constant, the value defaults to **#f**.

**type:** The value supplied should be a type specifier which limits the types of value that can be stored in the slot. This type specification is enforced by low-level mechanisms. Slots which are declared as **virtual** do not have their types enforced (they can be variously and dynamically typed). The default value for **type:** is **<object>** when the default is used, any value can be stored in the slot. The argument to this keyword is evaluated once (after the corresponding variable is defined and before the slot is first added to an instance).

**init-value:** This keyword supplies an initial value for the slot. The argument is evaluated once after the variable containing the class is defined and before the slot is first added to an instance. The resulting value is used as the initial value when an instance is created. If a new value is desired for each instance, **init-function:** should be used rather than **init-value:**. There is no default value for this keyword argument.

**init-function:** This keyword should be used in conjunction with a value which is a function of no arguments. The function is called to produce an initial value for the slot when a new instance is created. There is no default value for this argument. The function is evaluated once after the variable containing the class is defined and before the slot is first added to an instance. It is not permitted to specify **init-function:** together with **init-value:** in the definition of a slot.

**init-keyword:** The value supplied to this argument should be a keyword. **init-keyword:** permits an initial value for the slot to be passed to make as a keyword argument. The argument is not initialised. There is no default value for this argument.

**required-init-keyword:** This is similar to init-keyword:. The difference is that it indicates an init-keyword which must be provided when the class is instantiated. If **make** is called on the class and a required-init-keyword is not provided, an error is signalled. If a slot specifies **required-init-keyword:** or **init-keyword:**, **init-value:** and **init-function:** must not be specified.

### Initialisation Argument Specifications

An initialisation argument specification does not describe a slot. Instead, it describes how a particular initialisation argument is to be treated. It allows the type of the initialisation argument to be restricted, as well as allowing the initialisation argument to be declared. It allows the specification of a default value for an initialisation argument which is not required.

Dylan provides two kinds of initialisation argument specification: required and optional initialisation argument specifications.

A *required* initialisation argument specification has the form:

**required keyword** *keyword* **#key** *type*

A required initialisation argument specification asserts that the initialisation argument must always be present in a call to **make**. The default **make** method will signal an error if no such argument is passed to it when one is required.

An optional initialisation argument specification has the form:

**keyword** *keyword* **#key** *type init-value init-function*

An optional specification can be used to specify a default value for an initialisation argument. When a call to **make** does not specify the keyword, the default method for **make** using its default value is used in its place. The default value is used in computing the defaulted initialisation arguments. The default value is also indirectly used in initialising the slot.

The type argument has the same meaning for both kinds of argument specification. It restricts the type of that argument. This is *not* the same as restricting the type of the slot.

Here is an example class definition. It resembles the definition we gave for **<xy-point>**, but uses initialisation argument specifications:

```
define class <xy-point1> (<xy-point>)
      required keyword x:;
      keyword y:, init-value: 0.0;
end class <xy-point1>;
```

Here, the **x**: initialisation argument is required. When **make** is called, it will signal an error if **x**: is not supplied as an argument to it. The initialisation argument **y**: is optional. If **y**: is not specified in a call to **make**, the slot **y** will have an initial value of 0.0. Note that **<xy-point1>** is a subclass of **<xy-point>**; the slots being initialised are inherited from the superclass. The example shows how initialisation can be controlled in subclasses of Dylan classes.

It is possible for more than one keyword initialisable slot to be initialised from a single argument (i.e. more than one slot can specify the same *init-keyword*). An error is signalled if a single **define class** form has more than one initialisation argument specification for the same keyword. An error will also be signalled when a single define class form has keyword initialisable slots which specify **init-value:** or **init-function:** together with an initialisation argument specification for the same keyword which either requires a value (a required initialisation argument) or provides a default value with **init-value:** or **init-function:**. That is, the initial value specification of the slot can never be used.

### Inherited Slot Specifications

An inherited slot specification specifies a getter generic function. Optionally, it specifies an **init-value:** or **init-function:** slot option (but not both at the same time).

The syntax of an inherited slot specification is:

**inherited slot** *getter-name* **#key** *init-value init-function*

The value of *getter-name* identifies the slot (it is the slot's name in simpler terms). It must be the name of a variable (have the same syntax as a variable name, and must name a slot). A superclass of the class being defined must specify a slot with the same name (with the same getter).

Should neither **init-value:** nor **init-function:** be specified, the only function of the inherited slot specification is to require that some superclass of the class being defined has a slot with the same name. This feature might be of some use as documentation (perhaps). Because the slot options **init-value:** and **init-function:** are not permitted for virtual slots, the form without these specifications is the only valid form of inherited slot specification for virtual slots.

If either **init-value:** or **init-function:** is specified for a slot in a subclass, the **init-value:** or **init-function:** of the slot in the superclass is ignored, and the local one used to provide an initial value. This allows the default value of a slot to be different at different places in the inheritance hierarchy. The following example shows how this might be used:

```
define class <transport> (<object>)
       slot num-wheels, init-value:  4;
end class <transport>;

define class <bicycle> (<transport>)
       inherited slot num-wheels, init-value:  2;
end class <bicycle>;

define class <tricycle> (<transport>)
       inherited slot num-wheels, init-value:  3;
end class <tricyle>;

define class <unicycle> (<transport>)
       inherited slot num-wheels, init-value:  1;
end class <unicycle>;
```

In each subclass of **<transport>**, the initial value for num-wheels, the slot containing the number of wheels of the vehicle type in question, is different2.

### Filtered Slots

Sometimes, the value of a slot will be stored directly in instances of some class, but require some computation in at least one of its subclasses. The following example is taken from [6] (p. 76).

Consider the following class:

```
define class <view> (<object>)
       instance slot position;
       ...
end class <view>;
```

The **position** slot could be stored as a value in direct instances of **<view>**, while it requires some computation to be performed in direct instances of the subclass **<displaced-view>** of class **<view>**.

Both classes provide the same interface to **position** (the **position** generic function). If the implementor of either class decides to change the implementation, users of the two classes will not need to change or recompile code because there is no change to the interface.

In such a case, **<view>** supports **position** as an instance slot, while the **<displaced-view>** class supports **position** as a filtered slot. Methods for **position** and **position-setter** are added automatically by the slot definition in **<view>**; these two methods access the value actually stored in the instance. On the other hand, **<displaced-view>** must be implemented in such a way that methods are added to the setter and getter generic functions in order to modify their functionality. The **<displaced-view>** methods can call **next-method** to get or set the stored value of the slot.

Thus, given a definition of **<displaced-view>**:

```
define class <displaced-view> (<view>)
       ...
end class <displaced-view>;

define method position (v :: <displaced-view>)
       displace-transform(next-method(v))
end method position;

define method position-setter (new-position,
                               v :: <displaced-view>)
       next-method (undisplace-transform(new-position),v)
end method position-setter;
```

In other cases, the programmer can store a slot value in the instances of the class's instances, but will want to perform some auxiliary action whenever the slot is accessed. In such a case, the programmer should define two slots: an instance slot to allocate storage and a virtual slot to provide the interface. In general, the virtual slot will be the only one documented, for the instance slot will be an internal implementation used by the virtual slot for storage. An example (taken from [6], p. 77) is a slot that stores (caches) a value:

```
define class <shape> (<view>)
      virtual slot image;
      instance slot cached-image, init-value: #f;
      ...
end class <shape>;

define method image (shape :: <shape>) /* getter */
      cached-image (shape)
        | (cached-image(shape) := compute-image(shape))
end method image;

define method image-setter (new-image, shape :: <shape>)
      cached-image(shape) := new-image
end method image-setter;
```

Note that if one defines a virtual slot, it is necessary to define an internal instance slot in order to provide a value for the slot accessor function.

This approach can be used to implement such things as active values or daemons.

## 7.4 Instance Creation

### 7.4.1 Basic Mechanisms

Instances of classes must be created and initialised. This process is controlled by two generic functions called initialize and make. The make function has been mentioned a number of times. In this section, its functioning will be considered in some detail. This section is quite technical in content, but full understanding of instance creation is needed if the programmer is to override the standard methods on those occasions when a more specialised creation method is required for the classes being defined (when a *Meta-Object Protocol* [10] is defined for Dylan, this need will be even greater).

The instance creation process works as follows:

1. The user calls **make**, specifying a class and set of keywords and arguments.

2. If the system-defined **make** method is shadowed by a user-defined method specialised with a singleton specialiser, this user-supplied method is used to collect all the arguments to **make** and to provide the actual initialisations based on them. This user-defined method will typically use

**next-method** to perform the actual creation of the instance and to perform the new instance's initialisation (**next-method** will call the system-defined version of the **make** method).

3. Next, the default make method examines its keywords. The result of this is the *supplied initialisation arguments.* The next step is for **make** to produce a set of *defaulted initialisation arguments*; these are used in creating and initialising the instance, and augment the supplied initialisation arguments with additional arguments to hold default values defined by the class or by any of its superclasses.

4. The default **make** method allocates an instance and initialises all the slots for which it can provide values. Those slots which are keyword initialisable are initialised from the corresponding values of the defaulted initialisation arguments. Slots which are not keyword initialisable, but which have a default initial value specification, have the appropriate value assigned to them.

5. The default **make** function then calls initialize on the initialised instance and default initialisation arguments.

6. Each **initialise** method typically calls **next-method()**, and then performs whatever initialisations of which it is capable (the method uses **#key** to access the initialisation arguments it needs). Slots initialised in step 4 do not need further initialisation.

7. The default **make** method ignores the value of the call to initialize and returns the newly created instance as its value.

The **make** and **initialize** methods are now described in detail.

The generic function **make** has the following syntax:

**make** *class* **#key #all-keys** ⇒ *instance*

**make** returns an instance of class. The characteristics of the instance are supplied by the keyword-value pairs.

Dylan does not specify whether **make** must always return a newly created instance or whether it can return an instance which has previously been created. If a newly created instance is allocated, **make** will call **initialize** (as was seen above) on the instance before returning it.

The object which **make** returns is guaranteed to be a general instance of *class*, but it is not necessarily a direct instance of it. This permits make to be called on abstract classes (abstract classes are ones for which instance creation makes no sense). In such a case, **make** can instantiate and return a direct instance of one of the abstract class's concrete subclasses. However, the default method on **make** always returns a newly allocated direct instance of *class.*

Programmers are permitted to customise **make** for particular cases by defining methods specialised by singleton specialisers. Such methods can obtain the default make behaviour by calling **next-method** if the default behaviour is required. When no customisation is defined for a class, the default **make** method is called.

The default method for **make** is as follows:

**make** *class* **#rest** *supplied-initialisation-arguments* **#key** ⇒ *instance*

The default method signals an error if *class* is abstract. An instantiable abstract class must override this behaviour with its own method for **make**. Any deferred evaluations which have not yet been performed for class and its superclasses are performed before anything else. Next, if *supplied-initialisation-arguments* contains duplicate keywords, make uses the leftmost occurrence, a procedure which is consistent with the **#key** convention for function calls. Next, **make** starts with *supplied-initialisation-arguments* and constructs the set of defaulted initialisation arguments to be used in creating and initialising the instance, and augments it with any additional initialisation arguments for which default values are defined by *class* or any of its superclasses. **make** signals an error if any required initialisation argument is missing from the defaulted initialisation arguments, or if any of the defaulted initialisation arguments are invalid for the initialisation of class (i.e. some keyword is neither usable for the initialisation of a slot, nor recognised by some **initialize** method applicable to an instance of class). Init-functions used to construct the defaulted initialisation arguments are only invoked if the initialisation argument is missing from the supplied initialisation arguments.

The method then allocates an instance and initialises all slots for which it can compute values. If a slot is keyword initialisable, and if the corresponding initialisation argument is present in the defaulted initialisation arguments, the slot is set to that value. Otherwise, if the slot has a default initial value specification, it is used to furnish the initial value (this involves the use of **init-value:** or the invocation of **init-function:**). Should either of these provide a value which is not of an appropriate type to fill the slot, an error is signalled.

The precise order in which instance allocation and init-function invocation occur in the above sequence of operations is not defined by the language.

The **make** method calls **initialize** on the initialised instance and on the defaulted initialisation arguments. **initialize** performs any custom or complex initialisations. User-defined **initialize** methods can use **#key** parameters to access particular initialisation arguments, or **#rest** to access the whole set of them. If the entire set is examined, and if the supplied initialisation arguments contain duplicate keywords, it is undefined as to whether any entries other than the leftmost for each duplicated keyword will be present.

The **make** method returns the instance, ignoring any values returned by **initialize**.

The initialize generic function has the following form:

**initialize** *instance* **#key #all-keys**

The **initialize** generic function provides a way for users to handle initialisation of instances which cannot be expressed simply using init-values or init-functions. The reasons for the need to handle initialisation explicitly are that a computation requires inputs from init-args or slot values, or that a single computation needs to be used to initialise multiple slots.

By convention, all **initialize** methods should call **next-method** very early in their execution. The reason for this is to ensure that any initialisations from more general classes are performed first. Implementations can issue warnings about code style when processing **initialize** methods which do not call **next-method**.

The **initialize** generic function *permits* all keywords; it *requires* none. It does this for the reason that keyword argument checking has already been performed by the default method on **make**.

The default method on initialize has its interface defined as:

**initialize** *instance* :: **<object> #key**

The default **initialize** method does nothing. It is present so that the system-defined method **next-method()** can be used *ad lib.* by **initialize** methods written in a sensible, modular style.

### 7.4.2 Keyword Initialisation

Some slots are keyword initialisable. In such a case, it is possible to change the default value for the initialisation argument alone. There is no need to mention the slot. This case can be illustrated by the following example:

```
define class <person> (...)
      slot favourite-poet, init-value: "Shakespeare",
                           init-keyword: favourite-poet:;
      slot name required-init-keyword: name:;
end class <person>;

define class <welsh-person> (<person>)
      keyword favourite-poet: init-value "Dylan Thomas";
      keyword name: init-value: "Evan";
end class <welsh-person>;
```

Another common use is the supply of a default which is required in the superclass, as illustrated in the name: init-keyword in the above example. This makes the **name:** keyword no longer required when calling make on **<welsh-person>**.

Initialisation argument specification is defined by the following algorithm. There are four cases to consider:

1. A slot specification supplying an init-keyword $K$ requires that the keyword **required-init-keyword:** is treated as if the initialisation argument specification **required-init-keyword:** $K$ had been specified in the class definition. A slot specification supplying both init-keyword and init-value or init-function is *not* equivalent to an initialisation argument specification including the init-keyword and init-value or init-function. The former is used in order directly to provide a default value of the slot. It does not affect the defaulted initialisation arguments. The latter case is used to provide the default value of the slot; this is performed indirectly by affecting the defaulted initialisation arguments.

2. The initialisation argument is specified for the first time, and is not inherited from any superclass. There are three points to note:

   (a) The type: argument, whose defaults is **<object>**, specifies the type of the initialisation argument.

   (b) If the initialisation argument is specified using the keyword specifier **required-init-keyword:**, it is required; otherwise it is optional.

   (c) If the initialisation argument is specified using the **init-keyword:** specifier, it can provide an initial value specification for use by the default **make** method as a default value for the initialisation argument in the defaulted initialisation arguments. This is either a value specified using **init-value:** or a function (called each time a value is needed) can be specified by means of **init-function:**.

3. An initialisation argument specification is being specified for an initialisation argument which is inherited from a single superclass. There are three points to note:

   (a) The argument's type must be a subtype of the type of the inherited initialisation argument.

   (b) The initialisation argument is required if the overriding initialisation argument is specified in terms of **required-init-keyword:**. If the inherited initialisation argument specification is required and the overriding initialisation argument specification does not provide one of **init-value:** or **init-function:**, the initialisation argument is required. In the case in which the overriding initialisation argument specification employs **required-init-keyword:**, any init-value or init-function in the inherited initialisation argument specification is discarded. This means that a superclass can force an initialisation argument used by a superclass to become required. It cannot force a required initialisation argument to become optional without specifying a default value.

   (c) Otherwise, the initialisation argument is optional. If the overriding slot specification provides one of **init-value:** or **init-function:**, that value is used to compute the defaulted initialisation argument when the class is instantiated. Otherwise, the inherited initial value specification is used.

4. An initialisation argument specification is inherited from multiple superclasses. If the superclasses have exactly the same definition for the initialisation argument, that definition is merely inherited. If the definitions differ, the class which combines these other classes must provide an initialisation argument specification compatible with all of the inherited ones, as described above.

### 7.4.3 Class Allocated Slots

The initialisation of slots whose allocation is class or each-subclass works as follows. There are four cases to consider, depending upon whether the slot is keyword initialisable, and whether any way of computing a default value is specified.

1. The slot is not keyword initialisable, and there is no default value for the slot. In other words, no **init-value:** or **init-function:** is specified. The slot value is not changed, and if currently uninitialised it remains so.

2. The slot is not keyword initialisable, but there is a default value for it. In other words, either an **init-value:** or **init-function:** is specified. Either before or during the first call to **make** on a class which shares this slot, the init-value or value returned by the init-function is used to initialise the slot.

3. The slot is keyword initialisable, but the corresponding initialisation argument is absent from the defaulted initialisation arguments of the call to **make**. The slot is not changed, and if it is presently uninitialised, it remains so.

4. The slot is keyword initialisable, and the corresponding initialisation argument is present in the defaulted initialisation arguments of the call to **make**. The slot is unconditionally set to the value of that initialisation argument.

### 7.4.4 Testing the Initialisation of a Slot

It is possible within a program to test a slot to see whether it has been initialised. The following predicate performs this task:

**slot-initialised?** *instance getter* ⇒ *boolean*

This function returns true if the slot in *instance* which would be accessed by *getter* (in the normal run, the slot named by *getter*) is initialised. If the slot is uninitialised, false is returned.

**slot-initialised?** signals an error if the getter does not access a slot in *instance*. There is no mechanism for resetting a slot to the uninitialised state.

# 7.5 Inheritance

## 7.5.1 Inheritance and the Class Precedence List

Inheritance is performed on the basis of the *class hierarchy*. This hierarchy describes the relationships between the classes, both user- and system-defined, in a program. For any class, there is a class precedence list which determines the order in which its superclasses are examined when inheriting a slot or method. The class precedence list is computed from the superclasses of a given class. Its computation is complicated by the fact that multiple inheritance can be present.

The definition of a class defines a total ordering on that class and its direct superclasses. This ordering is called the *local precedence order*. In the local precedence order, the class precedes its direct superclasses, and each direct superclass precedes all other direct superclasses following it in the sequence of direct superclasses of the class definition.

The class precedence list of a class $C$ is a total ordering on $C$ and its superclasses. This ordering is consistent with the local precedence orders for each of $C$ and its superclasses.

It is sometimes the case that there are several possible total orderings on $C$ and its superclasses which are consistent with the local precedence orders for each of $C$ and its superclasses. Dylan uses a deterministic algorithm to compute the class precedence list. This algorithm selects one of the possible total orderings. The algorithm has the effect that the classes in a simple superclass chain (linear ordering) are adjacent in the class precedence list, and that classes in every relatively separated subgraph are adjacent in the class precedence list.

Occasionally, there is no possible total ordering on $C$ and its superclasses such that the ordering is consistent with the local precedence orders for each $C$ and its superclasses. In this case, Dylan signals an error because the class precedence list cannot be computed.

The computation of the class precedence list takes place as follows.

Let $S$ be the set of $C$ and all of its superclasses.

For each class $c$ in $S$, let:

$$R_c = \{(c, c_1), (c_1, c_2), \ldots, (c_{n-1}, c_n)\}$$

where $c_1, \ldots, c_n$ are the direct superclasses of $c$ in the order in which they are mentioned in the class definition of c (i.e. in the superclass list—this means that the order is the same as the order of the superclasses in the text of the class's superclass list).

Let $R$ be the union of all $R_c$, i.e.

$$R = \bigcup_{c \in S} R_c$$

The set $R$ might or might not generate a partial ordering, depending upon whether the $R_c$ are consistent. It is assumed that they are consistent and that

$R$ generates a partial ordering. When the $R_c$ are not consistent, $R$ is said to be *inconsistent.*

In order to compute the class precedence list of $C$, topologically sort $C$ and its superclasses with respect to $R$. This consists of the following steps:

1. Find a class $N$ in $S$ such that no other class precedes $N$ according to the elements of $R$. If there are several classes in $S$ with no predecessors, select the one that has a direct subclass rightmost in the partial class precedence list computed thus far. More precisely, let $\{N_1, \ldots, N_m\}$, $m \leq 2$, be the classes in $S$ with no predecessors.

   Let:
   $$(C_1, \ldots, C_n)$$
   where $n \geq 1$, be the partial class precedence list.

   Let $1 \leq j \leq n$ be the greatest number such that there exists some $i$ such that $1 \leq i \leq m$, and $N_i$ is a direct superclass of $C_j$. Choose $N_i$.

2. Place $N$ first in the result. Remove $N$ from $S$, and remove all pairs of the form $(N, M)$ such that $M$ is a member of $S$, from $R$.

3. Repeat the process, adding classes with no predecessors to the end of the result. Stop when no elements can be found that have no predecessor.

If $S$ is not empty, and the process has stopped, and $R$ is inconsistent because it contains a loop. In other words, there is a chain of classes $C_1, \ldots, C_n$ in $S$ such that $C_i$ precedes $C_{i+1}$, $1 \leq i < n$, and $C_n$ precedes $C_i$. When $R$ is inconsistent, there is no possible total ordering on $C$ and its superclass such that the ordering is consistent with the local precedence orders for each of $C$ and its superclasses, and an error is signalled.

### 7.5.2 Singletons

Singletons are not a type in the sense that classes are; they are, nevertheless, a type. In fact, singletons provide a mechanism for adding methods to single objects. Thus, an object (which is an instance of a class) can have methods associated with it. This mechanism allows programs to specialise a single object without needing to change other objects of the same class, and without defining an entire class just for the single object. In other words, when an object is made a singleton, the other instances of its class are unaffected; similarly, the class is unaffected by the definition.

A singleton is a type, but not a class. In [6], p. 68, the following is stated: 'A singleton is a type, but it is not a class. It is little more than a pointer to a single object.' The purpose of a singleton is to individuate that object so that a method can be created to specialise the object. By defining a method on an object, that object discriminates the object's type.

*Singleton methods are considered more specific than methods defined on an object's original class. Singletons are the most specific specialiser.*

Dylan provides a shorthand notation for singletons when used as method specialisers. The usual way to specialise an object is to use **singleton**, but == can be used instead, as the following example documents.

```
define method alarm? (alert-status :: singleton(#"red") )
       warn-user(emergency);
end method;
```

uses the singleton notation to convert alert-status into a singleton object; note that the syntax is identical to a normal specialisation. The following definition is:

```
define method (alter-status == #"red")
       ...
end method;
```

Here, the == is used, and the syntax is different from that used in a variable specialisation.

### 7.5.3 Method Specificity

It is now possible to state the conditions under which methods are chosen for execution; this is called *method dispatch.* Part of the story depends upon the class precedence list. Method dispatch occurs when a generic function is called. The generic function uses the classes and identities of the arguments to the call to determine which methods to call.

There are three phases in method dispatch:

1. All applicable methods are selected.

2. The applicable methods are sorted by specificity.

3. The most specific method is chosen for execution.

Step 2 often involves the class precedence list.

The most complex step is the second, so effort is concentrated upon it.

For any two methods A and B which are applicable to a generic function call, one method can be *more specific than* the other; alternatively, the methods can be *ambiguous.* To order the two methods A and B with respect to a particular set of arguments, the specialisers of A's arguments are compared with those of B. This process of comparison is performed argumentwise.

The details of the comparison are as follows:

1. If the specialisers are type equivalent, A and B are unordered at the current argument position. This argument position provides no information about the order of the two methods, therefore.

2. If the specialiser of A is a subtype of the specialiser of B, A precedes B at the current argument position. Conversely, B precedes A at this position if B's specialiser is a subtype of that of A.

3. If both specialisers are classes, their order in the class precedence list of the argument's class is used to determine which is more specific. If the specialiser of A precedes that of B in the class precedence list, A precedes B at the current argument position. Conversely, B precedes A in the current argument position if B's specialiser precedes that of A in the class precedence list. 4. If none of the above apply, the methods are ambiguous.

Method A is more specific than method B if and only if A precedes B or is unordered with respect to B in all required argument positions, and precedes B in at least one argument position. Conversely, B is more specific than A if and only if B precedes A or is unordered with respect to A in all required argument positions, and precedes A in at least one argument position. If neither case obtains (i.e. if neither method is more specific than the other), A and B are ambiguous methods.

When the applicable methods are sorted by specificity, the sorted list is divided into two parts, each of which can be empty. The first part contains methods more specific than every method following them. The second part (which cannot be sorted) begins at the first point of ambiguity. There are at least two methods which could be placed first in the second part. If the first part is empty, generic function dispatch signals an error to the effect that this is a case of ambiguous methods. If the last method in the first part calls next-method, the call signals an 'ambiguous next method error.'

### 7.5.4 Calling More General Methods

It is quite common for a subclass to need to alter the behaviour of a method rather than replace it. Whatever need be done involves the inherited behaviour. For example, in a FIFO queue, it is necessary to add an element to the queue. If a FIFO queue is defined as a subclass of stack, this could be done (as was done, albeit nastily) by first reversing the queue, calling the stack's method for adding an element, and then reversing the result. In this case, the FIFO class does not need to replace stack's add method, it needs to augment it. The way to augment the behaviour of the inherited method is to use **next-method**. **next-method** is a function which, when called, invokes the next most specific applicable method in the generic function. The **next-method** is the value of the **#next** parameter; this is the parameter kind omitted from discussion in Chapter 5. Normally, the **#next** parameter is named **next-method**, although it can have other, programmer-defined, names.

The following is the implementation of the add method for **<fifo>** expressed as a specialisation of that for **<stack>**. Thus, in the example at the start of this chapter:

```
define method add-element!(q :: <fifo>, e :: <object>)
      queue-element(q) := reverse!(queue-elements(q));
      next-method();
```

```
        queue-elements(q) := reverse!(queue-elements(q));
        #f
end method add-element!;
```

The method upon which the above is based is:

```
define method add-element!(q :: <stack>, e :: <object>)
        queue-elements(q) := pair(e,queue-elements(q));
end method add-element!;
```

This second method is the one called as a result of calling **next-method**. Before the call to **next-method**, **add** for FIFOs destructively reverses the elements of its queue. Next, **next-method** is called; it adds a new element to the front of the list of queue elements. Now, note that the front of the list of queue elements is the same as the end of the unreversed list. When next-method returns, the new element is on the front of the reversed list of elements; add for **<fifo>** destructively reverses the list, so that the new element is in the correct place.

A way of thinking about **next-method** is that it calls the method which would have been called if the caller to **next-method** had not been defined.

If there are no more available methods, the parameter **next-method** is bound to the value **#f** instead of to a method. Care must be taken in shallow hierarchies, therefore. What happens if arguments must be passed to the next method? Usually, **next-method** is called with no arguments. This is an indication that the arguments passed to the calling method should be directly passed to the next method. (In the example above, the fifo and **e** should be passed to the next method.) It is valid to supply arguments, including quite different ones, when calling **next-method**. However, if different arguments are passed, the new arguments must result in the same ordered sequence of applicable methods, in the same order, as the original arguments (that is, the arguments must respect method specificity). Otherwise, the behaviour exhibited by Dylan is undefined.

In some cases, the methods in a generic function accept different keyword arguments. In these cases, it is convenient for the methods also to accept a **#rest** parameter. By this device, all non-required arguments to the generic function are captured by the **#rest** parameter. By using **apply**, the next method can be invoked with the complete set of arguments.

The next method parameter is passed without explicit mention within a program. When a method is called by its generic function, the generic function dispatch mechanism automatically passes the appropriate value for the next method. There is no way for a user to specify the next method argument when a method is called.

If a method is created using **method** rather than **define method**, and it is desired that this method accept a next method parameter, a **#next** should be explicitly placed in the parameter list. This is done for a method that is explicitly to be added to a generic function, and when this method is to be able to call **next-method**. The next method parameter, **#next**, can also be supplied when using **define method** in cases where the programmer wishes to assign the parameter a name other than its default.

## 7.6 Classes and Types

In Dylan, classes define types. With the exception of booleans and singletons, all types are classes in this language.

The language contains a root class which is the superclass of all other classes; this class is called **<object>**. Anything of type **<object>** is of the most general possible type in the language. Every other type is a specialisation of **<object>**. Type **<object>** is the default type for all variables.

Dylan provides a class called **<type>**. All types, including **<type>** and ¡class¿ (see below) are general instances of **<type>**. The class **<type>** is a subclass of **<object>**; this is a meta-class.

The class **<class>** is a subclass of **<object>**. All classes, including the class **<class>**, are general instances of **<class>**. Class **<class>** is a subclass of **<type>**. Because **<class>** is an instance of itself, the Dylan type system is *impredicative.*

In most programs, the majority of classes are created using **define class**. There is nothing to prevent them from creating classes by calling, for example, **make** if they want to create a class without storing it in a module variable, or if run-time class creation is required. If **make** is used to create a new class, and if creating the class would violate any restrictions specified by directives concerning sealing, an error of type **<sealed-object-error>** is signalled.

The class **<class>** supports the following init-keywords:

- **superclasses:** Specifies the direct superclasses of the class. The value of **superclasses:** should be a class or sequence of classes. The default value is **<object>**. The meaning of the order of superclasses is the same as in **define class**.

- **slots:** A sequence of slot specifications; each slot specification is a sequence of keyword-value pairs. The following keywords and corresponding values are accepted by all implementations. Implementations can also define additional keywords and values.

  - **getter:** A generic function of one argument. Unless the allocation of the slot is virtual, the getter method for the slot will be added to this generic function. This is a required option.

  - **setter:** A generic function of two arguments. The setter method for the slot is added to this generic function unless the allocation of the slot is virtual. No default is provided.

  - **type:** A type. Values stored in the slot are restricted to this type. The default value is **<object>**.

- **deferred-type**: A function of no arguments. It returns a type and is called once in order to compute the type of the slot. This call is made inside the call to **make** which constructs the first instance of the class.
- **init-value**: This parameter supplies a default initial value for the slot. This option cannot be specified together with **init-function**:.
- **init-function**: A function of no arguments. This function is called in order to compute an initial value for the slot when new instances are created. This option cannot be specified together with **init-value**:.
- **init-keyword**: A keyword. This option allows an initial value for the slot to be passed to make as a keyword argument. There is no default value. This option cannot be specified together with **required-init-keyword**:.
- **required-init-keyword**: A keyword. This option is like the option **init-keyword**:, but indicates that an init-keyword must be provided when the class is instantiated. If **make** is called on the class and a required init-keyword is not provided, an error is signalled. There is no default for this option. This option cannot be specified when **init-keyword**:, **init-value**:, or **init-function**: is specified.
- **allocation**: This option can be bound to exactly one of the values: **instance**:, **class**:, **each-subclass**:, **constant**: or else to **virtual**:. As an alternative, **allocation**: can be bound to an implementation-defined keyword. The meaning of this option is the same as adding the corresponding adjective to a **define class** form.

The class **<singleton>** supports the **init-keyword**:

- **object**: The object that the singleton indicates. There is no default for this argument. If it is not supplied, an error will be signalled.

If a **singleton** for the specified object already exists, implementations are free to fold the two instances into one.

**singleton** *object* ⇒ *singleton*

**singleton** returns a singleton for *object*.
**singleton(***object***)** is equivalent to:

**make(<singleton>, object:** *object***)**

An examination of types would be incomplete if there were no discussion of type conversion. In Dylan, type conversion is referred to as *coercion*. The language provides a generic function, **as**, to perform coercion between types.

**as** *class object* ⇒ *instance*

The function **as** coerces *object* to *class*. In other words, it returns an instance of *class* that has the same contents as *object*.

If *object* is already an instance of *class*, it is returned unaltered.

Predefined methods allow coercion between numeric types, between integers and characters, between symbols and strings, and between collection types (e.g. conversion of vectors to lists and vice versa). No methods are defined for other classes.

When converting between collection types, the new collection (the object returned by **as**) has the same number of elements as the source collection (the object). If source and target are both subclasses of **<sequence>**, the elements will be in the same order. The individual elements can sometimes undergo conversions.

Finally, there are two functions for performing copies. They are the methods **shallow-copy** and **class-for-copy**, defined as follows.

**shallow-copy** *object* ⇒ *new-object*

This is a generic function which returns a new object with the same contents as *object*. The contents are not copied; they are the same objects contained in *object*. Dylan includes methods for copying collections. The method for **<collection>** creates a new object by calling **make** on the **class-for-copy** of object; for other classes, methods must be supplied by the programmer.

**class-for-copy** *object* ⇒ *class*

This generic function returns an appropriate collection class for creating mutable copies of the argument. For already mutable collections, the collection's actual class is the most appropriate, so the most general form of this method can be used (i.e. the method defined as `define method class-for-copy (object :: <object>)` is used).

The **class-for-copy** value of an explicit-key-collection should be a subclass of **<explicit-key-collection>**. In all cases, the value returned by this method must be a mutable collection.

## 7.7 Introspecting on Classes and Functions

It is occasionally necessary to obtain information about the current state of an object or about the superclasses of an object. Such operations are called introspective operations. It is more common to use introspective operations when constructing object systems similar to Dylan's, or when constructing a *Meta-Object Protocol* [10]. The functions provided by Dylan for introspecting on classes are given for completeness, and because they are sometimes needed. The first function, **instance?**, is quite frequently used, so these functions are not entirely esoteric.

In Dylan, and this might come as a surprise, functions of all kinds are also considered as objects. Thus, each function or method has a class, and class-based operations can be performed on them. It is possible, for example, to determine the number and type of the parameters of a function. Descriptions of these functions are also included, although they will, probably, be used even less frequently in the average program than the introspective functions for classes.

The following operations return information about types and objects.

- **instance?** *object type* ⇒ *boolean*

  **instance?** is true if *object* is a general instance of *type*.

- **subtype?** $type_1$ $type_2$ ⇒ *boolean*

  **subtype?** is true if $type_1$ is a subtype, whether direct or indirect, of $type_2$, or if $type_1$ and $type_2$ are the same type.

- **object-class** *object* ⇒ *class* **object-class** returns the class of which *object* is a direct instance.

- **all-superclasses** *class* ⇒ *sequence*

  **all-superclasses** returns all the superclasses of *class* in a sequence. The order of the classes in the sequence is significant. The first element in the sequence will always be *class*, and the class **<object>** will always be the last. The sequence returns should never be destructively modified. If destructive modification is performed, unpredictable program behaviour can result. If *class* is sealed, an implementation can choose to signal an error of type **<sealed-object-error>** rather than return the superclass sequence.

- **direct-superclasses** *class* ⇒ *sequence*

  **direct-superclasses** returns the direct superclasses of *class* in a sequence. The classes in the sequence are the classes passed to **make** or **define class** when *class* was created. The order in which the classes appear in the sequence is the same as the order in which they were passed to **define class** or **make** when class was created. The sequence which is returned should *never* be destructively modified, or else unpredictable program behaviour can result. If *class* is sealed, an implementation can choose to signal an error of type **<sealed-object-error>** rather than return the superclass sequence.

- **direct-subclasses** *class* ⇒ *sequence*

  **direct-subclasses** returns the direct subclasses of *class* in a sequence. The elements of the sequence are those classes which have class as a direct superclass. The order in which the classes appear in the sequence has no meaning or relevance. The returned sequence should *never* be destructively modified, for unpredictable program behaviour can otherwise result. (The pointer from a class to its subclasses is through a weak like, so subclasses can be garbage collected if there are no other references to them.) If *class* sealed, an implementation can choose to signal an error of type **<sealed-object-error>** rather than return the superclass sequence.

Before describing the reflective operations for functions, it is necessary to discuss the classes defined as standard for functions. Functions of all kinds (methods, generic functions, and general functions) are members of classes. The classes are **<function>**, **<generic-function>** and **<method>**.

The classes relating to functions and methods are now described.

- **<function>** The class **<function>** is the class of all objects which can be applied to arguments. It is the superclass of generic functions and methods. **<function>** inherits from **<object>**.

- **<generic-function>** The class **<generic-function>** is the class of functions which contain methods. **<generic-function>** inherits from **<function>**. The class **<generic-function>** supports the following keywords:

  - **required:** *number-or-sequence* This keyword represents the number of required parameters accepted by the generic function. If a sequence is supplied, the size of the sequence is the number of required arguments, and the elements of the sequence are the specialisers. If a number is supplied, it is the number of required arguments, and the specialisers default to **<object>**. If the argument is not supplied, or the supplied argument is neither a sequence nor a non- negative integer, an error is signalled.

  - **rest?:** *boolean* A value of true indicates that the generic function accepts a variable number of parameters. The keyword has a default of **#f**.

  - **key:** *collection-of-keywords-or-***#f** If the value supplied for this keyword is a collection, the generic function accepts keyword arguments and the collection specifies the set of mandatory keywords of the generic function. A value of **#f** indicates that the generic function accepts no keyword parameters. The default value for this keyword is **#f**.

  - **all-keys?:** *boolean* A value of true indicates that the generic function accepts all keyword arguments. The default value is **#f**.

  If the value of **rest?:** is true, and the value of **key:** is a collection, an error is signalled.

  If the value of **all-keys?:** is true and the value of key: is **#f**, an error is signalled. The new generic function has, initially, no methods. An error is signalled if the generic function is called before methods are added to it. Once a generic function is created, it can be given behaviours by adding methods; methods can be added by means of **add-method** or **define method**.

Generic functions are not usually directly created. The typical mode of creation is by the direct means of define generic, or by means of the indirect define method technique.

- **<method>** This is the class of methods and is a subclass of **<function>**.

With these definitions in mind, it is possible to move on to the description of the introspective functions defined for functional objects.

- **generic-function-methods** *generic-function* ⇒ *sequence*

  **generic-function-methods** returns a sequence of all of the methods in *generic-function*. The order in which the methods appear in the sequence is of no significance. The sequence returned should not be destructively modified, for unpredictable program behaviour can otherwise result. If *generic-function* is sealed, an implementation can opt not to return a sequence of methods, but to signal an error of type **<sealed-object-error>**.

- **add-method***generic-function method* ⇒ *new-method old-method*

  **add-method** adds *method* to *generic-function*. This operation modifies the generic function object. In general, it is not necessary to call **add-method** directly. It is called by **define method**. If a method is added to a generic function, and if that generic function already has a method with exactly the same specialisers, the old method is replaced by the new one. A single method can be added to any number of generic functions.

  **add-method** returns two values. The first is the new method. The second is either the method which has been replaced by *method*, or it is **#f** if no method is being replaced.

- **generic-function-mandatory-keywords** *generic-function*

  This function returns a collection of mandatory keywords for *generic-function*, provided that it accepts keyword arguments. The function returns false if *generic-function* accepts no mandatory keywords. The collection returned by this function should never be destructively modified; doing so can cause unpredictable program behaviour.

- **function-specializers***function* ⇒ *sequence* This function returns a sequence of the specialisers for *function*. The length of the sequence will be equal to the number of *function*'s required arguments. The first element of the sequence will be the specialiser of the first of *function*'s arguments; the second element the specialiser of the function's second argument, and so on.

- **function-arguments** *function* ⇒ *required-number rest-boolean kwd-sequence*

  This function returns three values:

  1. The number of required arguments which the function accepts.
  2. A boolean value indicating whether the function accepts a variable number of arguments.
  3. If the value of the third returned value is **#f**, the function does not accept keyword arguments; otherwise, the function accepts keyword parameters and the value is either a collection of the keywords permissible for any call to the function, or the symbol **all** if the function permits all keywords.

  Note that particular calls to a generic function can accept additional keyword arguments not included in the third returned value; this is because the additional keywords are recognised by applicable methods rather than by the generic.

- **applicable-method?** *function* **#rest** *sample-arguments* ⇒ *boolean*

  This function returns true if *function* is a method or contains a method which would be applicable to *sample-arguments.*

- **sorted-applicable-methods** *generic-function* **#rest** *sample-arguments* ⇒ *sequence*$_1$ *sequence*$_2$

  This generic function returns two sequences. Taken together, the two sequences contain the methods in *generic-function* which are applicable to *sample-arguments. sequence*$_1$ contains methods which are more specific than every method which follows them; *sequence*$_2$ (which itself cannot be sorted) begins at the first point of ambiguity. There are at least two methods which could equally occur first in *sequence*$_2$.

- **find-method** *generic-function specialiser-list* ⇒ {*method or* **#f**}

  **find-method** returns the method in *generic-function* which has the specialisers in *specialiser-list* as its specialisers. The specialisers must match exactly in order that a method be returned. If *generic-function* is sealed, an implementation has the option of signalling an error of type **<sealed-object-error>** (rather than return a value).

- **remove-method***generic-function method* ⇒ *method*

  This function removes *method* from *generic-method* and returns *method.* The function signals an error if *method* is not in *generic-function.* An error is signalled of type **<sealed-object-error>** if *generic-function* is sealed, or if *method* is a sealed method of *generic-function.*

## 7.8 Control of Dynamism

Dylan is an essentially dynamic language. Dynamism makes programming easier, but it comes at a cost. Dylan, therefore, provides mechanisms for controlling the dynamism of its classes and function. The mechanisms are:

- Declaring a class to be **sealed** or **open**.
- Declaring a class to be **abstract** or **concrete**.
- Declaring a class to be **primary** or **free**.
- Declaring a generic function to be **sealed** or **open**.
- Uing the **seal generic** form, or using the abbreviations **define sealed method** and **sealed slot**.

These declarations can usually be made using the adjectives of generic functions, methods, classes and slot specifications. The exception is of the **sealed generic** form.

The definition of a class can contain the adjectives **sealed**, **open**, **primary**, **free**, **abstract**, or **concrete**. The adjectives declare characteristics of the class. The following is a list of properties which are declared using the adjectives.

- A class can be declared to be either **sealed** or **open**. If a class is **sealed**, *no additional subclasses other than those explicitly defined in the same library* (see Chapter 9) can be created. It is, therefore, an error to define a subclass of a **sealed** class in a library other than the one in which the definition of the **sealed** class occurs, or to use **make** of **<class>** with a **sealed** class directly or indirectly in the superclasses (**make** of **<class>** dynamically creates a class). **Open** classes do not prohibit such operations. It is an error to define an **open** subclass of a **sealed** class.

  When explicitly defining a class, *the default is for the class to be sealed.* This can be overridden by an explicit **open** specification. A class created using **make** of **<class>** is **open**. There is no specified way to create a **sealed** class using **make**.

- An explicitly defined class can be declared as either **primary** or **free**. The default is for classes to be **free**. It is illegal for a class to have two **primary** superclasses unless one is a superclass of the other. A **primary** class is one which can be used only as the **primary** superclass in multiple inheritance. A **free** class is one which is not **primary**.

- An explicitly defined class can be defined as either **abstract** or **concrete**. The default is for classes to be **concrete**. Abstract classes are classes which cannot be instantiated (i.e. cannot have *direct* instances); they can only have general instances. The superclasses of an **abstract** class must be **abstract**. An **abstract** class does not usually have slots. Although it is not forbidden to define slots in an **abstract** class, it should be done with care, especially for instance-allocated slots.

A generic function definition can include the adjectives **sealed** or **open**. These adjectives declare whether the generic function is **sealed**. If a generic function is **sealed**, *no additional methods other than those explicitly defined in the same library* can be added to the generic function. It is, then, an error to define a new method for a **sealed** generic function in a library other than the one in which the **sealed** generic is defined. It is, furthermore, an error to apply **add-method** or **remove-method** to a **sealed** generic. An **open** generic function does not impose such prohibitions.

When explicitly defining a generic function, the default is for the generic function to be **sealed**. This can be overridden by the explicit stipulation that the function is **open**. A generic function with *no explicit definition*, but with implicit definitions provided by explicit definitions of generic function methods, is **sealed**. A generic function which is created using **make** of **<generic-function>** is **open**. There is no specified way to create a **sealed** generic function using **make**.

There is also a seal generic top-level form. It has the following syntax:

**seal generic** *function* ( *type*, ... ) ;

Where *function* must be a module variable referring to a generic function. The *types* must be expressions which evaluate to instances of **<type>**. The number of *types* must be the same as the number of required arguments accepted by the function.

A **seal generic** form for a generic function G with types $T_1, \ldots, T_n$ in a library L imposes the following constraints on programs:

1. A method M congruent to G and which is not an explicitly known method in L can be added to G if and only if *at least one* of the specialisers of M is disjoint from the corresponding type in the sealing form.

2. A method M can be removed from G if and only if *at least one* of the specialisers of M is disjoint from the corresponding type in the sealing form.

3. A class C with direct superclasses $D_1, \ldots, D_m$ and which is not an explicitly known class in L can be created if and only if:

   (a) None of the classes $D_1, \ldots, D_m$ are subtypes of the types $T_1, \ldots, T_n$ in the sealing form;

   (b) Or, for every method M in G with specialisers $S_1, \ldots, S_n$, if there exists an $i$ such that $S_i$ is disjoint from $T_i$, then M must satisfy condition 1 below, otherwise must satisfy condition 2 below:

i. There exists an $i$ such that $S_i$ is disjoint from $T_i$ and such that there exist no $j$ and $k$ such that $D_j$ is a subtype of $S_i$ and $D_k$ a subtype of $T_i$.

ii. There exist no $i$, $j$, and $k$, such that $D_j$ and $D_k$ are subtypes of $T_i$, $D_j$ is disjoint from $D_k$, $D_j$ is a subtype of $S_i$, and $D_k$ is not a subtype of $S_i$.

Dylan provides abbreviations for **`seal generic`**. The form **`define sealed method`** defines a normal method and then seals the generic function for the types that are the specialisers of the method.

The **`sealed`** slot option to **`define class`** defines a normal slot; it then seals the getter generic function for the class, and seals the setter generic function if there is one, first on **`<object>`** and then on the class.

# Chapter 8

# Conditions and Errors

## 8.1 Introduction

Programs do not always work as expected. Users input data that is not of the expected form or in the expected range. Sometimes data structures become tangled for various reasons (typically programmer error). Many programming languages ignore these issues. Dylan, like LISP and Ada, and like C and C++ to a certain extent, includes facilities for handling erroneous conditions. This contrasts strongly with Pascal, which provided no such facilities (the programmer frequently had to resort to tricks such as the passing of additional parameters to procedures or to non-local and irrevocable—jumps when handling errors).

The basic concept in Dylan is that of the condition. A condition is used to describe some situation which is considered abnormal. Conditions are notified by means of a signalling operation which notifies the system of the situation. When a condition has been signalled, it can be handled in various ways, most of which are under programmer control.

Dylan allows the user to signal errors in programs and to perform remedial action. Errors of all kinds, including those which cause termination of the program, can be signalled. This chapter is a relatively straightforward review of the condition and signalling facilities provided by Dylan. The material is adapted from [6]) with few illustrations. In the example program developed for this book, the only error function employed was `error`; the reason for this was that the kinds of error detected by the program are almost always of the kind that cannot be repaired or remediated.

## 8.2 The Dylan Exception Facility

Given that Dylan is essentially an object-oriented programming language, it should come as no surprise that the exception facility is also object-oriented. Exceptions are error abnormal states detected by programs and signalled by objects called conditions. The facility provides calling semantics (error conditions or exceptions are called like functions), and provides termination handlers to trap the exceptions or conditions and allow arbitrary computation to be performed on termination. The facility also provides formal recovery.

The Dylan exception facility is based upon the concept of a condition. Conditions are dynamically bound type-based mechanisms for finding and calling functions. When something exceptional occurs, or when an error is detected, it is indicated to the calling code by means of signalling a condition. The Dylan condition facility finds an applicable handler function and calls it. An applicable handler is one which matches the signalled condition by type and (optionally) by a test function associated with the handler. The condition system is merely a way for a signaller and a handler to connect to each other. Once signaller and handler have been connected, they communicate via ordinary function calls.

In exactly the same way as an ordinary function, a handler can return some value or values, or can perform a non-local exit. In each case, the handler is deemed to have handled the condition, and the act of signalling is deemed to be completed. A dynamic handler also has the option of declining to handle any given condition, passing the responsibility to a next-handler function which is passed to the dynamic handler as an argument. A default handler cannot decline because it is always the last applicable handler. Every signalled condition is handled. The system ensures that there is always an applicable default handler.

The simplest way to handle a condition is to terminate the signalling unit by performing a non-local exit established prior to establishing the handler. The exception clause of the block statement is provided for exactly this purpose. The signalling unit is that program unit (block, method, module) which detects the anomalous condition and which executes the signal operation to notify the system of the condition.

Instead of terminating, a handler can recover and return control to the signalling unit. By recovery are intended such actions as supplying default values, supplying reasonable values (on the basis of the computation up to the point where the condition was signalled), or of performing some other action (closing files or streams are also reasonable recovery actions). Recovery can be performed either by returning values which the signalling unit will understand, or by taking a non-local exit established in the state immediately prior to the point at which the signal was issued. Returns or exits can be performed directly, or a more formal recovery process can be undertaken. The advantage of the latter over the former is that a formal interface is present which provides greater assurance that the handler and the signalling unit agree on what they are doing, and provides some isolation of the handler from names and data internal to the signalling unit.

A handler restarts by signalling a restart. This is the formal recovery mechanism which is initiated by calling the `signal` primitive. Any values required for recovery are passed in the restart. The restart is handled by a restart handler which either returns or takes a non-local exit. If the restart handler returns values, **signal** returns those values; the handler which invoked signal also returns them. The call to **signal** from the signalling unit which signalled the original condition returns the same values; the signalling unit recovers as directed by those values.

For every condition class, there should be a 'recovery protocol' which defines what it means for a handler to handle an exception, what the meanings of the returned values are, and which restart handlers should be established by the signalling unit. The recovery protocol determines what is to be passed from the signaller to the handler. The protocol turns out to be the empty protocol for many handlers, and handling by returning is not permitted, no restart handlers are provided. In this case, handling by termination is the only option. The recovery protocol for a subclass should be compatible with that of one of its superclasses.

## 8.3 Specification

The following is a description of the condition classes and operations on them which the Dylan language makes available.

### 8.3.1 Format Strings

A 'format string' is a string template into which values of various types can be inserted in order to construct a message. The Dylan concept of a format string is similar to that found in C (e.g. fprintf) or Common LISP (format). The two-character sequences (format directives) **%d**, **%b**, **%o**, **%x**, **%**, **%s** and **%=** are replaced by the next element of an associated sequence of 'format arguments'. Upper- and lower-case letters are considered equivalent in format directives. The inserted value and its formatting are shown in Table 8.1.

The text printed by the The behaviour when a format argument is not of the type specified in the table is implementation-defined, as is the behaviour when too many or too few format arguments are supplied. The two character sequence There is no standard way defined in Dylan for a user-defined condition class to supply an error message when that class does not inherit from **<simple-error>**, **<simple-restart>**, or **<simple-warning>**.

### 8.3.2 Condition Classes

This subsection outlines the condition classes defined as part of the Dylan language. In addition, additional classes can be defined to suit users' or applications' needs. Figure 8.1 shows the class hierarchy.

**<condition>** Any condition is a general instance of this abstract class. It is an object which represents the occurrence of an exception. Conditions have indefinite extent and no special restrictions are placed on them.

| directive | argument type | textual format |
|---|---|---|
| %d | <integer> | decimal number |
| %b | <integer> | binary number |
| %o | <integer> | octal number |
| %x | <integer> | hexadecimal number |
| %c | <character> | character (with no quotes) |
| %s | <string> | string (with no quotes) |
| %s | <condition> | error message (with no quotes) |
| %= | <object> | unspecified but works for any object |
| %% | *none* | literal % |

Table 8.1: *Table 8.1 Format directives*

A program which does not encounter any exceptional situations will not implicitly allocate any conditions. There is a default handler for **<condition>**; this handler returns **#f**.

**<serious-condition>** . This is the abstract class of all conditions which cannot be ignored with impunity. There is a default handler for this class which calls the debugger (the call uses a mechanism which is not defined in the language).

**<error>** This is the abstract class of all conditions which represent something invalid about a program (rather than just indicating something about environmental conditions, for example). The abstract class **<error>** is a subclass of **<serious-condition>**. The condition **<error>** is distinct from **<serious-condition>** so that it is possible to establish a handler for errors which does not also trap unpredictable environmental exceptions (e.g. process problems, network interrupts, disk problems).

**<simple-error>** This is a concrete class. It is the class of error conditions which consist of just an error message constructed from a format string and arguments. It is a subclass of **<error>**. It has an empty recovery protocol. The initialisation arguments **format-string**: and **format-arguments**: are accepted.

Two accessor functions are defined: **condition-format-string** and **condition-format-arguments**.

**<type-error>** This is a concrete subclass of **<error>** used by check-type. The recovery protocol is empty. This class accepts initialisation arguments **value**: and **type**:.

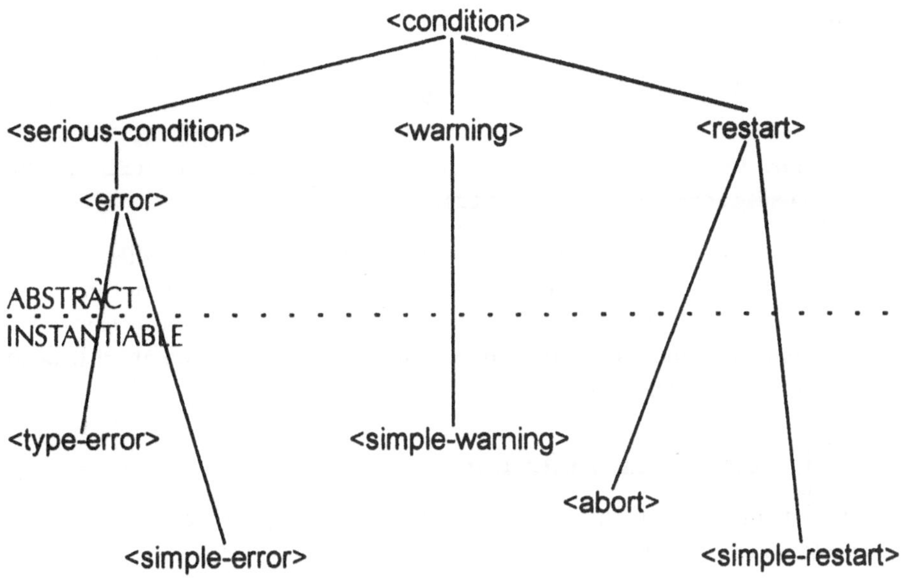


Figure 8.1: *The Dylan condition classes*

**type-error-value**: and **type-error-expected-type**: are the two accessor functions for this class.

**<sealed-object-error>** This is a subclass of **<error>**. It is concrete.

**<warning>** This is an abstract subclass of **<condition>**. The class has a default handler which displays the warning in a user interface-dependent fashion; it returns **#f**. The recovery protocol is that any value can be returned and will be ignored.

**<simple-warning>** This is a concrete subclass of **<warning>**. It is used by signal. The class's recovery protocol is the same as that for **<warning>**. The initialisation and accessor functions are the same as for condition class **<simple-error>**.

**<restart>** A restart is a general instance of the abstract class **<restart>**. This class is a subclass of **<condition>**. There is a default handler for **<restart>** which signals an error reporting an attempt to use a restart for which no restart handler is established. The recovery protocol concept is inapplicable to restarts. The initialisation argument condition:

is accepted, but ignored, by **<restart>**. Some subclasses save the value of this initialisation argument and use it to associate a restart with a particular condition from which the restart can recover. Other restarts do not do this; they can recover from any condition.

**<simple-restart>** This is a concrete subclass of **<restart>**. It is used by **cerror**. **<simple-restart>** accecpts the initialisation arguments **format-string:** and **format-arguments:**.

In order to describe the restart (among other things), this class defines two accessor functions called **condition-format-string:** and **condition-format-arguments:**.

**<abort>** This is a concrete subclass of **<restart>** whose handlers are expected to terminate the execution of the current application command, or similar unit of execution. They are expected to return control to something like a command loop. The precise details of an abort depend upon the environment.

## 8.3.3 The signal Function

The signal function is the basic operator for signalling on a condition. A call to signal has either the form:

**signal***condition* ⇒ *values*

or the form:

**signal***string argument1 argument2 ...* ⇒ *values*

A call to this function signals on the condition condition, trying each active dynamic handler in the order the most recent first. If all dynamic handlers decline, signal performs the call **default-handler(condition)**. If a handler returns, all the values returned by it are returned from signal. If signal returns when condition's recovery protocol does not allow it, some handler is in violation of the protocol; signal, however, does not check for this. If condition is a restart, the caller of signal must always assume that it could return.

The second form signals a condition of type ¡simple-warning¿.

## 8.3.4 Basic Handler

The most basic form of handler is lexically scoped. It is an extension of the let construct and defines a similar kind of scope. It has the form:

**let handler***condition* = *handler*

**let handler** establishes a condition handler during the dynamic extent of the evaluation of the remainder of the enclosing block. It is scoped as in let. *condition* should either be of the form:

*type*

or:

( *type* [, **test**: *test* ][ , **init-arguments**: *init-arguments* ] )

*type*, *handler*, *test* and *init-arguments* are evaluated before evaluation of the rest of the enclosing body begins.

The above arguments are interpreted as follows:

*type* The handler applies to conditions which are general instances of type.
test A function called with a condition which is a general instance of type and which returns true if this handler applies to this condition. The default is a function which is always true. An example use is a restart handler for restarting from a given condition object only, for example restarting from an unbound-slot error by setting the slot and retrying the invocation of the accessor associated with the slot. The **<set-and-continue>** restart condition will have the signalled **<unbound-slot>** condition in a slot, and the handler's test will check for it. (This example is an artificial one, and is to be found in [6], p. 157).

*handler* This is a function which is called to handle a condition which matches type and which passes test. The values of its arguments are the condition being signalled and the next handler function. The function handles the condition by taking a non-local exit and returns a value according to the condition's recovery protocol, or else by calling signal on a restart. The function can decline to handle the condition by calling **next-handler** with no arguments. The function must ensure that all the value values returned by the call are returned by the handler; not returning them cold interfere with the condition's recovery protocol.

*init-arguments* A sequence of alternating keywords and objects which can be used as initialisation arguments in the construction of an instance of type. This argument defaults to an empty sequence. This is probably only used in restart handlers.

*test* and *handler* are distinct. Thus, the applicability of handler can be tested without actually handling the condition (actually handling the condition might only involve a non-local exit). One use of this is in the construction of a list of available restart handlers. When executing handler, the set of available handlers is not reset to the handlers which were in effect when the let handler was entered. This last requirement is necessary in order to maintain the availability of restart handlers—they are required by other condition handlers.

### 8.3.5 Other Signalling Operators

**error** *condition* ⇒ never returns
**error** *string* $argument_1$ $argument_2$ ... ⇒ will never return

**error** resembles **signal** but never returns. If a handler returns, **error** directly exits into the debugger. **error** is used when a program does not expect to receive control again after signalling a condition. The second form signals a condition of type **<simple-error>**.

**cerror** *restart-description condition* ⇒ **#f**
**cerror** *restart-description string* $argument_1$ $argument_2$ ... ⇒ **#f**

**cerror** is a continuable error-signalling function. In its operation, it is similar to **error**, but first establishes a handler for **<simple-restart>**, with **init-arguments:** set to **format-string:** *restart-description*, and with the slot **format-ar-guments:** set to the sequence $argument_1$ ...

If the restart handler is invoked, **cerror** returns **#f**, otherwise cerror never returns. If **cerror** returns, the program should take the corrective actions stated in the restart- description. **cerror** is the standard way of signalling correctable errors when no special class of restart condition is required.

**break** [ *condition* ] ⇒ **#f**
**break** [ *string argument1 argument2* ... ] ⇒ **#f**

This is a function which accepts zero or more arguments. It gets a condition in the same way as signal, but then invokes the debugger immediately without first signalling on the condition. **break** establishes a **<simple-restart>** so that the debugger can continue execution of the program. This is useful for **break** points. **break** always returns **#f**.

When called with no arguments, a default message string is used.

**check-type***value type ...value*

This signals a **<type-error>** if **instance?(value, type)** is false.

**abort** calls **error(make(<abort>))**. This is a shortcut.

**default-handler***condition* ⇒*values*

The generic function **default-handler** is called if no dynamic handler handles a given condition. There are predefined methods for condition class **<condition>** which return the empty sequence; similarly the condition class **<serious-condition>** has a method which calls the debugger; class **<warning>** has one which prints the supplied message and returns **#f**; finally, the method for **<restart>** signals an error.

**restart-query***restart*

This generic function engages the interactive user in a dialogue and stores the results in the slots of *restart*. It is intended to be called from a handler, after making a restart and before signalling it. There is a default method for **<restart>** which does nothing.

**return-query***condition*

If the recovery protocol of condition permits the return of values, this function engages the interactive user in a dialogue and returns the results as an arbitrary number of values returned by the handler. **return-query** should not be called if **return-allowed?** returns **#f**. If a programmer defines a condition class whose recovery protocol allows the return of values, it is necessary to define a method for return-query unless the inherited method is suitable.

In addition, exception handling within Dylan's **block** statement establishes exception handlers during the dynamic extent of the evaluation of the body of the block. Any number of *cleanup-clauses* (see **block** in Section 5.8.2) are permitted, and they can be interleaved arbitrarily with exception-clauses. The syntax of an exception clause is:

**exception** ( *type* | *name* :: *type* **#key** *test init-arguments* )
*exception-body* [ ; ]

If one of these handlers is invoked, it never declines, but immediately takes a non-local exit, and executes the expression in the *exception-body*; it returns the values of the last expression in the *exception-body*, or, if the *exception-body* contains no expressions, returns **#f**. If the exception handlers are never invoked, **block** returns the values of the last expression in its *body* (or the values returned from the last expression in the last *cleanup-clause* if there are any). When the expressions in an *exception-body* are executed, the handler establishes that exception clause is no longer active.

The arguments *type*, *test* and *init-arguments* are the same as in let handler. The *name* argument, if present, is not evaluated, and is taken as the name of a variable to be bound to the condition around the expressions in the **block** *body*. The exception clauses are checked in the order in which they appear within the **block**; the first handler takes precedence over the second, and so on.

### 8.3.6 Introspection on Conditions and Handlers

Operations are provided by Dylan for introspecting on the condition system and its handlers. The standard functions are the following.

**do-handlers** *funarg*

This function applies *funarg* to all dynamically active handlers, first testing the most recently established. *funarg* is a function which receives four arguments: type, *test*, *function* and *init-arguments*. The arguments describe a dynamically active handler. All arguments have dynamic extent and must not be modified. test defaults to a function which is always **#t**. *init-arguments* is **#f** if the handler does not supply it.

**return-allowed?** *condition* ⇒ *boolean*

This generic function is a predicate which returns **#t** if the recovery protocol of *condition* allows values to be returned, and **#f** if it does not. A default method which always returns **#f** is defined for **<condition>**. If the programmer defines a condition class, it is necessary to define a method for **return-allowed?** unless the inherited one is appropriate.

**return-description***condition* ⇒ *description*

If the recovery protocol of *condition* permits the return of values, generic method **return-description** returns a description of the meaning of returning values. This description can be a restart, a string, or **#f**. **return-description** should not be called if **return-allowed?** returns **#f**. If the programmer defines a condition class whose recovery protocol permits the return of values, it is necessary to define a method for **return-description** unless the inherited one is appropriate.

# Chapter 9

# Modules and Libraries

## 9.1 Introduction

Given the structures considered so far, it is possible to construct programs of medium size. However, one issue which must be addressed by a modern programming language is how to provide facilities for the construction of large programs, and probably programs constructed by more than one person.

Part of the solution to the problem is the provision of modules. It was seen in Chapter 2 that the module concept is an old one. A module is a collection of routines and data that can be considered to be a logical entity. In a language like Dylan, the module concept can be interpreted as a collection of classes, instances and methods which can be considered a logical entity. The module construct provides mechanisms for defining and maintaining interfaces. By composing modules, programmer errors can be localised. Dylan provides a module construct which is somewhat more powerful than that found in some other languages. Dylan's modules can import and export things (the things are restricted to variables, as will be explained) and can perform such acts as aliasing, selective imports and exports. Dylan programs will typically be constructed by the composition of modules.

The module construct is an intermediate-level mechanism for the construction of programs. When programs become larger, or when they have considerably longer lives, or when they are considered to be parts that can be assembled into larger systems, other mechanisms must be used.

The problem of large programs or of multiple-author programs has an additional dimension in the current age of the microcomputer. Programs can be written which depend upon facilities that are provided by other people. Libraries in a conventional sense are an example of this; one group of programmers produce routines which other programmers use in their programs—the mathematics library or the input-output library in C are typical examples. However, the natural extension of this, somewhat limited, approach is to provide libraries of objects which can be used by other programmers in other programs. The reader might remember that it was stated in Chapter 2 that an editor or a database could be construed as an object of a particular kind; users might want to include an editor or a database intact in their programs.

The library concept goes part of the way in helping the programmer. A library in Dylan is a collection of modules and other libraries. Import, export, renaming etc. are supported by the library construct. The run-time system of the Dylan programming system itself is constructed as a library.

This chapter is concerned with both of these concepts. First, modules are described. Then, the library construct is outlined. The syntax of the latter is based on that of the former, and many of the concepts employed by the two constructs are similar.

The example program developed for this book does not use modules (it does not use libraries because it is too small). Our reason for doing this was to allow the reader to concentrate on the object-oriented and other more conventional concepts of the Dylan language. The reader could profitably reorganise the program so that it is adequately modularised.

## 9.2 Modules

A module defines a namespace which is disjoint from all other such spaces. Within a module, it is possible to have named entities which are not visible outside it. Two modules can, therefore, define entities with the same names, yet cause no naming conflict. Only names which are explicitly exported from a module are visible outside. When an object is exported from a module, it is made visible by the importing module, which can manipulate the object in the same way as locally defined objects. Exported objects can be bound to values in their exporting modules, and such values are typically visible in the importing one.

Modules export variables in order to make them accessible to other modules. Some languages support module systems which permit objects of different kinds to be exported. Some languages, for example, allow the export of functions, types, classes, variables, constants and so on from modules. Dylan is different; it only supports export of variables. Functions and classes are stored in variables within a module (with some variables being read-only), so a uniform interface is presented to the external world. Within modules, module variables (variables which hold objects defined at top level using **define constant**, **define variable**, **define generic**, **define method** or **define class** play the same role in Dylan as do global variables in other languages.

When a variable is exported, the object to which it is bound is also exported. Thus, if an exported variable is bound to a class, that class will be exported. This makes for a simple and uniform mechanism.

A module establishes a mapping between variable names and variables (memory locations which are bound to values). This mapping is established in one of two ways:

- the variable can be owned by the module
- the module can import variables exported by another module by using the other module

Within any module, a variable can refer to at most one object. It is an error to create or import two or more different variables with the same name in a single module. If a name refers to a variable, that variable is said to be *accessible* from the module. Each variable is owned by (i.e. is defined inside) *exactly one* module. Variables can be accessible from many modules.

Owned variables are created by a *create clause* in a **define module**, and in some cases by definitions associated with a module. The definitions permitted by Dylan are:

- The *explicit* definitions provided by the constructs:
  - **define constant**
  - **define variable**
  - **define generic**

  and the class name in **define class**.
- The *implicit* definitions provided by **define method** and the slot specifications of **define class**.

There must be *exactly one* explicit definition for each module variable, with the exception that the explicit definition can be omitted when there are one or more implicit definitions. Any module variable whose value is a generic function can have any number of implicit definitions.

A Dylan program is composed of expressions. Each expression is associated with a module. Within an expression, variables are referenced by variable name. The module associated with the expression provides the mapping from variable name to location. An error is signalled if a name is employed which does not name a variable.

Module declarations are expressions. Like other forms of definition, module declarations are allowed only at the top level or inside **begin** blocks. The variable names in module declarations are relative either to the module being declared or to the module which it uses. A module declaration can be associated with any module where **define module** has its normal meaning. Before an expression can be compiled, the module declaration for the module associated with the expression must be compiled and made available to the development environment in some implementation-dependent fashion.

Modules are defined by define module:

```
define module module-name
       [module-clauses]
end [ module ] [ module-name ]
```

where each *module-clause* is a *use* clause, a *create* clause, or an export clause (these are described below).

The above form defines a module with the given name. It describes which modules are used by the module being defined, which variables are imported from the used modules, and which variables are exported by the module being defined.

*module-name* has the same syntax as a variable name. Module names have a scope which is a library. The namespace of module names is distinct from that of variables. No variable with the name module-name is created.

Typically, one or more use-clauses exist for each module used by a module being defined. Each use-clause has the form:

`use` *module-name* [ , *module-use-options* ] ;

*module-name* is the name of a module to be used. By default, all variables exported from the used module are imported by the module being defined. They are imported under the same name they have in the used module.

When the same module has more than one use clause, the set of imported variables is the union of those specified in all the use clauses. It is possible for the same variable tobe imported by more than one variable name.

Circular use relationships between modules are strictly forbidden. The graph of the module-uses-module relation *must* be acyclic.

The various use options to a use clause are as follows.

`import:` This can have the value all, meaning that all the variables exported by the module are to be imported. Alternatively, it can have the form:

*import* , *imports*

where an *import* is either a *variable-name* or of the form:

*variable-name* `=>` *variable-name*

(*imports* is a comma-separated list of *imports*.) In the latter case, when $\Rightarrow$ appears in an import option, the imported variable is being renamed. Thus:

```
import: {foo => bar}
```

is an abbreviation for:

```
import: {foo}, rename: {foo => bar}
```

In the case of:

```
import: {foo}
```

the variable is imported without renaming.

The next option is the `exclude:` option. It indicates those variables which should not be imported. This option can only be included if `import: all` is specified. The default value for the `exclude:` keyword is {}. The syntax of the `exclude:` option is as follows:

**exclude**: {*variable-name-set*}

where *variable-name-set* is an optional comma-separated list of variable names (as its name suggests, a variable name can only appear once in the set).

The following option specifies a string which is used to prefix the names of variables as they are imported from the module. The option can be overridden for a particular variable by using the **rename**: keyword option (described next). The default for the **prefix**: keyword is the empty string, "". The syntax is:

**prefix**:*string*

where *string* is the prefixing string.

The **rename**: option is used to override the **import**:, **exclude**:, and **prefix**: keywords.

The variables named are imported regardless of whether the keywords **import**: and **export**: indicate that they should be imported. The syntax is:

**rename**: { *rename-specs*}

where *rename-specs* is an optional list of comma-separated entries of the form:

*old-name* $\Rightarrow$ *new-name*

where *old-name* indicates the name of the variable in the module being used, and *new-name* indicates the name to be used for the variable in the module currently being defined. The **prefix**: keyword of the use-clause is ignored for variables specified by the **rename**: keyword. The default value for rename: is {}.

The final option is the **export**: option. It takes either the form:

**export**: **all**

or the form:

**export**: *variable-name-set*

where *variable-name-set* is a set of variable-names, each name separated by a comma from the next (as for **exclude**:). This option specifies variables which should be exported from the module being defined. Each of the variables must have been imported into the module being defined by this use clause. Each *variable-name* is the name of the variable in the module being defined. It allows for the same *variable-name* to appear more than once, as this can be useful for documentation. The value all indicates that all the variables imported by this use-clause should be exported. The default value for this keyword is {}.

It is possible also to export owned variables. This is done using the *module export* clause; it has the following syntax:

**export** *variable-names*

This option specifies that the named variables are to be exported from the module currently being defined. Each *variable-name* is the name of a variable to be exported. The variables must have been defined by a defining form in the module. It is an error for any imported variables to be included in this list. For reasons of documentation, a name is permitted to appear more than once in the list.

Finally, there is the module *create clause*. It has the following syntax:

**create** *variable-names*

This option specifies that the named variables are to be created in and exported from the module currently being defined. A *variable-name* is the name of a variable to be created and exported. The variables which appear in *variable-names* must not be created or defined by a defining form in the module being defined, and they must be defined by a module which uses the one being defined. It is an error for any of the variables imported from other sources to appear in *variable-names*. For reasons of documentation, a name is permitted to appear more than once in the list.

## 9.3 Libraries

Libraries provide the largest unit of abstraction and collection in Dylan. Libraries collect modules together. A library is given a formal description by language constructs. A library description consists of the following parts:

- A single library declaration form. This specifies the name of the library: a set of modules which are to be exported from the library and which are for the use of other libraries. It can also include a set of modules to be imported from other libraries for use by the library being defined. Library declaration forms are described below.

- The association of source code with the library. Implementations define their own mechanisms for associating code and library.

- The association of executable code with the library. Implementations define their own mechanisms for associating executable code and library. The mechanism for invoking the compiler to produce code is also implementation-dependent.

- The association of library export information with the library. Implementations define their own mechanisms for this. The mechanism for invoking the compiler in order to produce code is also an implementation-dependent matter, as are the contents of the library export information, but it comprises the content of the information required to process the source code of some other library which imports this library.

Library export information is the only part of a Dylan library needed to permit other libraries to import it. A library exporting modules does not have any additional declarations to provide information to the compiler when it is processing the code of a library importing those modules. Any such needed information is can be obtained via some implementation-specific mechanism.

The syntax of library declarations exactly matches the syntax of module declaration, with the exception that the word `library` replaces the word `module`, and that library declarations do not have create clauses.

Exporting a module from a library makes all of the variables exported by the module available for import by modules in other libraries. There are two ways in which a module can be exported from a library:

1. If the module is defined in the library, it is exported by including a *library-export-clause* which names the module in the library declaration. Each *module-name* in a *library-export-clause* is the name of a module exported by the library.

2. If the module is imported from some other library, it is exported by including an *export-option* specifying the module (either by name or implicitly by using `export:` all) in a *library-use-option* which imported the module.

Importing a module into a library allows the module to be used by modules defined in the importing library. A module is imported into a library by including a *library-use-clause* in the library declaration which includes the module in the set of modules imported from the used library. All exported modules from the used library are, by default, imported by the library being defined; they have the same names in the importing library as in the used one.

The set of imported modules is the union of those specified by all of the use clauses when there are multiple use clauses using the same library. Sometimes modules will be imported under more than one module name; this is permitted.

The options in a use clause are to prevent some modules from being imported, to give some or all the imported modules different names in the new library and so on; the functions are similar to those in the corresponding constructs for modules (the difference, of course, being that they deal with libraries and not with modules).

Every implementation provides a library called `dylan` which exports a module called `dylan`. This module exports those variables which comprise the Dylan language. Additional features will be added to the `dylan` module by some implementations.

Library declarations are expressions as far as Dylan is concerned. Like all other defining forms, they can only appear at the top level or within a `begin` block. The names in a library declaration are not module variable names; they are not affected by the library declarations associated module. A library declaration can be associated with any module in which `define library` has its intended (normal) interpretation.

Macros can be expanded into library declarations. This happens during the compilation of the library declaration.

The module named **dylan-user** is implicitly defined in each library. This module contains all the variables specified by the Dylan language; they are accessible using their specified names. Additional variables will be provided by some implementations.

# Appendix A

# Example Program Listing

## A.1 Introduction

In this Appendix, the code of the example program, the shopping list database is presented. With the exception of the font (here `typewriter` is used) and a little formatting (to make it more readable), the code is exactly as it is on disk, warts and all.

The code is divided into separate files, each of which begins with a module specification `module: Dylan-User`. This says that the code is to be executed within the default module and library, and thus ensures that the interpreter will find all the necessary standard bindings.

## A.2 Money

```
module: Dylan-User

//
// Class amount.
// This represents the cost of an item in terms
// of pounds and pence.
//

//
// Should the slots both be constants?
//


define class <amount> (<object>)
       slot pounds :: <integer>, init-keyword: pounds:,
                                 init-value: 0;
       slot pence :: <integer>, required-init-keyword: pence:;
end class <amount>;
```

```
define method amount? (x)
      instance?(x,<amount>)
end method amount?;

//
// show crudely prints the amount on the screen.
//

define method show (amount :: <amount>)
      print(format("Amount: %d pounds and %d pence.",
                   pounds(amount),
                   pence(amount)))
end method show;

//
// make-amount is for external consumption only.
// Internally, we do things a little more quickly.
//

define method make-amount (#key pounds (0), pence (0))
      if (pounds < 0)
         error("Cannot make amount with negative pounds")
      elseif (pence < 0)
         error("Cannot make amount with negative pence")
      end if;
      make(<amount>,pounds: pounds, pence: pence)
end method make-amount;

//
// print-amount prints the amount.
//

define method print-amount (amnt :: <amount>)
      print(format("%d.%d",pounds(amnt),pence(amnt)))
end method print-amount;

//
// pence-only? returns true if the amount is < 100 pence.
//

define method pence-only? (amount :: <amount>)
      pounds(amount) = 0
end method pence-only?;

//
// pounds-to-pence converts a sum in pounds and pence to
// one in pence -- useful for comparison operators.
//
```

```
define method pounds-to-pence (amount :: <amount>)
      (100 * pounds(amount)) + pence(amount)
end method pounds-to-pence;

//
// pence-to-pounds converts pence to pounds.
// Return a <amount>.
//

define method pence-to-pounds (amount :: <integer>)
      let pounds = 0;
      let pence = amount;
          while (pence > 99)
               pence := pence - 100;
               pounds := pounds + 1;
          end while;
          make(<amount>,pounds: pounds,pence: pence)
end method pence-to-pounds;

//
// Perform addition, subtraction, multiplication and division
// on <amount>.
//

//
// Return a amount and a remainder.
//

define method divide-amount (amount :: <amount>,
                             dividend :: <integer>)
      let amnt = pounds-to-pence(amount);
      let div = amnt / dividend;
      let rem = 0;
          if ((dividend * div) ~= amnt)
             rem := amnt - (dividend * div)
          end if;
          values(pence-to-pounds(div),rem)
end method divide-amount;

//
// Does amount1 = amount2?
//

define method \< (amount1 :: <amount>, amount2 :: <amount>)
      pounds-to-pence(amount1) < pounds-to-pence(amount2)
end method \<;
```

```
define method \= (amount1 :: <amount>, amount2 :: <amount>)
       pounds-to-pence(amount1) = pounds-to-pence(amount2)
end method \=;



define method \~= (amount1 :: <amount>,
                   amount2 ::<amount>)
       ~(amount1 = amount2)
end method \~=;


define method \<= (amount1 :: <amount>,
                   amount2 :: <amount>)
       (amount1 < amount2) | (amount1 = amount2)
end method \<=;

//
// Is amount1 <= amount2?
//

/*
//
// Greater-than:
//

define method \> (amount1 :: <amount>,
                  amount2 :: <amount>)
       amount2 < amount1
end method

//
// Greater-than-or-equal
// define method \>=(amount1 :: <amount>,
                     amount2 :: <amount>)
          (amount1 > amount2) | (amount1 = amount2)
end method \>=; */
//
// minus? is true if the amount is negative.
//
```

## A.3 Time

```
module: Dylan-User
//
// Dates for calculating periods.
```

```
// Dates are represented as dd/mm/yy
// as well as dd/yy
//

define class <purchase-date> (<object>)
      slot day :: <integer>, init-keyword: dd:;
      slot month :: <symbol>, init-keyword: mm:;
      slot year :: <integer>, init-keyword: yy:;
      slot dayno :: <integer>;
      slot monthno :: <integer>;
end class <purchase-date>;

define method show (pd :: <purchase-date>)
      print(format("Date: %d/%s/%d.",
      day(pd),as(<string>,month(pd)),year(pd)))
end method show;

define method \= (pd1 :: <purchase-date>,
                  pd2 :: <purchase-date>)
      (year(pd1) == year(pd2))
          & (dayno(pd1) == dayno(pd2))
          & (monthno(pd1) == monthno(pd2))
end method \=;

//
// Creation function:
//

define method make-purchase-date (day :: <integer>,
                                  month :: <symbol>,
                                  year :: <integer>,
                                  #key leap-year?(#f))
      if (year < 1995)
         error(
         "Cannot make date: year must start at 1995 (%d).",
         year)
      end if;
      if ((day < 1) | (day > 31))
       error(
       "Cannot make date: days must be in range 1..31 (%d).",
       day)
      end if;
      let mnumber = calc-monthno(month);
      let dynumber = calc-dayno(month,day,
                                leap-year?:
                                leap-year?);
      let pdate = make(<purchase-date>,
```

```
                        dd:  day,
                        mm:  month,
                        yy:  year);
          dayno(pdate) := dynumber;
          monthno(pdate) := mnumber;
          pdate
end method make-purchase-date;

define constant $year-info =
       #( #(#"january",1,31),
       #(#"february",2,28),
       #(#"march",3,31),
       #(#"april",4,30),
       #(#"may",5,31),
       #(#"june",6,30),
       #(#"july",7,31),
       #(#"august",8,31),
       #(#"september",9,30),
       #(#"october",10,31),
       #(#"november",11,30),
       #(#"december",12,31));

define method month-name (minfo ::  <list>)
       head(minfo)
end method month-name;
define method month-number (minfo ::  <list>)
       head(tail(minfo))
end method month-number;
define method days-in-month (minfo ::  <list>)
       head( tail( tail(minfo)))
end method days-in-month;

define method valid-month? (month-name ::  <symbol>)
       member?(month-name,
              #( #"january", #"february",#"march",
              #"april", #"may", #"june",
              #"july", #"july", #"august",
              #"september", #"october", #"november"),
              test:  \=)
end method valid-month?;

define method calc-monthno (m-name ::  <symbol>)
       if (~valid-month?(m-name))
          error(
          "Cannot calculate month number:  unknown month %s.",
          as(<string>, m-name))
```

```
      end if;
      let mno :: <integer> = 0;
      let year-data = $year-info;
      let month-data = head(year-data);
         while (month-name(month-data) ~= m-name)
              year-data := tail(year-data);
              month-data := head(year-data)
         end while;
      month-number(month-data)
end method calc-monthno;

define method calc-dayno (m-name :: <symbol>,
                          day :: <integer>,
                          #key leap-year?(#f))
  local method calc ()
        let month-infos = tail($year-info);
        let month-data = head($year-info);
        let days-tot = 0;
            while (month-name(month-data) ~= m-name)
                 if (month-name(month-data) == #"february")
                    if (leap-year?)
                       days-tot := days-tot + 29
                    else
                       days-tot := days-tot + 28
                    end if
                 else
                    days-tot :=
                      days-tot + days-in-month(month-data)
                 end if;
                 month-data := head(month-infos);
                 month-infos := tail(month-infos)
            end while;
        days-tot + day
  end;
  if (~valid-month?(m-name))
     error(
     "Cannot calculate day number:  unknown month %s.",
     as(<string>,m-name))
  end if;
  calc()
end method calc-dayno;

//
// Is time1 before time2?
// If the yearnos are the same, dayno1 < dayno2.
//
```

```
define method before? (time1 :: <purchase-date>,
                       time2 :: <purchase-date>)
       if (year(time1) < year(time2))
          #t
       elseif (year(time1) == year(time2))
             dayno(time1) < dayno(time2)
       else #f
       end if
end method before?;

define method after? (time1 :: <purchase-date>,
                      time2 :: <purchase-date>)
       if (year(time1) > year(time2))
          #t
       elseif (year(time1) == year(time2))
             dayno(time1) > dayno(time2)
       else #f
       end if
end method after?;
```

## A.4 Physical Quantities

```
module: Dylan-User

//
// Quantity.dylan
// This file contains code to manipulate quantities of
// shopping.
//

define abstract class <quantity>(<object>)
end class <quantity>;

define generic compute-unit-cost (quant, cost);

define class <number-quantity> (<quantity>)
       slot amount :: <integer>, init-keyword: amnt:;
end class <number-quantity>;

n define method show (a :: <number-quantity>)
         print(format("No. = %d.",amount(a)))
end method show;

define method make-number-quantity (q :: <integer>)
       if (q <= 0)
          error("Cannot make negative quantity -- %d", q)
```

```
      else
         make(<number-quantity>,amnt: q)
      end if
end method make-number-quantity;

define method \= (nq1 :: <number-quantity>,
                  nq2 :: <number-quantity>)
      amount(nq1) == amount(nq2)
end method \=;

define method compute-unit-cost (quant :: <number-quantity>,
                                 amnt :: <amount>);
      let pence = pounds-to-pence(amnt);
      let rounded = round(pence / amount(quant));
         pence-to-pounds(rounded)
end method compute-unit-cost;

define class <mass-quantity> (<quantity>)
      slot mass-in-grams :: <integer>, init-keyword: mig:;
end class <mass-quantity>;

define method show (mq :: <mass-quantity>)
      print(format("Amount = %= kg.",
                   mass-in-grams(mq) / 1000.0))
end method show;

define method \= (mq1 :: <mass-quantity>,
                  mq2 :: <mass-quantity>)
      mass-in-grams(mq1) == mass-in-grams(mq2)
end method \=;

// mass in kilos and grams:

define method make-mass (mass)
      if (mass < 0)
         error("Cannot make mass: mass negative (%d)", mass)
      else
         make(<mass-quantity>,mig: mass)
      end if
end method make-mass;

define method compute-unit-cost (quant :: <mass-quantity>,
                                 amnt :: <amount>)
      let pence = pounds-to-pence(amnt);
      let rounded = round(pence / mass-in-grams(quant));
         pence-to-pounds(rounded)
end method compute-unit-cost;
```

```
define class <volume-quantity> (<quantity>)
       slot mil :: <integer>, init-keyword: milvol:;
end class <volume-quantity>;

define method show (vq :: <volume-quantity>)
       print(format("Volume = %=.", mil(vq) / 1000.0))
end method show;

define method \= (vq1 :: <volume-quantity>,
                  vq2 :: <volume-quantity>)
       mil(vq1) == mil(vq2)
end method \=;

define method make-volume (vol)
       if (vol < 0)
          error("Cannot make volume: volume negative (%d)",vol)
       else
          make(<volume-quantity>,milvol: vol)
       end if
end method make-volume;

define method compute-unit-cost (quant :: <volume-quantity>,
                                 amnt :: <amount>)
       let pence = pounds-to-pence(amnt);
       let rounded = round(pence / mil(quant));
           pence-to-pounds(rounded)
end method compute-unit-cost;
```

## A.5 Foodstuffs

```
//
// Module foodstuffs.
// This file contains the definitions of the various classes
// of foodstuff available from the shops.

module: Dylan-User
//

define constant $food-category =
       > #( #"meat",
       #"fish",
       #"vegetable",
       #"fruit",
       #"bread",
       #"dairy-product");
```

```
define constant $packing-kind =
      #( #"fresh",
      #"canned-product",
      #"dairy-product",
      #"bread",
      #"frozen-food",
      #"paper-goods");

define variable *vegetables* =
      #( #"potatoes",
      #"onions",
      #"carrots",
      #"cabbage",
      #"cauliflower",
      #"parsnips",
      #"leeks",
      #"lettuce",
      #"artichoke",
      #"chillies",
      #"garlic",
      #"root-ginger",
      #"turnip",
      #"swede",
      #"fennel",
      #"celery",
      #"celeriac",
      #"broad-beans",
      #"string-beans",
      #"french-beans");

define variable *fruit* =
      #( #"apple",
      #"orange",
      #"banana",
      #"grapefruit",
      #"melon",
      #"lemon",
      #"lime",
      #"apricot",
      #"peach",
      #"nectarine",
      #"tomato",
      #"pepper",
      #"aubergine",
      #"strawberry");

define variable *dairy-products* =
```

```
      #( #"milk",
      #"cheese",
      #"creme-fraiche",
      #"single-cream",
      #"double-cream",
      #"yoghurt");

define variable *breads* =
      #( #"loaf",
      #"rolls",
      #"baguettes",
      #"biscuits");

define variable *meat* =
      #( #"beef",
      #"lamb",
      #"pork",
      #"veal",
      #"liver",
      #"kidney",
      #"pork-chops",
      #"lamb-chops",
      #"sausages");

define variable *fish* =
      #( #"cod",
      #"haddock",
      #"sole",
      #"coli",
      #"kipper",
      #"salmon",
      #"trout",
      #"sea-bass",
      #"monk-fish",
      #"sardines",
      #"tuna",
      #"pichards",
      #"anchovies",
      #"crab",
      #"lobster");

//
// type-of-food returns the type of a purported foodstuff.
// An error is raised if there

define method type-of-food (x :: <symbol>)
  case
```

```
        member?(x,*meat*,test:  \==) => #"meat";
        member?(x,*fish*,test:  \==) => #"fish";
        member?(x,*vegetables*,test:  \==) => #"vegetable";
        member?(x,*fruit*,test:  \==) => #"fruit";
        member?(x,*breads*,test:  \==) => #"bread";
        member?(x,*dairy-products*,test:  \==)
                                         => #"dairy-product";
  otherwise =>
        error("type-of-food:  unrecognised food kind %d.",
              as(<string>,x))
  end case; end method type-of-food;

//
// Class definitions for database.
//

define abstract class <foodstuff-info> (<object>)
       slot packing-kind ::  <symbol>;
       slot food-category ::  <symbol>;
       slot foodname ::  <symbol>;
end class <foodstuff-info>;

define method show (fs ::  <foodstuff-info>)
       print(format("Packaging:  %s.",
                    as(<string>,packing-kind(fs))));
       print(format("Category:  %s.",
                    as(<string>,food-category(fs))));
       print(format("Name:  %s.",
                    as(<string>,foodname(fs))))
end method show;

define method \= (fsi1 ::  <foodstuff-info>,
                  fsi2 ::  <foodstuff-info>)
       (packing-kind(fsi1) == packing-kind(fsi2))
        & (food-category(fsi1) == food-category(fsi2))
        & (foodname(fsi1) == foodname(fsi2))
end method \ =;

define class <foodstuff-with-mass> (<foodstuff-info>)
       slot mass ::  <mass-quantity>;
end class <foodstuff-with-mass>;

define method show (fsm ::  <foodstuff-with-mass>,
                    #next next-method)
       next-method();
       show(mass(fsm))
end method show;
```

```
define method \= (fsm1 :: <foodstuff-with-mass>,
                  fsm2 :: <foodstuff-with-mass>,
                  #next next-method)
       (mass(fsm1) = mass(fsm2))
            & next-method()
end method \=;

define class <foodstuff-with-volume> (<foodstuff-info>)
       slot volume :: <volume-quantity>;
end class <foodstuff-with-volume>;

define method show (fsv :: <foodstuff-with-volume>,
                    #next next-method)
       next-method();
       show(volume(fsv))
end method show;

define method \= (fsv1 :: <foodstuff-with-volume>,
                  fsv2 ::<foodstuff-with-volume>,
                  #next next-method)
       (volume(fsv1) = volume(fsv2))
              & next-method()
end method \=;

define class <counted-foodstuff> (<foodstuff-info>)
       slot number :: <number-quantity>;
end class <counted-foodstuff>;

define method show (cf :: <counted-foodstuff>,
                    #next next-method)
       next-method();
       print(number(cf))
end method show;
define method \= (cf1 :: <counted-foodstuff>,
                 cf2 :: <counted-foodstuff>,
                 #next next-method)
      (number(cf1) = number(cf2))
            & next-method()
end method \=;

define class <branded-foodstuff-with-mass>(<foodstuff-with-mass>)
       slot brandname :: <string>
end class <branded-foodstuff-with-mass>;

define method show (bfm :: <branded-foodstuff-with-mass>,
                    #next next-method)
       next-method();
```

```
        print(format("Brand:  %s.",brandname(bfm)))
end method show;

define method \= (b1 ::  <branded-foodstuff-with-mass>,
                  b2 ::  <branded-foodstuff-with-mass>,
                  #next next-method)
        (brandname(b1) = brandname(b2))
                  & next-method()
end method \=

define class <branded-foodstuff-with-volume>
                      (<foodstuff-with-volume>)
        slot brandname ::  <string>
end class <branded-foodstuff-with-volume>;

define method show (bfv ::  <branded-foodstuff-with-volume>,
                    #next next-method)
        next-method();
        print(format("Brand:  %s.",brandname(bfv)))
end method show;

define method \= (b1 ::  <branded-foodstuff-with-volume>,
                  b2 ::  <branded-foodstuff-with-volume>,
                  #next next-method)
        (brandname(b1) = brandname(b2))
                  & next-method()
end method ;

define class <counted-branded-foodstuff>(<counted-foodstuff>)
        slot brandname ::  <string>
end class <counted-branded-foodstuff>;

define method show (cfm ::  <counted-branded-foodstuff>,
                    #next next-method)
        next-method();
        print(format("Brand:  end method show;

define method \= (b1 ::  <counted-branded-foodstuff>,
                  b2 ::  <counted-branded-foodstuff>,
                  #next next-method)
        (brandname(b1) = brandname(b2))
                  & next-method()
end method \=;

//
// The above classes are used to define a purchase:
//
```

```
define class <purchase> (<object>)
      slot shopname :: <string>;
      slot item-purchased :: <foodstuff-info>;
      slot date-purchased :: <purchase-date>;
      slot total-cost :: <amount>;
      slot unit-price :: <amount>,
           init-function:
                method()
                     make(<amount>,pence: 0)
                end
end class <purchase>;

define method show (p :: <purchase>)
      print(format("Shop: %s.",shopname(p)));
      show(item-purchased(p));
      show(date-purchased(p));
      print("Total cost:");
      show(total-cost(p));
      print("Unit price:");
      show(unit-price(p));
end method show;

//
// An equality predicate can be defined for <purchase>.
//

define method \= (p1 :: <purchase>, p2 :: <purchase>)
      (shopname(p1) = shopname(p2))
                & (total-cost(p1) = total-cost(p2))
                & (unit-price(p1) = unit-price(p2))
                & (date-purchased(p1) = date-purchased(p2))
                & (item-purchased(p1) = item-purchased(p2))
end method \=
```

## A.6 Food-table and The Database

```
module: Dylan-User

//
// This file contains the definition of the operations
// on the various tables that the database uses.
//

define class <food-table> (<object>)
      slot entries :: <object-table>,
           init-function: // no setter needed
```

```
                method () make(<object-table>) end;
      slot valid-food-kinds :: <list>,
           init-keyword: valid-foods:; // constant slot
end class <food-table>;

define method make-food-table (kinds :: <list>)
      let ft = make(<food-table>,valid-foods: kinds);
          for (fk in valid-food-kinds(ft))
              element(entries(ft),fk) := #()
          end for;
      ft end method make-food-table;

define method add-valid-food! (ft :: <food-table>,
                               fk :: <symbol>)
      if (~valid-food?(ft,fk))
         valid-food-kinds(ft) := pair(fk,valid-food-kinds(ft));
         element(entries(ft),fk) := #()
      end if
end method add-valid-food!;

define method valid-food? (ft :: <food-table>,
                           food-kind :: <symbol>)
      member?(food-kind,valid-food-kinds(ft),test: \==)
end method valid-food?;

define method add-food-purchase! (ft :: <food-table>,
                                  food-kind :: <symbol>,
                                  info :: <object>)
      // info :: <object> for now.
      if (~valid-food?(ft,food-kind))
         error("Cannot add purchase: invalid food (%s).",
               as(<string>, food-kind))
      end if;
      element(entries(ft),food-kind)
             := pair(info,element(entries(ft),food-kind))
end method add-food-purchase!;

define method purchases-of-kind (ft :: <food-table>,
                                 food-kind :: <symbol>)
  if (~valid-food?(ft,food-kind))
     error(
       "Cannot retrieve purchases of kind %s -- invalid kind.",
       as(<string>,food-kind))
  end if;
  let buys = element(entries(ft),food-kind);
      buys
end method purchases-of-kind;
```

```
define method current-food-kinds (ft :: <food-table>)
       key-sequence(entries(ft))
end method current-food-kinds;

define method purchased-food-kinds (ft :: <food-table>)
       let kinds = #();
           for (kind in current-food-kinds(ft))
               if (element(entries(ft),kind) ~= #())
                  kinds := pair(kind,kinds)
               end if
           end for;
           kinds end method purchased-food-kinds;

define method all-purchases (ft :: <food-table>)
       let kinds = purchased-food-kinds(ft);
       let purchases = #();
           for (kind in kinds)
               purchases :=
                         concatenate(purchases,
                                     purchases-of-kind(ft,kind))
           end for;
           purchases
end method all-purchases;

define method filter-purchases (ft :: <food-table>,
                                kind :: <symbol>,
                                filter :: <function>)
       let purchases = purchases-of-kind(ft,kind);
       let filtered = #();
           for (purchase in purchases)
               if (filter(purchase))
                  filtered := add(filtered,purchase)
               end if
           end for;
           filtered
end method filter-purchases;

define method filter-all-purchases (ft :: <food-table>,
                                    filter :: <function>)
       let all-purchased-items = all-purchases(ft);
       let filtered = #();
           for (purchase in all-purchased-items)
               if (filter(purchase))
                  filtered := add(filtered,purchase)
               end if
           end for;
```

```
        filtered
end method filter-all-purchases;
```

## A.7 Shopping

```
module: Dylan-User

//
// Shopping.
//

//
// Supermarkets and shops.
// The program maintains a list of supermarkets and shops inside
// an object. This object is the main database and also contains
// slots to hold information about what was bought and where.
// This constitutes the main bank of information about shopping.
//

define class <shopping-info> (<object>)
      slot shops :: <list>, init-value: #();
      slot meat-items :: <food-table>,
           init-function:method ()
                          make-food-table(*meat*)
           end;
      slot fish-items :: <food-table>,
           init-function:method ()
                          make-food-table(*fish*)
           end;
      slot veg-items :: <food-table>,
           init-function:method ()
                          make-food-table(*vegetables*)
           end;
      slot fruit-items :: <food-table>,
           init-function:method ()
                          make-food-table(*fruit*)
           end;
      slot dairy-items :: <food-table>,
           init-function:method ()
                          make-food-table(*dairy-products*)
           end;
      slot bread-items :: <food-table>,
           init-function:method ()
                          make-food-table(*breads*)
           end;
```

```
end class <shopping-info>;

define method known-shop? (sn :: <string>,
                           si :: <shopping-info>)
      member?(sn, shops(si), test: \ =)
end method known-shop?;

define method add-shopname! (sn :: <string>,
                             si :: <shopping-info>)
      if (~ known-shop?(sn,si))
         shops(si) := pair(sn,shops(si))
      end if;
      sn
end method add-shopname!;

define method add-purchased-item!
                           (purchased-item :: <purchase>,
                           shop-where-purchased :: <string>,
                           item-kind :: <symbol>,
                           food-kind :: <symbol>,
                           si :: <shopping-info>)
  if (~known-shop?(shop-where-purchased,si))
     error("Do not know this shop: %s.",shop-where-purchased)
  end if;
  select (item-kind)
        #"meat"=>
              add-food-purchase!(meat-items(si),
                                 food-kind,
                                 purchased-item);
        #"fish" =>
              add-food-purchase!(fish-items(si),
                                 food-kind,
                                 purchased-item);
        #"vegetable" =>
                   add-food-purchase!(veg-items(si),
                                      food-kind,
                                      purchased-item);
        #"fruit" =>
               add-food-purchase!(fruit-items(si),
                                  food-kind,
                                  purchased-item);
        #"bread" =>
               add-food-purchase!(bread-items(si),
                                  food-kind,
                                  purchased-item);
        #"dairy-product"=>
```

```
                    add-food-purchase!(dairy-items(si),
                                       food-kind,
                                       purchased-item);
        otherwise =>
         error("add-purchased-item!:  cannot recognise %s.",
              as(<string>,item-kind))
  end select
end method add-purchased-item!;

define method purchases-of-kind (si ::  <shopping-info>,
                                 fk ::  <symbol>)
  let purchases = #();
      select(fk)
            #"meat" =>
              purchases := all-purchases(meat-items(si));
            #"fish" =>
              purchases := all-purchases(fish-items(si));
            #"vegetable" =>
              purchases := all-purchases(veg-items(si));
            #"fruit" =>
              purchases := all-purchases(fruit-items(si));
            #"bread" =>
              purchases := all-purchases(bread-items(si));
            #"dairy-product" =>
              purchases := all-purchases(dairy-items(si));
      otherwise =>
       error(
         "purchases-of-kind:  unrecognised food kind %s.",
         as(<string>,fk))
  end select;
end method purchases-of-kind;

//
// Every purchase returns a list of all the purchases in
// the database.
//

define method every-purchase (db ::  <shopping-info>)
       let all-purchases = #();
           for (kind in #( #"meat", #"fish",
               #"vegetable", #"fruit",
               #"bread", #"dairy-product"))
               let purchases = purchases-of-kind(db,kind);
               if (purchases ~= #())
                  all-purchases := add(all-purchases,purchases)
               else
```

```
                all-purchases :=
                   add(all-purchases,list("nothing for",kind))
             end if
          end for;
       all-purchases
end method every-purchase;

//
// Routines to select items and to produce sets of items
// satisfying some predicate.
//

define method filter-purchases (si :: <shopping-info>,
                                food-kind :: <symbol>,
                                filter :: <function>)
       let purchases-of-kind = purchases-of-kind(si,food-kind);
       let filtered = #();
          for (purchase in purchases-of-kind)
             if (filtered(purchase))
                filtered := add(filtered,purchase)
             end if
          end for;
          filtered
end method filter-purchases;
```

## A.8 Shopping Lists

```
module: Dylan-User

//
// Interface to the shopping list.
// The class defined below is constructed when the shopping list
// is read and parsed.
//

define class <shopping-list> (<object>)
       slot shop :: <string>, init-keyword: shop-name:;
       slot date :: <purchase-date>,
                   init-keyword: shopping-date:;
       slot items-purchased :: <list>, init-value: #()
end class <shopping-list>;

define method show (sl :: <shopping-list>)
       print(format("Shop: %s.",shop(sl)));
       show(date(sl));
       for (item in items-purchased(sl))
```

```
          show(item)
      end for
end method show;

define class <shopping-item> (<object>)
   slot item-name :: <symbol>, init-keyword: item-name:;
   slot quantity :: <quantity>, init-keyword: amount-bought:;
   slot cost :: <amount>, init-keyword: item-cost:;
   slot packing :: <symbol>, init-keyword: packaging:;
   slot brandname :: <string>, init-value: ""
end class <shopping-item>;

define method show (si :: <shopping-item>)
      print("------------------");
      print(format("Item name: %s.",
                   as(<string>,item-name(si))));
      show(quantity(si));
      show(cost(si));
      print(format("Packaging: %s.",
                   as(<string>,packing(si))));
      if (brandname(si) ~= "")
         print(format("Brand: %s.",brandname(si)));
      end if
end method show;

define method shopping-item-to-purchase
                     (si :: <shopping-item>,
                     shop :: <string>,
                     date :: <purchase-date>)
  let purchase-record = make(<purchase>);
  let food-name = item-name(si);
  let branded? = #f;
  let how-packed = packing(si);
  let item = #f;
      shopname(purchase-record) := shop;
      date-purchased(purchase-record) := date;
      total-cost(purchase-record) := cost(si);
      if (brandname(si))
         branded? := #t
      end if;
      unit-price(purchase-record)
           := compute-unit-cost(quantity(si),cost(si));
      // Now store the item, unit and amount
      // in the most appropriate object.
      select(quantity(si) by instance?)
        <number-quantity> =>
```

```
          if (branded?)
             item := make(<counted-branded-foodstuff>);
             brandname(item) := brandname(si)
          else
             item := make(<counted-foodstuff>)
          end if;
          number(item) := quantity(si);
       <mass-quantity> =>
          if (branded?)
             item := make(<branded-foodstuff-with-mass>);
             brandname(item) := brandname(si)
          else
             item := make(<foodstuff-with-mass>)
          end if;
          mass(item) := quantity(si);
       <volume-quantity> =>
          if (branded?)
             item := make(<branded-foodstuff-with-volume>);
             brandname(item) := brandname(si)
          else
             item := make(<foodstuff-with-volume>)
          end if;
          volume(item) := quantity(si);
       otherwise =>
          error(
             "Unrecognised quantity.  %=")
     end select;
     food-category(item) := type-of-food(food-name);
     foodname(item) := food-name;
     packing-kind(item) := how-packed;
     item-purchased(purchase-record) := item;
     purchase-record
end method shopping-item-to-purchase;

//
// For testing only:
//

define method shopping-to-purchase-list (sl :: <shopping-list>)
  let pl = #();
     for (item in items-purchased(sl))
         pl := add(pl,
                   shopping-item-to-purchase(item,shop(sl),date(sl)))
     end for;
  pl end method shopping-to-purchase-list;

define method store-shopping-list (sl :: <shopping-list>,
```

```
                                      db :: <shopping-info>)
  let shopname = shop(sl);
  let date = date(sl);
     for (item in items-purchased(sl))
        let purchase =
           shopping-item-to-purchase(item,shopname,date);
           add-purchased-item!
              (purchase,
               shopname,
               food-category(item-purchased(purchase)),
               foodname(item-purchased(purchase)),
               db)
     end for;
  values()
end method store-shopping-list;

define method make-shopping-item (name :: <symbol>,
                                  quantity :: <quantity>,
                                  cost :: <amount>,
                                  packing :: <symbol>,
                                  #key brand-name(""))
      if (~member?(packing,$packing-kind,test: =))
         error("Unknown packaging (%s).",
               as(<string>,packing))
      end if;
      let food-kind = type-of-food(name);
      let sitem = make(<shopping-item>,
                        item-name: name,
                        amount-bought: quantity,
                        item-cost: cost,
                        packaging: packing);
      if (brand-name ~= "")
         brandname(sitem) := brand-name
      end if;
      sitem
end method make-shopping-item;

define method add-shopping-item (sl :: <shopping-list>,
                                 name :: <symbol>,
                                 quantity :: <quantity>,
                                 cost :: <amount>,
                                 packing :: <symbol>,
                                 #key brand-name (""))
  items-purchased(sl)
       := add(items-purchased(sl),
              make-shopping-item(name,quantity,cost,packing,
```

```
                brand-name:  brand-name));
  values()
end method add-shopping-item;

//
// Shopping lists are actual lists when input to the program.
// They have the format:
// #("Shopname" #(dd month yy)
// #(foodname quantity cost packing | brandname))
// The following routines unpack the data.
//

define method list-shopname (sl ::  <list>)
       head(sl)
end method list-shopname;

define method list-date (sl ::  <list>)
       head(tail(sl))
end method list-date;

define method list-purchases (sl ::  <list>)
       tail(tail(sl))
end method list-purchases;

//
// The components of the list have to be picked out and converted
// to the shopping list:
//

define method add-list-item (sl ::  <shopping-list>,
                             li ::  <list>)
       let name = head(li);
       let quant = head(tail(li));
       let cost = head(tail(tail(li)));
       let packing = head(tail(tail(tail(li))));
       local method convert-quant(q)
             let units = head(q);
             let num = head(tail(q));
                 select (units)
                 #"kg" => make-mass(num);
                 #"num" => make-number-quantity(num);
                 #"ltr" => make-volume(num);
                 otherwise =>
                    error("unrecognised physical unit:  %s.",
                          as(<string>,units))
                 end select
       end;
```

```
      if (size(li) == 5)
         add-shopping-item(sl,name,convert-quant(quant),
                           make-amount(pounds: head(cost),
                           pence: head(tail(cost))),
                           packing,
                           brand-name: last(li))
      else
          add-shopping-item(sl,name,convert-quant(quant),
                            make-amount(pounds: head(cost),
                            pence: head(tail(cost))),
                            packing)
      end if
end method add-list-item;

define method convert-shopping-list (li :: <list>)
      let shop :: <string> = list-shopname(li);
      let date :: <list> = list-date(li);
      let purchases :: <list> = list-purchases(li);
      let shopping-list :: <shopping-list>
            = make(<shopping-list>,
                   shop-name: shop,
                   shopping-date:
                      make-purchase-date(head(date),
                   head(tail(date)),
                   head(tail(tail(date)))));
      for (item in purchases)
          add-list-item(shopping-list,item)
      end for;
      shopping-list
end method convert-shopping-list;
```

## A.9 The Main Method

```
module: Dylan-User

// foodname quantity cost packing | branded

define variable *shopping* =
      #("tesco", #(7, #"november", 1995),
      #(#"beef", #(#"kg", 2500), #(5,45), #"fresh"),
      #(#"trout",#(#"num",2), #(2, 99), #"frozen-food"),
      #(#"potatoes",#(#"kg",1500), #(0,82),#"fresh"),
      #(#"milk",#(#"ltr",1250), #(1,44),#"fresh"));

define variable *shlist* = #();
define variable *database* = make(<shopping-info>);
```

```
define method main (arg, #rest ignore)
       *shlist* := convert-shopping-list(*shopping*);
       add-shopname!("tesco",*database*);
       store-shopping-list(*shlist*,*database*);
       for (purchases in every-purchase(*database*))
           if (instance?(head(purchases),<string>))
              print(purchases)
           else
              for (purchase in purchases)
                  show(purchase)
              end for
           end if
       end for;
       print("Bye")
end method main;
```

End of code.

# Bibliography

[1] Allen, John, *The Anatomy of LISP*, McGraw-Hill, New York, 1978.

[2] Birtwistle, Graham M., et al., *Simula Begin*, Chartwell-Bratt, 1979.

[3] Bobrow, D., et al., *The LOOPS Manual*, Xerox Parc, 1983.

[4] Booch, Grady, *Object-Oriented Design*, Benjamin/Cummings, CA, 1991.

[5] Charniak, E., Riesbeck, C., McDermott, D., and Meehan, J., *Artifical Intelligence Programming*, 2nd ed., Lawrence Erlbaum, Hillsdale, NJ, 1987.

[6] Dylan Group, *Dylan Interim Reference Manual*, Apple Computer, June, 1994.

[7] Goldberg A. and Robson, D., *Smalltalk80: The Language and its Implementation*, Addison-Wesley, Reading, MA, 1983.

[8] Harbison, Samuel P., *Modula-3*, Prentice-Hall, Englewood Cliffs, NJ, 1992.

[9] Hudak, Paul and Wadler, Philip (eds.), *Report on the Programming Language Haskell*, Computer Science Departments, Yale and Glasgow Universities.

[10] Kiczales, G., des Rivieres, Jim, and Bobrow, Daniel G., *The Art of the Meta-object Protocol*, MIT Press, Cambridge, MA, 1991.

[11] Kernigham, Brian W. and Richie, Dennis M., *The C Programming Language*, 2nd ed., Prentice-Hall, Englewood Cliffs, NJ, 1988.

[12] Lieberman, H., Using Prototypical Objects to Implement Shared Behaviour in Object Oriented Systems, *Proc. First ACM Conference on Object-Oriented Programming Systems*, 1986.

[13] Milner, Robin and Tofte, Mads, *The Definition of ML*, MIT Press, 1990.

[14] Naur, Peter, et al., Revised Report on the Algorithmic Language Algol60, *Communications of the ACM*, Vol. 6, no. 1, pp. 1-17, 1963.

[15] Padget, Julian, (ed.), *Programming Language Eulisp*, Versrion 0.99, School of Mathematical Sciences, University of Bath, 1994.

[16] Roberts, R.B. and Goldstein, I.P., *The FRL Manual*, AI Laboratory, Memo 409, MIT, Cambridge, MA, 1977.

[17] See chapter 28 of [18]

[18] Steele, Guy L., *Common LISP The Language*, 2nd ed., Digital Press, Bedford, MA, 1990.

[19] Stefik, M. J., An examination of a frame-structured representation system, *Proc. IJCAI-79*, pp. 846-852, 1979.

[20] Stroustrup, Bjarne, *The C++ Programming Language*, 2nd ed., Addison-Wesley, Reading, MA, 1991.

[21] Sun Microsystems, *The JAVA Language Specification*, 1995.

[22] Ungar, David and Smith, Randall B., Self: The Power of Simplicity, *Proc. OOPSLA-87*, pp.227-242, 1987.

# Index